Vegetarian
Mediterranean
180 fresh and healthy recipes
from sun-drenched cuisines
in 195 fantastic photographs
Cooking

BEVERLEY JOLLANDS

southwater

This edition is published by Southwater,
an imprint of Anness Publishing Ltd,
Hermes House,
88–89 Blackfriars Road,
London SE1 8HA;
tel. 020 7401 2077; fax 020 7633 9499
www.southwaterbooks.com; www.annesspublishing.com

If you like the images in this book and would like to investigate
using them for publishing, promotions or advertising, please visit
our website www.practicalpictures.com for more information.

UK distributor: Book Trade Services; tel. 0116 2759086;
fax 0116 2759090; uksales@booktradeservices.com;
exportsales@booktradeservices.com

North American distributor: National Book Network;
tel. 301 459 3366; fax 301 429 5746; www.nbnbooks.com

Australian distributor: Pan Macmillan Australia; tel. 1300 135 113;
fax 1300 135 103; customer.service@macmillan.com.au

New Zealand distributor: David Bateman Ltd; tel. (09) 415 7664;
fax (09) 415 8892

Publisher: Joanna Lorenz
Editorial Director: Helen Sudell
Project Editors: Rosie Gordon, Amy Christian
Proofreading Manager: Lindsay Zamponi
Production Controller: Christine Ni

Ethical trading policy
At Anness Publishing we believe that business should be conducted
in an ethical and ecologically sustainable way, with respect for the
environment and a proper regard to the replacement of the natural
resources we employ.
As a publisher, we use a lot of wood pulp in high-quality paper for
printing, and that wood commonly comes from spruce trees. We are
therefore currently growing more than 750,000 trees in three
Scottish forest plantations: Berrymoss (130 hectares/320 acres),
West Touxhill (125 hectares/305 acres) and Deveron Forest
(75 hectares/185 acres). The forests we manage contain more than
3.5 times the number of trees employed each year in making paper
for the books we manufacture.
Because of this ongoing ecological investment programme, you, as
our customer, can have the pleasure and reassurance of knowing
that a tree is being cultivated on your behalf to naturally replace the
materials used to make the book you are holding.
Our forestry programme is run in accordance with the UK
Woodland Assurance Scheme (UKWAS) and will be certified by the
internationally recognized Forest Stewardship Council (FSC). The
FSC is a non-government organization dedicated to promoting
responsible management of the world's forests. Certification ensures
forests are managed in an environmentally sustainable and socially
responsible way. For further information about this scheme, go to
www.annesspublishing.com/trees

A CIP catalogue record for this book is available from the
British Library.

Previousuly published as part of a larger volume,
Mediterranean: 500 Classic Recipes

Notes
Bracketed terms are intended for American readers.

For all recipes, quantities are given in both metric and imperial
measures and, where appropriate, in standard cups and spoons.
Follow one set of measures, but not a mixture, because they are
not interchangeable.

Standard spoon and cup measures are level.
1 tsp = 5ml, 1 tbsp = 15ml. 1 cup = 250ml/8fl oz

Australian standard tablespoons are 20ml. Australian readers should
use 3 tsp in place of 1 tbsp for measuring small quantities.

American pints are 16fl oz/2 cups. American readers should use
20fl oz/2.5 cups in place of 1 pint when measuring liquids.

Electric oven temperatures in this book are for conventional
ovens. When using a fan oven, the temperature will probably
need to be reduced by about 10–20°C/20–40°F. Since ovens
vary, you should check with your manufacturer's instruction
book for guidance.

Nutritional information
The nutritional analysis given for each recipe is calculated per
portion (i.e. serving or item), unless otherwise stated. If the recipe
gives a range, such as Serves 4–6, then the nutritional analysis will
be for the smaller portion size, i.e. 6 servings. Measurements for
sodium do not include salt added to taste.
Medium (US large) eggs are used unless otherwise stated.

Main front cover image shows Leek, Pepper and Spinach Frittata,
for recipe see page 39.

Publisher's note
Although the advice and information in this book are believed to
be accurate and true at the time of going to press, neither the
authors nor the publisher can accept any legal responsibility or
liability for any errors or omissions that may have been made nor
for any inaccuracies nor for any loss, harm or injury that comes
about from following instructions or advice in this book.

Contents

Introduction

The sun-drenched Mediterranean is well known for its wonderful cuisine, with a strong emphasis on fresh and healthy produce. Numerous nations and communities can be found

around the Mediterranean's rocky coast and on its islands, and all have distinctive and thriving culinary traditions. This is a region that brings together the diverse cultures of Europe, Africa and Asia, and where every village seems to boast its own speciality. This book contains a fantastic selection of the best vegetarian recipes from all over the Mediterranean, from classic Italian pasta dishes to Spanish paella, Greek stuffed vine leaves to spicy Moroccan couscous.

For many centuries, Mediterranean farmers and smallholders have eked a living from a region where small patches of cultivated land are scattered between mountains, forest and shore. The soil is stony and shallow, the weather hot and dry in summer, stormy and unpredictable in winter. But while it has always been difficult to grow arable crops on a large scale, fruit trees and vegetables thrive, providing crops that are unrivalled anywhere in the world.

The "Mediterranean diet", which is now hailed as a key to good health and long life, stems from a traditional reliance on the area's abundance of vegetables, fruit, pulses, herbs, nuts and grains, with relatively little dairy produce. Mediterranean cooks are frugal, but the flavours they create are generous and memorable. Vegetarians will find many delicious dishes to tempt them. Vegetables are stewed in olive oil, salads are laced with garlicky dressings, and everything is fragrant with herbs and spices. Summer visitors to the region have their senses awakened by its dazzling light and colour, and the intense flavours of its food have a comparable effect, which can be quite addictive.

The lands of the Mediterranean have been repeatedly invaded and colonized since Phoenician traders criss-crossed the sea 3,000 years ago, carrying foodstuffs, cooking techniques and recipes from port to port. The whole area was at the heart of the Roman Empire, and was later dominated by the Byzantine Empire. In the 8th century it came under Islamic influence, and the Arabs, who remained in Spain until the 15th century, established orchards and gardens, introduced irrigation technology, and planted many crops new to Europe, including rice, sugar cane, oranges, spinach and dates. Other ingredients that are now considered staples of Mediterranean cooking, such as tomatoes, peppers and chillies, came from the New World.

Successive incomers stamped their own styles of cooking on the region, and ideas spread along the trade routes they set up. As a result, similar dishes can often be found in the cuisines of different countries: soups, pizzas and tarts, vegetable stews and nut-thickened sauces and dips occur in many guises but are recognizable as variations on ancient and well-loved themes.

This book brings together a huge selection of vegetarian recipes collected from all over the Mediterranean, ranging from simple snacks and ideas for quick family meals to full-on festive feasts. Many are faithful versions of traditional dishes, carefully adapted where necessary for today's kitchens and ingredients. Others are modern recipes, though still just as authentic, because despite its respect for tradition, the cooking of the region is constantly evolving.

There are many tantalizing pictures of the finished dishes and ingredients to inspire you and whet your appetite. An important part of the attraction of Mediterranean food is its visual impact. Its colours are as sparkling as its flavours, and its vivid reds, greens and yellows are drawn from the same bright palette as the deep blue of the summer sky and the clear turquoise of the sea.

Finally, all the recipes have been analysed by a nutritionist, and the energy, fat, carbohydrate and protein count, and levels of fibre, calcium and sodium, are detailed under each entry. This information helps you to plan meals that are both delicious and nutritious.

Cannellini Bean Bruschetta

This traditional Italian dish is a sophisticated version of beans on toast. The beans make these appetizers filling and substantial, but they are low in fat.

Serves 6
150g/5oz/¾ cup dried
  cannellini beans
5 tomatoes
10ml/2 tsp olive oil
2 sun-dried tomatoes in oil,
  drained and finely chopped
2 garlic cloves
30ml/2 tbsp chopped
  fresh rosemary
12 slices Italian-style bread,
  such as ciabatta
salt and freshly ground
  black pepper
fresh basil leaves, to garnish

1 Soak the beans in water overnight. Drain, rinse, place in a pan and cover with water. Boil rapidly for 10 minutes then reduce the heat and simmer for 50–60 minutes. Drain.

2 Meanwhile, place the tomatoes in a bowl, cover with boiling water, leave for 30 seconds, then refresh in cold water. Skin, seed and chop the flesh.

3 Heat the oil in a pan and add the fresh and sun-dried tomatoes. Crush 1 garlic clove and add with the rosemary. Cook for 2 minutes. Add the mixture to the cooked cannellini beans, season to taste with salt and ground black pepper, and mix well. Heat through gently.

4 Preheat the grill (broiler) to high. Cut the remaining garlic clove in half and rub the bread slices with it. Toast the bread lightly on both sides.

5 Spoon the cannellini bean mixture on top of the toast. Garnish with basil leaves and serve immediately.

> **Variation**
> Canned beans can be used instead of dried; use 275g/10oz/ 2 cups drained, canned beans, rinse well, drain and add to the tomato mixture in step 4.

Buñuelos

The name of these cheese puffs literally means "puffballs". In Spain, they are usually deep-fried, but baking is easier when you are entertaining, and it gives wonderful results. The dough is made in the same way as French choux pastry, and the buñuelos should be eaten within a few hours of baking.

Serves 4
50g/2oz/¼ cup butter, diced
1.5ml/¼ tsp salt
250ml/8fl oz/1 cup water
115g/4oz/1 cup plain
  (all-purpose) flour
2 whole eggs, plus 1 yolk
2.5ml/½ tsp Dijon mustard
2.5ml/½ tsp cayenne pepper
50g/2oz/1/2 cup finely grated
  Manchego, Gruyère or
  Cheddar cheese

1 Preheat the oven to 220°C/425°F/Gas 7. Place the butter and salt in a pan, then add the water. Bring the liquid to the boil. Meanwhile, sift the flour on to a sheet of baking parchment.

2 Working quickly, pour the flour into the pan of boiling liquid in one go and stir it in immediately.

3 Beat the mixture vigorously with a wooden spoon until it forms a thick paste that binds together and leaves the sides of the pan clean. Remove the pan from the heat.

4 Gradually beat the eggs and yolk into the mixture, then add the mustard, cayenne pepper and cheese.

5 Place teaspoonfuls of mixture on a non-stick baking sheet and bake for 10 minutes. Reduce the temperature to 180°C/350°F/Gas 4. Cook for 15 minutes until well browned. Serve hot or cold.

> **Cook's Tip**
> Manchego is a semi-hard Spanish cheese made with sheep's milk. It has a firm, creamy texture and a nutty, piquant flavour that is very distinctive.

Bruschetta: Energy 284kcal/1203kJ; Protein 12.7g; Carbohydrate 49.7g, of which sugars 5.3g; Fat 5g, of which saturates 0.7g; Cholesterol 0mg; Calcium 127mg; Fibre 5.1g; Sodium 376mg.
Buñuelos: Energy 296kcal/1237kJ; Protein 9.9g; Carbohydrate 22.5g, of which sugars 0.6g; Fat 19g, of which saturates 10.5g; Cholesterol 185mg; Calcium 156mg; Fibre 0.9g; Sodium 223mg.

Pimiento Tartlets

These pretty Spanish tartlets are filled with strips of roasted sweet peppers and a creamy, cheesy custard. They make a perfect snack to serve with drinks.

Serves 4
1 red (bell) pepper
1 yellow (bell) pepper
175g/6oz/1½ cups plain
   (all-purpose) flour
75g/3oz/6 tbsp chilled
   butter, diced
30–45ml/2–3 tbsp cold water
60ml/4 tbsp double
   (heavy) cream
1 egg
15ml/1 tbsp grated
   Parmesan cheese
salt and ground black pepper

1 Preheat the oven to 200°C/400°F/Gas 6, and heat the grill (broiler). Place the peppers on a baking sheet and grill for 10 minutes, turning occasionally, until blackened. Cover with a dish towel and leave for 5 minutes. Peel away the skin, then discard the seeds and cut the flesh into very thin strips.

2 Sift the flour and a pinch of salt into a bowl. Add the butter and rub it in until the mixture resembles fine breadcrumbs. Stir in enough of the water to make a firm, not sticky, dough.

3 Roll the dough out thinly on a lightly floured surface and line 12 individual moulds or a 12-hole tartlet tin (muffin pan). Prick the bases with a fork and fill the pastry cases with crumpled foil. Bake for 10 minutes, then remove the foil and divide the pepper strips among the pastry cases.

4 Whisk the cream and egg in a bowl. Season and pour over the peppers. Sprinkle each tartlet with Parmesan and bake for 15–20 minutes until firm. Cool for 2 minutes, then remove from the moulds and transfer to a wire rack. Serve warm or cold.

> **Variation**
> Use strips of grilled aubergine (eggplant) mixed with sun-dried tomatoes in place of the roasted peppers.

Half-Moon Cheese Pies

These delicious small Greek pies, which are called *skaltsounakia*, always dazzle people and are a favourite at every meze table. In Crete, where they are very popular, there are several variations, including one with a filling of sautéed wild greens. Serve them freshly baked, hot from the oven or while still warm.

Makes 12–14
1 egg, plus 1 egg yolk for glazing
150g/5oz feta cheese, chopped
   and crumbled
30ml/2 tbsp milk
30ml/2 tbsp chopped fresh
   mint leaves
15ml/1 tbsp raisins
15ml/1 tbsp pine nuts,
   lightly toasted
a little vegetable oil,
   for greasing
a few sprigs of fresh mint,
   to garnish

For the pastry
225g/8oz/2 cups self-raising
   (self-rising) flour
45ml/3 tbsp extra virgin olive oil
15g/½oz/1 tbsp butter, melted
90g/3½oz/scant ½ cup Greek
   (US strained) yogurt

1 To make the pastry, put the flour in a bowl and mix in the oil, butter and yogurt by hand. Cover and rest in the refrigerator for 15 minutes.

2 Meanwhile, make the filling. Beat the egg lightly in a bowl. Crumble in the cheese, then mix in the milk, mint, raisins and pine nuts.

3 Preheat the oven to 190°C/375°F/Gas 5. Cut the pastry into two pieces and cover one with clear film (plastic wrap) or a dish towel. Thinly roll out the remaining piece of pastry and cut out 7.5cm/3in rounds.

4 Place a heaped teaspoonful of filling on each round and fold the pastry over to make a half-moon shape. Press the edges to seal, then place the pies on a greased baking sheet. Repeat with the remaining pastry.

5 Brush the pies with egg yolk and bake for 20 minutes, or until golden. Serve hot.

Half-Moon Pies: Energy 160Kcal/669kJ; Protein 5g; Carbohydrate 16.4g, of which sugars 2.5g; Fat 8.8g, of which saturates 3.4g; Cholesterol 31mg; Calcium 129mg; Fibre 0.7g; Sodium 270mg.
Tartlets: Energy 427kcal/1778kJ; Protein 8.4g; Carbohydrate 40g, of which sugars 6.4g; Fat 27g, of which saturates 16.1g; Cholesterol 112mg; Calcium 131mg; Fibre 2.8g; Sodium 180mg.

Filo Cigars with Feta and Herbs

These classic cigar-shaped Turkish pastries are popular snack and meze food, and they are also good as nibbles with drinks. In this version they are filled with cheese and herbs, but other popular fillings include baked aubergine (eggplant) and cheese, or mashed pumpkin, cheese and dill. The filo pastry can be folded into triangles, but cigars are the most traditional shape. They can be prepared in advance and kept under a damp dish towel in the refrigerator until you are ready to fry them in sunflower oil at the last minute.

Serves 3–4
225g/8oz feta cheese
1 egg, lightly beaten
1 small bunch each of fresh flat leaf parsley, mint and dill, finely chopped
4–5 sheets of filo pastry
sunflower oil, for deep-frying
dill fronds, to garnish (optional)

Feta Pastries

Known as *börek* in Turkey, these crisp, cheese-filled pastries are a common feature of street food throughout much of the Mediterranean, where they are often eaten with aperitifs. They are quite easy to make at home, though they require a little time and patience.

Makes 10
250g/9oz feta cheese, crumbled
2.5ml/1/2 tsp freshly grated nutmeg
30ml/2 tbsp each chopped fresh parsley, dill and mint
10 filo pastry sheets, each about 30 x 18cm/12 × 7in, thawed
75g/3oz/6 tbsp melted butter or 90ml/6 tbsp olive oil
ground black pepper

1 Preheat the oven to 190°C/375°F/Gas 5. Mix the feta cheese, nutmeg and fresh herbs in a bowl. Add pepper to taste and mix.

2 Brush a sheet of filo pastry lightly with butter or oil, place another on top of it and brush that too.

3 Cut the buttered sheets in half lengthways to make 10 strips, each 30 × 9cm/12 × 3½in. Place 5ml/1 tsp of the cheese filling at the base of a long strip, fold the corners in diagonally to enclose it, then roll the pastry up into a cigar shape.

4 Brush the end with a little butter or oil to seal, then place join-side down on a non-stick baking sheet. Repeat with the remaining pastry and filling. Brush the pastries with more butter or oil and bake for 20 minutes, or until crisp and golden. Cool on a wire rack.

1 In a bowl, mash the feta with a fork. Beat in the egg and fold in the herbs. Working with one sheet at a time, cut the filo into strips about 10–13cm/4–5in wide, and pile them on top of each other. Keep the strips covered with a damp dish towel.

2 Place a heaped teaspoon of the cheese filling along one of the short ends of a strip. Roll the end over the filling, quite tightly to keep it in place, then tuck in the sides to seal in the filling and continue to roll until you get to the other end.

3 Brush the tip with a little water to help seal the roll. Place the filled cigar, join-side down, on a plate and cover with a damp dish towel to keep it moist. Continue with the remaining sheets of filo and filling.

4 Heat enough oil for deep-frying in a wok or other deep-sided pan, and deep-fry the filo cigars in batches for 5–6 minutes until crisp and golden brown. Lift out of the oil with a slotted spoon and drain on kitchen paper. Serve immediately, garnished with dill fronds if you like.

Cook's Tip
When using filo pastry, it is important to keep the sheets from drying out. Cover the pile with a damp dish towel, and take out one sheet at a time to brush with butter. The quantities for filo pastry in this recipe are approximate, as the size of filo sheets varies. Any unused pastry will keep in the refrigerator for a week or so, if it is well wrapped.

Feta Pastries: Energy 171kcal/713kJ; Protein 5.5g; Carbohydrate 12.2g, of which sugars 0.8g; Fat 11.5g, of which saturates 7.4g; Cholesterol 33mg; Calcium 121mg; Fibre 0.7g; Sodium 407mg.
Filo Cigars: Energy 311kcal/1291kJ; Protein 12.4g; Carbohydrate 11.2g, of which sugars 1.6g; Fat 24.4g, of which saturates 9.5g; Cholesterol 92mg; Calcium 278mg; Fibre 1.7g; Sodium 838mg.

Potato Tortilla

The classic tortilla can be found in every tapas bar in Spain. The size of a large cake, it is dense and very satisfying. It can be eaten in wedges with a fork – a meal in itself with salad – or cut up into chunks and speared, to be enjoyed as a snack with drinks.

Serves 6
450g/1lb small waxy
    potatoes, peeled
1 Spanish onion
45ml/3 tbsp vegetable oil
4 large eggs
salt and ground black pepper
fresh flat leaf parsley or tomato
    wedges, to garnish

1 Using a sharp knife, cut the potatoes into thin slices and slice the onion into thin rings. Heat 30ml/2 tbsp of the oil in a 20cm/8in heavy frying pan.

2 Add the potatoes and the onions to the pan and cook over a low heat for 20 minutes, or until the potato slices are just tender. Stir from time to time to prevent the potatoes sticking. Remove from the heat.

3 In a large bowl, beat together the eggs with a little salt and pepper. When the cooked potatoes and onion have cooled a little, stir them into the eggs.

4 Clean the frying pan with kitchen paper then heat the remaining oil and pour in the potato mixture. Cook very gently for 5–8 minutes until set underneath. During cooking, lift the edges of the tortilla with a spatula, and allow any uncooked egg to run underneath. Shake the pan from side to side, to prevent sticking.

5 Place a large heatproof plate upside-down over the pan, invert the tortilla on to the plate and then slide it back into the pan. Cook for 2–3 minutes more, until the underside of the tortilla is golden brown.

6 Cut the tortilla into wedges and serve immediately or leave until warm or cold. Serve garnished with fresh flat leaf parsley or tomato wedges.

Yogurt Cheese in Olive Oil

Sheep's milk is widely used in cheese-making in the eastern Mediterranean, particularly in Greece where sheep's yogurt is hung in muslin to drain off the whey before patting into balls of soft cheese. Here it's bottled in extra virgin olive oil with chilli and herbs – an appropriate gift for a friend who enjoys Greek cuisine.

Fills two 450g/1lb jars
750g/10oz/1¼ cups Greek
    sheep's yogurt
2.5ml/½ tsp salt
10ml/2 tsp crushed dried chillies
    or chilli powder
15ml/1 tbsp chopped
    fresh rosemary
15ml/1 tbsp chopped fresh thyme
    or oregano
about 300ml/½ pint/1¼ cups
    olive oil, preferably
    garlic flavoured

1 Sterilize a 30cm/12in square of muslin (cheesecloth) by steeping it in boiling water. Drain and lay over a large plate.

2 Mix the yogurt with the salt and tip on to the centre of the muslin. Bring up the sides of the muslin and tie firmly with string. Hang the bag of yogurt over a large bowl to catch the whey and leave in a cool place for 2–3 days, or until the whey stops dripping.

3 Wash thoroughly and dry two 450g/1lb glass preserving jars or jam jars. Sterilize them by heating them in an oven preheated to 150°C/300°F/Gas 2 for 15 minutes.

4 Mix together the chilli and herbs. Take teaspoonfuls of the cheese and roll into balls with your hands. Lower into the jars, sprinkling each layer with the herb mixture.

5 Pour the olive oil over the soft cheese balls until they are completely covered. Mix gently with the handle end of a wooden spoon in order to blend the flavourings through the olive oil, making sure that you do not break up the cheese balls. Store in the refrigerator for up to 3 weeks.

6 To serve the cheese, spoon out of the jars with a little of the flavoured olive oil and spread on to lightly toasted bread.

Tortilla: Energy 163kcal/681kJ; Protein 5.8g; Carbohydrate 14.7g, of which sugars 2.9g; Fat 9.5g, of which saturates 1.9g; Cholesterol 127mg; Calcium 32mg; Fibre 1.2g; Sodium 56mg.
Yogurt Cheese: Energy 1331kcal/5488kJ; Protein 24g; Carbohydrate 7.5g, of which sugars 7.5g; Fat 138.2g, of which saturates 33.8g; Cholesterol 0mg; Calcium 563mg; Fibre 0g; Sodium 758mg.

Marinated Pimientos

Pimiento is simply another word for sweet peppers, which in this recipe are cooked and skinned, then marinated in a garlicky oil and vinegar dressing that goes well with their smoky flavour. You can buy preserved peppers in cans or jars, but they are very much tastier when homemade. They create a delicious, healthy appetizer, on their own or with other antipasti, and can also be used to top crostini or mini-pizzas.

Serves 4
3 red (bell) peppers
2 small garlic cloves, crushed
45ml/3 tbsp chopped
   fresh parsley
15ml/1 tbsp sherry vinegar
25ml/1½ tbsp olive oil
salt, to taste

1 Preheat the grill (broiler) to high. Place the peppers on a baking sheet and grill (broil) for 8–12 minutes, turning occasionally, until the skins have blistered and blackened. Remove the peppers from the heat, cover them with a clean dish towel or place in a plastic bag and leave for 5 minutes so that the steam softens the skin and makes it easier to peel.

2 Make a small cut in the bottom of each pepper and squeeze out the juice into a bowl. Peel away the skin and cut the peppers in half. Remove and discard the core and seeds.

3 Using a sharp knife, cut each pepper in half lengthways into 1cm/½in-wide strips. Place them in a bowl.

4 Whisk the garlic, parsley, vinegar and oil into the pepper juices. Add salt to taste. Pour over the pepper strips and toss well. Cover and chill, but, if possible, bring the peppers back to room temperature before serving.

> **Cook's Tip**
> *The marinated pimientos can be stored in the refrigerator for up to 2 weeks covered in olive oil in a screw-top jar. The flavours will blend and improve with keeping.*

Aubergine, Garlic and Red Pepper Pâté

Serve this Italian-style chunky, garlicky pâté of smoky baked aubergine and red peppers, on a bed of salad, accompanied by crisp toasts. Baking the ingredients imparts a wonderful smoky flavour.

Serves 4
3 aubergines (eggplants)
2 (bell) red peppers
5 garlic cloves
7.5ml/1½ tsp pink peppercorns
   in brine, drained and crushed
30m/2 tbsp chopped fresh
   coriander (cilantro)

1 Preheat the oven to 200°C/400°F/Gas 6. Arrange the whole aubergines, peppers and garlic cloves on a baking sheet. Bake for 10 minutes, then remove the garlic cloves and set aside. Turn over the aubergines and peppers, return to the oven and bake for a further 20 minutes.

2 Meanwhile, peel the garlic cloves and place them in a blender or food processor.

3 Remove the charred peppers from the oven and place in a plastic food bag. Set aside to cool. Return the aubergines to the oven and bake for a further 10 minutes.

4 Split each aubergine in half and scoop out the flesh into a sieve (strainer) placed over a bowl. Discard the skin. Press the flesh with a spoon to remove the bitter juices. Discard the juices. Add the aubergine to the garlic in the blender or food processor and process until smooth. Put the mixture in a bowl.

5 Skin, core and seed the red peppers and finely chop the flesh; stir into the aubergine mixture. Mix in the peppercorns and chopped coriander until thoroughly combined. Spoon into a serving dish and serve immediately.

> **Variation**
> *Use orange or yellow (bell) peppers in place of the red ones.*

Pimientos: Energy 84kcal/349kJ; Protein 1.7g; Carbohydrate 8.7g, of which sugars 8.3g; Fat 4.9g, of which saturates 0.8g; Cholesterol 0mg; Calcium 33mg; Fibre 2.7g; Sodium 9mg.
Pâté: Energy 69kcal/292kJ; Protein 3.5g; Carbohydrate 11.8g, of which sugars 10g; Fat 1.3g, of which saturates 0.3g; Cholesterol 0mg; Calcium 31mg; Fibre 6.2g; Sodium 8mg.

Smoked Aubergine and Yogurt Purée

One of the most popular Turkish meze dishes, this garlic-flavoured purée varies from house to house and from region to region. It is sometimes made with a heavy hand of garlic, with a kick of chilli, or with the fresh taste of dill, mint or parsley. The purée is heavenly when it is freshly made, served with chunks of warm crusty bread for scooping it up.

Serves 4
2 large, plump aubergines (eggplants)
30ml/2 tbsp olive oil, plus extra for drizzling
juice of 1 lemon
2–3 garlic cloves, crushed
225g/8oz/1 cup thick natural (plain) yogurt
salt and freshly ground black pepper
a few fresh dill fronds, to garnish
lemon wedges, to serve

1 Put the aubergines directly on the gas flame on top of the stove, or under a conventional grill (broiler), and turn them from time to time until the skin is charred on all sides and the flesh feels soft.

2 Place the aubergines in a plastic bag and leave for a few minutes to soften the skin.

3 Hold each aubergine by the stalk under cold running water and gently peel off the charred skin until you are left with just the smooth bulbous flesh. Squeeze the flesh between your hands to get rid of any excess water and place it on a chopping board.

4 Chop the aubergine flesh to a pulp, discarding the stalks. Put the flesh in a bowl and add 30ml/2 tbsp oil, the lemon juice and garlic. Beat well to mix, then beat in the yogurt and season with salt and pepper.

5 Transfer the mixture to a bowl, drizzle with olive oil and garnish with dill. Serve at room temperature, with lemon wedges for squeezing.

Chilli Aubergine Peppers

This is a lovely Turkish dish of smoked aubergine and peppers with a refreshing lemony tang. Its Arabic name is Acvar, and it is traditionally served warm with lemon wedges to squeeze over it as part of a meze. Here the dish is accompanied by toasted pitta with which to scoop it up, but you could increase the quantities and serve it as a main dish with yogurt and bread.

Serves 4
2 red (bell) peppers
1 fat aubergine (eggplant)
30–45ml/2–3 tbsp olive oil
1 red onion, cut in half lengthways and finely sliced along the grain
1 fresh red chilli, seeded and finely sliced
2 garlic cloves, chopped
5–10ml/1–2 tsp sugar
juice of 1 lemon
dash of white wine vinegar
a large handful of fresh flat leaf parsley, roughly chopped
salt and ground black pepper
lemon wedges and toasted pitta bread, to serve

1 Place the peppers and aubergine under a conventional grill (broiler), or on a rack over the hot coals of a barbecue. Turn them from time to time until the skin is charred on all sides and the flesh feels soft. Place them in a plastic bag and leave for a few minutes to soften the skin.

2 One at a time, hold the charred vegetables under cold running water and peel off the skins.

3 Place the vegetables on a chopping board and remove the stalks. Halve the peppers lengthways and scoop out the seeds, then chop the flesh to a pulp. Chop the aubergine flesh to a pulp too.

4 Put the oil into a wide, heavy pan and toss in the onion, chilli, garlic and sugar. Cook over a medium heat for 2–3 minutes, until they begin to colour.

5 Toss in the pulped peppers and aubergine, stir in the lemon juice and vinegar and season with salt and pepper. Toss in the parsley and serve with lemon wedges and toasted pitta bread.

Purée: Energy 103kcal/431kJ; Protein 4.4g; Carbohydrate 7.7g, of which sugars 6.4g; Fat 6.5g, of which saturates 1.2g; Cholesterol 1mg; Calcium 118mg; Fibre 2.3g; Sodium 49mg.
Aubergine Peppers: Energy 102kcal/425kJ; Protein 1.8g; Carbohydrate 10.5g, of which sugars 9.8g; Fat 6.2g, of which saturates 1g; Cholesterol 0mg; Calcium 19mg; Fibre 3.1g; Sodium 6mg.

Poached Eggs with Garlic Yogurt

This dish of poached eggs on a bed of garlic-flavoured yogurt is surprisingly delicious. It is called Cilbur in Turkey, where it is served as a meze dish or snack, but it works equally well for supper with a green salad. Hen's or duck's eggs can be used, and you can poach or fry them. Spiked with Turkish red pepper or paprika, and served with ciabatta or flat bread, it is simple and satisfying.

Serves 2
500g/1¼lb/2¼ cups thick
    natural (plain) yogurt
2 garlic cloves, crushed
30–45ml/2–3 tbsp
    white wine vinegar
4 large (US extra large) eggs
15–30ml/1–2 tbsp butter
5ml/1 tsp Turkish red pepper
    or paprika
a few dried sage leaves, crumbled
salt and ground black pepper

1 Beat the yogurt with the garlic and seasoning. Spoon into a serving dish or on to individual plates, spreading it flat to create a thick bed for the eggs.

2 Fill a pan with water, add the vinegar to seal the egg whites, and bring to a rolling boil. Stir the water with a spoon to create a whirlpool and crack in the first egg. As the egg spins and the white sets around the yolk, stir the water for the next one. Poach the eggs for 2–3 minutes so the yolks are still soft.

3 Lift the eggs out of the water with a slotted spoon and place them on the yogurt bed.

4 Quickly melt the butter in a small pan. Stir in the red pepper or paprika and sage leaves, then spoon the mixture over the eggs. Eat immediately.

Cook's Tip
Leave the yogurt at room temperature to form a contrast with the hot eggs, or heat it by placing the dish in a cool oven, or by sitting it in a covered pan of hot water.

Stuffed Vine Leaves

This popular Greek dish keeps moist when cooked slowly in a casserole or clay pot. Fresh vine leaves are best, but preserved or canned will also work well.

Serves 4
12 fresh vine leaves
30ml/2 tbsp olive oil
1 small onion, chopped
30ml/2 tbsp pine nuts
1 garlic clove, crushed
115g/4oz/1 cup cooked long
    grain rice
2 tomatoes, skinned, seeded and
    finely chopped
15ml/1 tbsp chopped fresh mint
1 lemon, sliced
150ml/¼ pint/⅔ cup dry
    white wine
200ml/7fl oz/scant 1 cup
    vegetable stock
salt and ground black pepper
extra virgin olive oil, lemon wedges
    and mint sprigs, to garnish

1 Soak the clay pot in cold water for 20 minutes, then drain. Blanch the vine leaves in a pan of boiling water for about 2 minutes or until they darken and soften. Rinse the leaves under cold running water and leave to drain.

2 Heat the olive oil and fry the onion for 5–6 minutes, stirring frequently, until softened. Add the pine nuts and crushed garlic and cook, stirring, until the onions and pine nuts are golden. Stir the onion mixture into the rice, then add and stir in the chopped tomatoes and fresh mint. Season to taste with salt and freshly ground black pepper.

3 Place a dessertspoonful of the rice mixture at the stalk end of each vine leaf. Fold the sides of the leaf in over the filling and roll up tightly. Place the stuffed vine leaves close together, seam side down, in the clay pot. Place the lemon slices on top and in between the stuffed vine leaves. Pour over the white wine and sufficient stock just to cover the rolls and lemon slices.

4 Cover the dish and place in an unheated oven. Set the oven to 200°C/400°F/Gas 6 and cook for 30 minutes. Reduce to 160°C/325°F/Gas 3 and cook for a further 30 minutes. Serve hot or cold as a starter or as part of a meze table, drizzled with fruity extra virgin olive oil and garnished with lemon wedges and a few sprigs of fresh mint.

Poached Eggs: Energy 345kcal/1438kJ; Protein 25.4g; Carbohydrate 19.1g, of which sugars 19.1g; Fat 19.8g, of which saturates 8.3g; Cholesterol 400mg; Calcium 534mg; Fibre 0.1g; Sodium 393mg.
Vine Leaves: Energy 188Kcal/782kJ; Protein 2.9g; Carbohydrate 13.6g, of which sugars 4.1g; Fat 11.3g, of which saturates 1.3g; Cholesterol 0mg; Calcium 37mg; Fibre 1.4g; Sodium 9mg.

Courgette Rissoles

This ingenious recipe makes a sharply appetizing dish.

Serves 6

500g/1¼lb courgettes (zucchini)
120ml/4fl oz/½ cup extra virgin olive oil
1 large onion, finely chopped
2 spring onions (scallions), green and white parts finely chopped
1 garlic clove, crushed
3 medium slices of bread (not from a pre-sliced loaf)
2 eggs, lightly beaten
200g/7oz feta cheese, crumbled
50g/2oz/½ cup freshly grated Greek Graviera or Italian Parmesan cheese
45–60ml/3–4 tbsp finely chopped fresh dill or 5ml/1 tsp dried oregano
50g/2oz/½ cup plain (all-purpose) flour
salt and ground black pepper
lemon wedges, to serve

1 Bring a pan of lightly salted water to the boil. Slice the courgettes into 4cm/1½in lengths and add them to the pan. Cover and cook for about 10 minutes. Drain and cool.

2 Heat 45ml/3 tbsp of the olive oil in a pan, add the onion and spring onions and sauté until translucent. Add the garlic and as soon as it becomes aromatic remove the pan from the heat.

3 Squeeze the courgettes to extract as much water as possible, then place them in a large bowl. Add the fried onion and garlic mixture and mix well.

4 Toast the bread, discard the crusts, then break up the toast and crumb it in a food processor. Add to the courgette mixture, with the eggs, feta and Graviera or Parmesan cheese. Stir in the dill or oregano and add salt and pepper to taste. If the mixture seems too wet, add a little flour.

5 Take a heaped tablespoon of the courgette mixture, roll it into a ball, using your hands, and press it lightly to make a rissole shape. Make more rissoles in the same way. Coat them lightly in the flour. Heat the remaining extra virgin olive oil in a large, non-stick frying pan, then fry the rissoles in batches until they are crisp and brown, turning them over once. Drain on kitchen paper and serve with the lemon wedges.

Chickpea Rissoles

This is one of the classic meze dishes that are typically found on a Greek table. It is an inexpensive dish, but very appetizing.

Serves 4

300g/11oz/scant 1½ cups chickpeas, soaked overnight in water to cover
105ml/7 tbsp extra virgin olive oil
2 large onions, chopped
15ml/1 tbsp ground cumin
2 garlic cloves, crushed
3–4 fresh sage leaves, chopped
45ml/3 tbsp chopped flat leaf parsley
1 egg, lightly beaten
45ml/3 tbsp self-raising (self-rising) flour
50g/2oz/½ cup plain (all-purpose) flour
salt and ground black pepper
radishes, rocket (arugula) and olives, to serve

1 Drain the chickpeas, rinse under cold water and drain again. Tip them into a large pan, cover with plenty of fresh cold water and bring them to the boil. Skim the froth from the surface of the water with a slotted spoon until the liquid is clear.

2 Cover the pan and cook for 1¼–1½ hours, or until the chickpeas are very soft. Set aside a few tablespoons of cooking liquid, then strain the chickpeas, discarding the rest of the liquid. Transfer them to a food processor, add 30–45ml/2–3 tbsp of the reserved liquid and process to a velvety mash.

3 Heat 45ml/3 tbsp of the olive oil in a large frying pan, add the onions, and sauté until they are light golden. Add the cumin and the garlic and stir for a few seconds until their aroma rises. Stir in the chopped sage leaves and the parsley, and set aside.

4 Scrape the chickpea mash into a large bowl and add the egg, the self-raising flour, and the fried onion and herb mixture. Season and mix well. Take large walnut-size pieces and flatten them so that they look like thick, round mini-hamburgers.

5 Coat the rissoles lightly in the plain flour. Heat the remaining olive oil in a large frying pan and fry them in batches until they are crisp and golden on both sides. Drain on kitchen paper and serve hot with the radishes, rocket and olives.

Courgette Rissoles: Energy 343Kcal/1,424kJ; Protein 14.7g; Carbohydrate 18.5g, of which sugars 4.9g; Fat 23.9g, of which saturates 8.6g; Cholesterol 95mg; Calcium 301mg; Fibre 2.2g; Sodium 668mg.
Chickpea Rissoles: Energy 532Kcal/2231kJ; Protein 19.7g; Carbohydrate 63.6g, of which sugars 8.1g; Fat 23.9g, of which saturates 3.2g; Cholesterol 0mg; Calcium 222mg; Fibre 10.7g; Sodium 77mg.

Marinated Vegetable Antipasto

Antipasto means "before the meal" and traditionally consists of a selection of several different small dishes such as these marinated vegetables. Serve antipasto in attractive bowls, with plenty of fresh crusty bread.

Serves 4
For the peppers
3 red peppers
3 yellow peppers
4 garlic cloves, sliced
handful fresh basil, plus extra
    to garnish
extra virgin olive oil
salt and ground black pepper

For the mushrooms
450g/1lb open cap mushrooms
60ml/4 tbsp extra virgin olive oil
1 large garlic clove, crushed
15ml/1 tbsp chopped fresh
    rosemary
250ml/8fl oz/1 cup dry white wine
fresh rosemary sprigs, to garnish

For the olives
1 dried red chilli, crushed
grated rind of 1 lemon
120ml/4fl oz/1/2 cup extra virgin
    olive oil
225g/8oz/1 1/3 cups black olives
30ml/2 tbsp chopped fresh flat
    leaf parsley
1 lemon wedge, to serve

1 Grill (broil) the peppers, turning occasionally, until they are blackened and blistered all over, then place in a large plastic bag. When cool, remove the skin and seeds.

2 Cut the pepper flesh into strips lengthways and place in a bowl with the garlic and basil. Add salt to taste, cover with oil and marinate for 3–4 hours, tossing occasionally. When serving, garnish with more basil leaves.

3 Slice the mushrooms and place in a bowl. Heat the oil and add the garlic, rosemary and wine. Bring to the boil, then lower the heat and simmer for 3 minutes. Season and pour over the mushrooms. Mix well and leave until cool, stirring occasionally. Cover and marinate overnight. Serve at room temperature, garnished with rosemary sprigs.

4 To prepare the olives, place the chilli and lemon rind in a small pan with the oil. Heat gently for about 3 minutes. Add the olives and heat for 1 minute more. Tip into a bowl and leave overnight. Sprinkle with parsley and serve with a lemon wedge.

Aubergine Fritters

The aubergine is popular all over the Mediterranean and appears in many recipes. These simple and delicious fritters make a superb starter or supper dish.

Serves 4
1 large aubergine (eggplant),
    about 675g/1 1/2lb, cut into
    1cm/1/2in thick slices
30ml/2 tbsp olive oil
1 egg, lightly beaten
60ml/4 tbsp chopped fresh parsley
2 garlic cloves, crushed

130g/4 1/2oz/2 1/4 cups fresh
    white breadcrumbs
90g/3 1/2oz/generous 1 cup grated
    Parmesan cheese
90g/3 1/2oz/generous 1 cup feta
    cheese, crumbled
45ml/3tbsp plain
    (all-purpose) flour
sunflower oil, for shallow frying
salt and ground black pepper

To serve
natural yogurt, flavoured with fried
    red chillies and cumin seeds
lime wedges

1 Preheat the oven to 190°C/375°F/Gas 5. Brush the aubergine slices with the olive oil, then place them on a baking sheet and bake for about 20 minutes until golden and tender.

2 Remove from the oven and chop the aubergine slices finely. Place them in a bowl with the egg, parsley, garlic, breadcrumbs, Parmesan and feta. Add salt and pepper to taste, and mix well. Leave the mixture to rest for about 20 minutes. If the mixture looks very sloppy, add some more breadcrumbs.

3 Divide the mixture into eight balls and flatten them slightly. Place the flour on a plate and season with salt and pepper. Coat the fritters in the flour, shaking off any excess.

4 Shallow-fry in batches for 1 minute on each side, until the fritters are golden brown. Drain on kitchen paper and serve with the flavoured yogurt and lime wedges.

> **Cook's Tip**
> *Aubergines can be bitter. To avoid this, slice, sprinkle with salt and leave to drain for an hour. Rinse and squeeze dry before cooking.*

Vegetable Antipasto: Energy 449kcal/1857kJ; Protein 5.6g; Carbohydrate 18g, of which sugars 16.9g; Fat 35.4g, of which saturates 5.3g; Cholesterol 0mg; Calcium 93mg; Fibre 7.7g; Sodium 1289mg.
Aubergine Fritters: Energy 508kcal/2122kJ; Protein 20.7g; Carbohydrate 38.3g, of which sugars 5g; Fat 31.4g, of which saturates 10.4g; Cholesterol 86mg; Calcium 458mg; Fibre 5.1g; Sodium 842mg.

TAPAS, ANTIPASTI & APPETIZERS

Grilled Aubergine in Honey

Hot, spicy, sweet and fruity flavours are a classic combination in this delicious Moroccan dish. Many different kinds of aubergine are grown in the Mediterranean, in all sizes and ranging from white to purple and black. Baby ones are effective for this recipe as you can slice them in half lengthways and hold them by their stalks to eat.

Serves 4
2 aubergines (eggplants), thickly sliced, or 8 baby aubergines, halved lengthways
25ml/1½ tbsp olive oil
2–3 garlic cloves, crushed
5cm/2in piece fresh root ginger, peeled and grated
5ml/1 tsp ground cumin
5ml/1 tsp harissa
75ml/5 tbsp clear honey
juice of 1 lemon
salt, to taste

1 Preheat the grill (broiler) or a griddle. Lightly brush each aubergine slice with olive oil and cook under the grill or in a griddle pan. Turn the slices during cooking so that they are lightly browned on both sides.

2 In a wide non-stick frying pan, fry the garlic in the remaining oil for a few seconds, then stir in the ginger, cumin, harissa, honey and lemon juice. Add enough water to cover the pan's base and to thin the mixture, then lay the aubergine slices in the pan.

3 Cook the aubergines gently for about 10 minutes, or until they have absorbed all the sauce.

4 Add a little extra water, if necessary, season to taste with salt, and serve at room temperature, with chunks of fresh bread to mop up the juices.

> **Variation**
> *If you want to make a feature out of this sumptuous dish, serve it on a platter accompanied by other grilled (broiled) vegetables and fruit, such as (bell) peppers, chillies, tomatoes, oranges, pineapples and mangoes.*

Mozzarella Skewers

These crunchy appetizers have stacks of flavour and contrasting textures – layers of oven-baked mozzarella, tomatoes, basil and bread infused with fruity olive oil.

45ml/3 tbsp olive oil
225g/8oz mozzarella cheese, cut into 5mm/¼in slices
3 plum tomatoes, cut into 5mm/¼in slices
15g/½oz/½ cup fresh basil leaves, plus extra to garnish
salt and ground black pepper
30ml/2 tbsp chopped fresh flat leaf parsley, to garnish

Serves 4
12 slices white bread (not from a pre-sliced loaf), each about 1cm/½in thick

1 Preheat the oven to 220°C/425°F/Gas 7. Trim the crusts from the bread and cut each slice into four equal squares. Arrange on a baking sheet and brush on one side (or both sides) with half the olive oil. Bake for 3–5 minutes until the squares are pale gold.

2 Remove from the oven and place the bread squares on a board with the other ingredients.

3 Make 16 stacks, each starting with a square of bread, then a slice of mozzarella topped with a slice of tomato and a basil leaf. Sprinkle with salt and pepper, then repeat, ending with a square of bread.

4 Push a skewer through each stack and place on the baking sheet. Drizzle with the remaining oil and bake for 10–15 minutes until the cheese begins to melt. Garnish the stacks with fresh basil leaves and serve scattered with chopped fresh flat leaf parsley.

> **Cook's Tips**
> • *If you use wooden skewers, soak them in water first, to prevent them scorching in the oven.*
> • *Use country bread with a full flavour and an open texture. Day-old bread will crisp more quickly.*

Grilled Aubergine: Energy 151kcal/631kJ; Protein 1.4g; Carbohydrate 17.6g, of which sugars 17.3g; Fat 8.9g, of which saturates 1.3g; Cholesterol 0mg; Calcium 16mg; Fibre 3g; Sodium 5mg.
Mozzarella Skewers: Energy 1693kcal/7107kJ; Protein 71.6g; Carbohydrate 169.4g, of which sugars 18.1g; Fat 85.9g, of which saturates 36g; Cholesterol 131mg; Calcium 1222mg; Fibre 8.6g; Sodium 2606mg.

Roast Pepper Terrine

This terrine is perfect for a dinner party because it tastes better if made ahead. Prepare the salsa a few hours before serving. Serve with hot Italian bread.

Serves 8

8 (bell) peppers
675g/1½lb/3 cups mascarpone
   or ricotta cheese
3 eggs, separated
30ml/2 tbsp each roughly
   chopped flat leaf parsley
   and shredded basil
2 large garlic cloves, chopped
2 red, yellow or orange (bell)
   peppers, chopped
30ml/2 tbsp extra virgin olive oil
10ml/2 tsp balsamic vinegar
a few basil sprigs
pinch of sugar
salt and freshly ground
   black pepper

1 Place the peppers under a hot grill (broiler) for 8–10 minutes, turning frequently until charred and blistered on all sides. Put the peppers in plastic bags and leave to cool. Rub off the skins and remove the seeds, then cut 7 of the peppers lengthways into thin, even-sized strips.

2 Put the mascarpone cheese in a bowl with the egg yolks, herbs and half the garlic. Add salt and pepper to taste and beat well. In a separate bowl, whisk the egg whites to a soft peak, then fold into the cheese mixture until evenly incorporated.

3 Preheat the oven to 180°C/350°F/Gas 4. Line the base of a lightly oiled 900g/2lb loaf tin (pan). Put one-third of the cheese in the tin and spread level. Arrange half the pepper strips on top and repeat until all the cheese and peppers are used. Cover with foil and place in a roasting pan. Pour in boiling water to come halfway up the sides. Bake for 1 hour. Leave to cool in the water bath, then lift out and chill overnight.

4 To make the salsa, place the remaining roast pepper and fresh peppers in a food processor. Add the remaining garlic, oil, vinegar and basil, keeping a few leaves for garnishing. Process until finely chopped. Add salt and pepper to taste and mix well. Tip into a bowl, cover and chill until ready to serve. Turn out the terrine, peel off the paper and slice thickly. Garnish with the basil leaves and serve cold, with the salsa.

Chickpea Pasta Parcels

Somewhere between a dumpling and pasta, this is a popular Turkish snack.

Serves 4–6

450g/1lb/4 cups plain (all-
   purpose) flour
2.5ml/½ tsp salt
1 egg, beaten with 1 egg yolk
salt and ground black pepper

For the filling

400g/14oz can chickpeas,
   drained and thoroughly rinsed
5ml/1 tsp cumin seeds, crushed
5ml/1 tsp paprika

For the yogurt

about 90ml/6 tbsp thick natural
   (plain) yogurt
2–3 garlic cloves, crushed

For the sauce

15ml/1 tbsp olive oil
15ml/1 tbsp butter
1 onion, finely chopped
2 garlic cloves, finely
   chopped
5ml/1 tsp Turkish red pepper,
   or 1 fresh red chilli, seeded and
   finely chopped
5–10ml/1–2 tsp granulated
   (white) sugar
5–10ml/1–2 tsp dried mint
400g/14oz can chopped
   tomatoes, drained
600ml/1 pint/2½ cups
   vegetable stock
1 small bunch each of fresh
   flat leaf parsley and
   coriander (cilantro),
   roughly chopped

1 To make the dough, sift the flour and salt into a wide bowl and make a well in the middle. Pour in the beaten egg and 50ml/2fl oz/¼ cup water. Using your fingers, draw the flour into the liquid and mix to a dough. Knead the dough for 10 minutes, then cover the bowl with a damp dish towel and leave to rest for 1 hour.

2 Meanwhile, prepare the filling and yogurt. In a bowl, mash the chickpeas with a fork. Beat in the cumin, paprika and seasoning. In another bowl, beat the yogurt with the garlic and season with salt and pepper.

3 To make the sauce, heat the oil and butter in a heavy pan and fry the onion and garlic until softened. Add the red pepper or chilli, sugar and mint, then stir in the tomatoes and cook gently for about 15 minutes. Season and remove from the heat.

4 Preheat the oven to 200°C/400°F/ Gas 6. Roll out the dough as thinly as possible on a lightly floured surface. Using a sharp knife, cut the dough into small squares (roughly 2.5cm/1in).

5 Spoon a little chickpea mixture into the middle of each square and bunch the corners together to form a little pouch. Place the filled pasta parcels in a greased ovenproof dish, stacking them next to each other. Bake, uncovered, for 15–20 minutes, until golden brown.

6 Pour the stock into a pan and bring to the boil. Take the pasta parcels out of the oven and pour the stock over them. Return the dish to the oven and bake for a further 15–20 minutes, until almost all the stock has been absorbed. Meanwhile, reheat the tomato sauce.

7 Transfer to a serving dish and spoon the yogurt over them. Top the cool yogurt with the hot tomato sauce and sprinkle with the chopped herbs.

Roast Pepper Terrine: Energy 276kcal/1145kJ; Protein 12.5g; Carbohydrate 16.8g, of which sugars 16.1g; Fat 18g, of which saturates 8.9g; Cholesterol 107mg; Calcium 41mg; Fibre 3.8g; Sodium 37mg.
Chickpea Pasta Parcels: Energy 416kcal/1760kJ; Protein 14.8g; Carbohydrate 73.7g, of which sugars 5.9g; Fat 9g, of which saturates 2.6g; Cholesterol 71mg; Calcium 179mg; Fibre 5.9g; Sodium 360mg.

Spicy Walnut Dip

This popular, spicy walnut dip, called Muhammara in Arabic, is usually served with toasted flat bread or crusty bread. It can also be served as a dip for raw vegetables. The ingredients vary a little – mashed chickpeas or carrots may be used instead of bread, grated feta or yogurt may be added for a creamy texture, and garlic may be included in liberal quantities – but the general aim is to create a fiery dip spiked with Turkish red pepper or chillies. The dip is traditionally made with pomegranate syrup, but contemporary recipes often use lemon juice instead. The parsley leaves at the end help to cut the heat, so add more if you like.

Serves 4–6

175g/6oz/1 cup broken shelled walnuts
5ml/1 tsp cumin seeds, dry-roasted and ground
5–10ml/1–2 tsp Turkish red pepper, or 1–2 fresh red chillies, seeded and finely chopped, or 5ml/1 tsp chilli powder
1–2 garlic cloves (optional)
1 slice of day-old white bread, sprinkled with water and left for a few minutes, then squeezed dry
15–30ml/1–2 tbsp tomato purée (paste)
5–10ml/1–2 tsp granulated sugar
30ml/2 tbsp pomegranate syrup or juice of 1 lemon
120ml/4fl oz/½ cup olive or sunflower oil, plus extra for serving
salt and ground black pepper
a few sprigs of fresh flat leaf parsley, to garnish
strips of pitta bread, to serve

1 Using a mortar and pestle, pound the walnuts with the cumin seeds, red pepper or chilli and garlic (if using). Add the soaked bread and pound to a paste, then beat in the tomato purée, sugar and pomegranate syrup.

2 Now slowly drizzle in 120ml/4fl oz/½ cup oil, beating all the time until the paste is thick and light. Season with salt and pepper, and spoon into a bowl. Splash a little olive oil over the top to keep it moist, and garnish with parsley leaves. Serve at room temperature.

Feta and Roast Pepper Dip with Chillies

This is a familiar meze in Greece, called *htipiti* and often served as a snack with a glass of ouzo. Its Greek name means "that which is beaten" and it has a tart, spicy flavour. If you chill the mixture before serving the texture will become firmer.

Serves 4

1 yellow or green elongated or bell-shaped pepper
1–2 fresh green chillies
200g/7oz feta cheese, cubed
60ml/4 tbsp extra virgin olive oil
juice of 1 lemon
45–60ml/3–4 tbsp milk
ground black pepper
finely chopped fresh flat leaf parsley, to garnish
slices of toast or toasted pitta bread, to serve

1 Scorch the pepper and chillies by threading them on to metal skewers and turning them over a flame or under the grill (broiler), until blackened and blistered all over.

2 Put the pepper and chillies into a plastic bag to loosen the skin and set aside until cool enough to handle.

3 Peel off as much of the skins as possible and wipe off the blackened parts with kitchen paper. Slit the pepper and chillies and discard the seeds and stems.

4 Put the pepper and chilli flesh into a food processor. Add the feta cheese, olive oil, lemon juice and milk, and blend well. Add a little more milk if the mixture is too stiff, and season with black pepper. Spread the dip on slices of toast, sprinkle a little fresh parsley over the top and serve.

> **Variation**
> *The dip is also excellent served with a selection of vegetable crudités, such as carrot, cauliflower, green or red (bell) pepper and celery.*

Spicy Walnut Dip: Energy 339kcal/1399kJ; Protein 4.8g; Carbohydrate 5.1g, of which sugars 2.8g; Fat 33.4g, of which saturates 3.5g; Cholesterol 0mg; Calcium 34mg; Fibre 1.2g; Sodium 32mg.
Roast Pepper Dip: Energy 245Kcal/1,014kJ; Protein 8.7g; Carbohydrate 4.5g, of which sugars 4.3g; Fat 21.5g, of which saturates 8.6g; Cholesterol 36mg; Calcium 198mg; Fibre 0.8g; Sodium 727mg.

Tzatsiki with Courgettes and Aubergines

Tzatsiki is a cool dip made with yogurt, cucumber and mint, which is extremely well suited to the heat of the summer. It can be served with chopped raw vegetables such as carrots or (bell) peppers, but is also perfect with freshly fried slices of courgettes and aubergines.

Serves 4
3 courgettes (zucchini)
1 aubergine (eggplant)
25g/1oz/¼ cup plain
   (all-purpose) flour
sunflower oil, for frying
salt and ground black pepper

For the tzatsiki
15cm/6in piece of cucumber
200g/7oz Greek (US strained
   plain) yogurt
1 or 2 garlic cloves, crushed
15ml/1 tbsp extra virgin olive oil
30ml/2 tbsp thinly sliced
   fresh mint leaves, plus extra
   to garnish

1 Start by making the tzatsiki. Peel the cucumber, grate it coarsely into a colander, and press out most of the liquid. Add to the yogurt with the garlic, olive oil and mint. Stir in salt to taste, cover and chill.

2 Trim the courgettes and aubergine, rinse and pat dry. Cut them lengthways into long, thin slices and coat lightly with flour.

3 Heat the oil in a large frying pan and add as many courgette slices as it will hold in one layer. Cook for 1–2 minutes, then turn over and brown the other side. Lift the slices out, drain them on kitchen paper and keep them hot while cooking the remaining courgettes and then the aubergines.

4 Pile the fried slices in a warmed bowl, season and serve immediately with the chilled tzatsiki garnished with mint leaves.

Cook's Tip
If you are making the tzatsiki several hours before serving, don't add the salt until later, as it will make the yogurt watery.

Salad of Puréed Aubergines

In the heat of high summer, *melitzanosalata* makes a surprisingly refreshing meze. To be strictly authentic, the aubergines should be grilled over charcoal, but baking them gives a very satisfactory result.

Serves 4
3 large aubergines (eggplants),
   total weight about 900g/2lb
15ml/1 tbsp chopped onion
2 garlic cloves, crushed
juice of ½ lemon, or a little more
90–105ml/6–7 tbsp extra virgin
   olive oil
1 ripe tomato, peeled, seeded and
   finely diced
salt and ground black pepper
finely chopped fresh flat leaf
   parsley, to garnish
chicory (Belgian endive), and black
   and green olives, to serve

1 Preheat the oven to 180°C/350°F/Gas 4. Prick the aubergines and lay them directly on the oven shelves. Roast them for 1 hour, or until soft, turning them over twice.

2 When the aubergines are cool enough to handle, cut them in half. Spoon the flesh into a food processor and add the onion, garlic and lemon juice. Season with salt and ground black pepper and process until smooth.

3 With the processor motor running, gradually drizzle in the olive oil through the feeder tube, until the mixture forms a smooth, light paste. Taste the mixture and adjust the seasoning if necessary, then spoon the purée into a bowl and stir in the diced tomato.

4 Cover and chill for 1 hour before serving. Garnish with chopped fresh flat leaf parsley and serve with fresh, washed chicory leaves and bowls of black and green olives.

Cook's Tip
If you wish to barbecue the aubergines instead of using the oven, prick them and barbecue over a low to medium heat for at least 1 hour.

Tzatsiki: Energy 247Kcal/1,020kJ; Protein 7.6g; Carbohydrate 11g, of which sugars 5.5g; Fat 19.9g, of which saturates 4.6g; Cholesterol 0mg; Calcium 149mg; Fibre 3.2g; Sodium 41mg.
Puréed Aubergines: Energy 190Kcal/788kJ; Protein 2.3g; Carbohydrate 6.7g, of which sugars 5.9g; Fat 17.5g, of which saturates 2.6g; Cholesterol 0mg; Calcium 28mg; Fibre 4.9g; Sodium 7mg.

Cannellini Bean Purée with Grilled Chicory

The slightly bitter flavours of chicory and radicchio make a wonderful marriage with the creamy bean purée to create this low-fat appetizer or snack.

Serves 4
400g/14oz can cannellini beans
45ml/3 tbsp sour cream

finely grated rind and juice of
  1 large orange
15ml/1 tbsp finely chopped
  fresh rosemary
4 heads of chicory
  (Belgian endive)
2 heads of radicchio
10ml/2 tsp walnut oil
longer shreds of orange rind, to
  garnish (optional)

1 Drain the beans, then rinse and drain them again. Place the beans in a blender or food processor with the sour cream, orange rind and juice and chopped rosemary and process until smooth and well mixed. Set aside.

2 Cut the heads of the chicory in half lengthways. Cut each radicchio head into 8 even wedges using a sharp knife. Preheat the grill (broiler) to medium.

3 Lay the chicory and radicchio on a baking sheet and brush lightly with the walnut oil. Grill (broil) for 2–3 minutes. Serve with the bean purée and garnish with orange shreds, if using.

> **Variation**
> Serve the dip with olives and pitta or as part of a meze table.

> **Cook's Tip**
> The dip can be made using dried cannellini beans, which must first be soaked in cold water for 5–6 hours. Place the drained beans in a pan, cover with fresh water and boil briskly for 10 minutes, then lower the heat and simmer for 1–1½ hours until tender. Drain and cool a little before puréeing.

Hummus

This classic chickpea dip from the eastern Mediterranean is a firm favourite everywhere. It is flavoured with garlic and tahini – sesame seed paste. For extra flavour, a little ground cumin can be added, and olive oil can also be stirred in to enrich the hummus, if you like. It is lovely served with wedges of toasted pitta or with crudités as a delicious dip.

Serves 4-6
400g/14oz can chickpeas,
  drained
60ml/4 tbsp tahini
2–3 garlic cloves, chopped
juice of ½–1 lemon
salt and ground black pepper
a few whole chickpeas reserved,
  to garnish

1 Reserving a few for garnish, coarsely mash the chickpeas in a mixing bowl with a fork. If you like a smoother purée, process the chickpeas in a food processor or blender until a smooth paste is formed.

2 Mix the tahini into the bowl of chickpeas, then stir in the chopped garlic cloves and lemon juice. Season to taste and garnish the top with the reserved chickpeas. Serve the hummus at room temperature.

> **Variations**
> • Process 2 roasted red (bell) peppers with the chickpeas, then continue as above. Serve sprinkled with lightly toasted pine nuts and paprika mixed with a little extra virgin olive oil.
> • Add a pinch of cayenne to the mixture.
> • Instead of chickpeas, top with a drizzle of olive oil and a dusting of paprika.

> **Cook's Tip**
> Add more lemon juice to taste if necessary when seasoning.

Purée: Energy 129kcal/542kJ; Protein 6.8g; Carbohydrate 17.3g, of which sugars 3.3g; Fat 4.9g, of which saturates 1.9g; Cholesterol 7mg; Calcium 48mg; Fibre 5.5g; Sodium 427mg.
Hummus: Energy 210Kcal/880kJ; Protein 10.3g; Carbohydrate 16.9g, of which sugars 0.6g; Fat 11.8g, of which saturates 1.6g; Cholesterol 0mg; Calcium 146mg; Fibre 5.5g; Sodium 223mg.

Fresh Vegetable Medley

This Turkish meze dish is a refreshing and colourful mixture of chopped fresh vegetables. Along with cubes of honey-sweet melon and feta, or plump, juicy olives spiked with red pepper and oregano, this is meze at its simplest and best. Popular in kebab houses, it dish makes a tasty snack or appetizer, and is good served with chunks of warm, crusty bread or toasted pitta.

Serves 4
2 large tomatoes, skinned,
    seeded and finely
    chopped
2 Turkish green peppers
    or 1 green (bell) pepper,
    finely chopped
1 onion, finely chopped
1 green chilli, seeded and
    finely chopped
1 small bunch of fresh flat leaf
    parsley, finely chopped
a few fresh mint leaves,
    finely chopped
15–30ml/1–2 tbsp olive oil
salt and ground black pepper

1 Put all the finely chopped ingredients in a bowl and mix well together.

2 Toss the mixture with the olive oil to bind the ingredients, and season to taste with salt and pepper.

3 Leave the dish to sit for a short time for the flavours to blend. Serve at room temperature, in individual bowls or one large dish.

Variations
• The salad can be turned into a paste. When you bind the chopped vegetables with the olive oil, add 15–30ml/1–2 tbsp tomato purée (paste) with a little extra chilli and 5–10ml/1–2 tsp sugar. The mixture will become a tangy paste to spread on fresh, crusty bread or toasted pitta, and it can also be used as a sauce for simple pasta or rice dishes.
• Try adding different herbs to the mixture, such as basil, and other salad vegetables, such as chopped cucumber and spring onions (scallions).

Pea Purée

This fresh-tasting spicy dip is similar to guacamole, but uses peas as a main ingredient instead of avocado. It's a really unusual dip to serve as tapas. Serve with crisp fruit and vegetable crudités.

Serves 6
350g/12oz/3 cups frozen
    peas, thawed
1 garlic clove, crushed
2 spring onions (scallions),
    trimmed and chopped
5ml/1 tsp finely grated lime rind
juice of 1 lime

2.5ml/½ tsp ground cumin
dash of Tabasco sauce
15ml/1 tbsp reduced-calorie
    mayonnaise
30ml/2 tbsp chopped fresh
    coriander (cilantro)
salt and ground black pepper
pinch of paprika and lime slices,
    to garnish

For the crudités
6 baby carrots
2 celery sticks
1 red-skinned eating apple
1 pear
15ml/1 tbsp lemon or lime juice
6 baby corn

1 Put the peas, garlic clove, spring onions, lime rind and juice, cumin, Tabasco sauce, mayonnaise and salt and ground black pepper in a blender or food processor and process for a few minuts, or until smooth.

2 Add the chopped fresh coriander and process for a further few seconds. Carefully spoon all of the mixture into a small serving bowl, cover with clear film (plastic wrap) and refrigerate for 30 minutes, to let the flavours develop.

3 Meanwhile, prepare the crudités. Trim and peel the carrots, cut in half, then quarter lengthways. Halve the celery sticks lengthways and trim into sticks the same length as the carrots. Quarter, core and thickly slice the apple and pear, then dip the slices into the lemon or lime juice to prevent any discolouration.

4 Arrange the crudités with the baby corn on a serving platter. Remove the pea purée from the refrigerator and place on the serving platter. Sprinkle a little paprika over the top of the purée and serve garnished with slices of fresh lime.

Fresh Vegetable Medley: Energy 101kcal/420kJ; Protein 2.3g; Carbohydrate 9.3g, of which sugars 8g; Fat 6.3g, of which saturates 0.9g; Cholesterol 0mg; Calcium 66mg; Fibre 2.7g; Sodium 15mg.
Pea Purée: Energy 93kcal/386kJ; Protein 5.2g; Carbohydrate 14.7g, of which sugars 9g; Fat 1.9g, of which saturates 0.3g; Cholesterol 1mg; Calcium 41mg; Fibre 5.1g; Sodium 232mg.

Carrot and Caraway Purée

Long, thin carrots that are orange, yellow, red and purple are a colourful feature in vegetable markets throughout Turkey. Used mainly in salads, lentil dishes and stews, they are also married with garlic-flavoured yogurt for meze – sliced and deep-fried, drizzled with yogurt, grated and folded in, or steamed and puréed, then served with the yogurt in the middle, as in this recipe. Try serving the carrot purée while it is still warm, with chunks of crusty bread or warm pitta to scoop it up.

Serves 4
6 large carrots, thickly sliced
5ml/1 tsp caraway seeds
30–45ml/2–3 tbsp olive oil
juice of 1 lemon
225g/8oz/1 cup thick natural
  (plain) yogurt
1–2 garlic cloves, crushed
salt and ground black pepper
a few fresh mint leaves,
  to garnish

1 Steam the carrots for about 25 minutes, until they are very soft. While they are still warm, mash them to a smooth purée, or whizz them in a blender.

2 Beat the caraway seeds into the carrot purée, followed by the oil and lemon juice. Season to taste with salt and ground black pepper.

3 In a separate bowl, beat the yogurt with the garlic and season with salt and pepper.

4 Spoon the warm carrot purée around the edge of a serving dish, or pile into a mound and make a well in the middle. Spoon the yogurt into the middle, and garnish with mint.

> **Cook's Tip**
> It is always better to steam, rather than boil, vegetables, so that they retain more of their taste, texture and goodness. This purée would not taste nearly as good if the carrots were boiled and watery.

Sesame and Lemon Dip

This delightful little dip comes from Turkey, where it is often served in outdoor cafés and restaurants as a meze dish on its own – a sort of whetting of the appetite while you wait for the assortment of exciting dishes to come. Sometimes you will see groups of old men drinking rakı or refreshing tea, sharing a plate of *tahin tarama* or a bowl of roasted chickpeas while they play cards or backgammon. The dip is sweet and tangy, and is delicious mopped up with chunks of crusty bread or toasted pitta bread.

Serves 2
45ml/3 tbsp light sesame
  paste (tahin)
juice of 1 lemon
15–30ml/1–2 tbsp clear
  honey
5–10ml/1–2 tsp dried mint
lemon wedges, to serve

1 Beat the sesame paste and lemon juice together in a bowl.

2 Add the honey and mint and beat again until thick and creamy, then spoon into a small dish.

3 Serve at room temperature, with lemon wedges for squeezing.

> **Cook's Tip**
> Tahin or tahini, made from ground sesame seeds, is available "hulled" or "unhulled". The latter is made with the whole seed and is more nutritious, but can be bitter.

> **Variation**
> Popular in Turkey for breakfast or as a sweet snack is tahin pekmez. Combine 30–45ml/2–3 tbsp tahini with 30ml/2 tbsp grape molasses (pekmez) to form a sweet paste, then scoop it up with chunks of bread. If you can't find pekmez, substitute date syrup, from Middle Eastern and health food stores.

Carrot Purée: Energy 157Kcal/651kJ; Protein 4.2g; Carbohydrate 15.3g, of which sugars 13.6g; Fat 9.2g, of which saturates 1.6g; Cholesterol 1mg; Calcium 140mg; Fibre 3.3g; Sodium 78mg.
Sesame and Lemon Dip: Energy 160kcal/664kJ; Protein 4.3g; Carbohydrate 6.4g, of which sugars 6.2g; Fat 13.3g, of which saturates 1.9g; Cholesterol 0mg; Calcium 155mg; Fibre 1.8g; Sodium 6mg.

Gazpacho

This classic chilled Spanish soup is deeply rooted in Andalusia. The soothing blend of tomatoes, sweet peppers and garlic is sharpened with sherry vinegar, and enriched with olive oil. Serving it with a selection of of garnishes has virtually become a tradition. In Spain, very ripe tomatoes are used: if necessary, add a pinch of sugar to sweeten the soup slightly.

Serves 4

1.3–1.6kg/3–3½lb ripe tomatoes
1 green (bell) pepper,
   roughly chopped
2 garlic cloves, finely chopped
2 slices stale bread,
   crusts removed
60ml/4 tbsp extra virgin olive oil
60ml/4 tbsp sherry vinegar
150ml/¼ pint/⅔ cup
   tomato juice
300ml/½ pint/1¼ cups
   iced water
salt and ground black pepper
ice cubes, to serve (optional)

For the garnishes

30ml/2 tbsp olive oil
2–3 slices stale bread, diced
1 small cucumber, peeled and
   finely diced
1 small onion, finely chopped
1 red (bell) and 1 green (bell)
   pepper, finely diced
2 hard-boiled eggs, chopped

1 Skin the tomatoes, then quarter them and remove the cores and seeds, saving the juices. Put the pepper in a food processor and process for a few seconds. Add the tomatoes, reserved juices, garlic, bread, oil and vinegar and process. Add the tomato juice and blend to combine.

2 Season the soup, then pour into a large bowl, cover with clear film (plastic wrap) and chill for at least 12 hours.

3 Prepare the garnishes. Heat the olive oil in a frying pan and fry the bread cubes for 4–5 minutes until golden brown and crisp. Drain well on kitchen paper, then arrange in a small dish. Place each of the remaining garnishes in separate small dishes.

4 Just before serving, dilute the soup with the ice-cold water. The consistency should be thick but not too stodgy. If you like, stir a few ice cubes into the soup, then spoon into serving bowls and serve with the garnishes.

Chilled Avocado Soup with Cumin

Andalusia in Spain is home to both avocados and gazpacho, so it is not surprising that this chilled avocado soup, also known as green gazpacho, was invented there.

Serves 4

3 ripe avocados
1 bunch spring onions (scallions),
   white parts only, trimmed and
   roughly chopped
2 garlic cloves, chopped
juice of 1 lemon
1.5ml/¼ tsp ground cumin
1.5ml/¼ tsp paprika
450ml/¾ pint/scant 2 cups
   vegetable stock
300ml/½ pint/1¼ cups iced
   water
salt and freshly ground black
   pepper
roughly chopped fresh flat leaf
   parsley, to serve

1 Starting several hours ahead, put the flesh of one avocado in a food processor or blender. Add the spring onions, garlic and lemon juice and purée until smooth.

2 Add the second avocado and purée, then the third, with the spices and seasoning. Purée until smooth.

3 Gradually add the vegetable stock. Pour the soup into a metal bowl and chill.

4 To serve, stir in the iced water, then season to taste with plenty of salt and black pepper. Garnish with chopped parsley and serve immediately.

Cook's Tips

- *Hass avocados, with bumpy skin that turns purplish black when ripe, generally have the best flavour. They should be perfectly ripe for this recipe.*
- *Avocado flesh blackens when exposed to air, but the lemon juice in this recipe preserves the colour of the soup.*

Gazpacho: Energy 356kcal/1494kJ; Protein 7.6g; Carbohydrate 41.9g, of which sugars 21.5g; Fat 18.8g, of which saturates 2.9g; Cholesterol 0mg; Calcium 90mg; Fibre 6.7g; Sodium 346mg.
Avocado Soup: Energy 151kcal/623kJ; Protein 2.1g; Carbohydrate 2.6g, of which sugars 1.1g; Fat 14.6g, of which saturates 3.1g; Cholesterol 0mg; Calcium 19mg; Fibre 3g; Sodium 6mg.

Yogurt and Cucumber Soup

Yogurt is frequently used in Greek cookery, and it is usually made at home. Sometimes it is added at the end of cooking a dish, to prevent it from curdling, but in this cold soup the yogurt is one of the basic ingredients. It makes a cool and refreshing first course for a hot summer's day.

Serves 4

1 large cucumber
300ml/½ pint/1¼ cups single
 (light) cream
150ml/¼ pint/⅔ cup natural
 (plain) yogurt
2 garlic cloves, crushed
30ml/2 tbsp white wine vinegar
15ml/1 tbsp chopped fresh mint
salt and ground black pepper
4 sprigs of fresh mint,
 to garnish

1 Peel the cucumber and grate coarsely. This can be done in a food processor or blender, or you can do it by hand using the coarse side of a grater.

2 Place the cream, yogurt, garlic, vinegar and chopped mint in a large bowl. Add the grated cucumber and stir well to mix. Season to taste.

3 Put the soup in the refrigerator and allow to chill for at least 2 hours. Stir well before serving in individual bowls, garnished with the sprigs of mint.

> **Variation**
> *Mint is the traditional herb used to flavour this classic dish, but other fresh herbs such as dill, parsley, basil or lemon thyme would also work well.*

> **Cook's Tips**
> • *In Greece, a rich and creamy yogurt is made from sheep's milk. This soup is equally good made with low-fat or whole milk varieties of yogurt.*
> • *If the soup is too thick, you can thin it by adding a little milk.*

Chilled Almond Soup with Grapes

Called *ajo blanco* – white garlic soup – this is a Moorish recipe of ancient origin. It is a perfect balance of crushed almonds, garlic and vinegar in a smooth purée enriched with oil.

Serves 6
115g/4oz stale white bread
115g/4oz/1 cup blanched
 almonds

2 garlic cloves, sliced
75ml/5 tbsp olive oil
25ml/1½ tbsp sherry vinegar
salt and ground black pepper

For the garnish
toasted flaked almonds
green and black grapes,
 halved and seeded
chopped fresh chives

1 Break the bread into a bowl and pour in 150ml/¼ pint/⅔ cup cold water. Leave to soak for about 5 minutes, then squeeze the bread dry.

2 Put the almonds and garlic in a food processor or blender and process until very finely ground. Add the soaked white bread and process again until thoroughly combined.

3 Continue to process, gradually adding the oil until the mixture forms a smooth paste. Add the sherry vinegar, followed by 600ml/1 pint/2½ cups cold water and process until the mixture is smooth.

4 Transfer the soup to a bowl and season with salt and pepper, adding a little more water if the soup is very thick. Cover with clear film (plastic wrap) and chill for 2 hours or more.

5 Ladle the soup into bowls. Scatter the almonds, halved grapes and chopped chives over to garnish.

> **Cook's Tip**
> *To accentuate the flavour of the almonds, dry-roast them in a frying pan until they are lightly browned before grinding them. This will produce a slightly darker soup.*

Yogurt and Cucumber Soup: Energy 77kcal/322kJ; Protein 6.9g; Carbohydrate 10.3g, of which sugars 10.1g; Fat 1.3g, of which saturates 0.6g; Cholesterol 2mg; Calcium 255mg; Fibre 0.3g; Sodium 106mg.
Almond Soup: Energy 165kcal/683kJ; Protein 3.9g; Carbohydrate 7.4g, of which sugars 0.9g; Fat 13.5g, of which saturates 1.5g; Cholesterol 0mg; Calcium 45mg; Fibre 1.2g; Sodium 68mg.

Leek Soup with Feta, Dill and Paprika

Creamy leek soup is a popular home-cooked dish in Turkey. Flavoured with dill and topped with crumbled white cheese, this one is warming and satisfying. The saltiness of feta is good in this soup, but you could just as well use Roquefort or Parmesan, both of which are equally salty, and you could substitute croûtons for the cheese. Serve with chunks of fresh, crusty bread.

Serves 3–4

30ml/2 tbsp olive or sunflower oil
3 leeks, trimmed, roughly chopped and washed
1 onion, chopped
5ml/1 tsp sugar
1 bunch of fresh dill, chopped, with a few fronds reserved for the garnish
300ml/½ pint/1¼ cups milk
15ml/1 tbsp butter (optional)
115g/4oz feta cheese, crumbled
salt and ground black pepper
paprika, to garnish

1 Heat the oil in a heavy pan and stir in the chopped leeks and onion. Cook for about 10 minutes, or until the vegetables are soft but not coloured.

2 Add the sugar and dill, and pour in 600ml/1 pint/2½ cups water. Bring to the boil, lower the heat and simmer for about 15 minutes.

3 Leave the liquid to cool a little, then process in a blender until smooth.

4 Return the puréed soup to the pan, pour in the milk and stir over a gentle heat until it is hot (don't let it come to the boil or the texture will be spoiled).

5 Season with salt and pepper, bearing in mind that the feta is salty. If using the butter, drop it onto the surface of the soup and let it melt.

6 Ladle the soup into warmed bowls and top with the crumbled feta. Serve immediately, garnished with a little paprika and the dill fronds.

Broad Bean and Potato Soup

In Spain, *habas* are fresh broad beans, and are a great deal nicer than the dried variety, known as *favas*. The latter word has now vanished from the Spanish dictionary and the rather indigestible dried bean has all but disappeared from Spanish cookery as well. This fresh soup uses a modern herb, too – coriander is not a common Spanish ingredient, but it adds a delicious flavour.

Serves 4

30ml/2 tbsp olive oil
2 onions, chopped
3 large floury potatoes, peeled and diced
450g/1lb fresh shelled broad (fava) beans
1.75 litres/3 pints/7½ cups vegetable stock
1 bunch fresh coriander (cilantro), roughly chopped
150ml/¼ pint/⅔ cup single (light) cream, plus a little extra, to garnish
salt and ground black pepper

1 Heat the oil in a large pan and fry the onions, stirring, for 5 minutes until soft.

2 Add the potatoes, most of the beans (reserving a few to garnish the soup) and the stock, and bring to the boil. Simmer for 5 minutes, then add the coriander and simmer for a further 10 minutes.

3 Blend the soup in batches in a food processor or blender, then return to the rinsed pan.

4 Stir in the cream, season, and bring to a simmer. Serve garnished with coriander, beans and cream.

Cook's Tip
The broad bean is the native European bean, and was an important staple food for centuries before the arrival of the haricot bean from America. Very young broad beans are often eaten raw, especially in Italy. It would be best to make this soup in early summer before the beans toughen and get over-large, but you could alternatively use frozen beans.

Leek Soup: Energy 203kcal/844kJ; Protein 10g; Carbohydrate 10.9g, of which sugars 9.4g; Fat 13.5g, of which saturates 5.7g; Cholesterol 25mg; Calcium 259mg; Fibre 4.1g; Sodium 454mg.
Broad Bean Soup: Energy 263kcal/1113kJ; Protein 13.9g; Carbohydrate 47g, of which sugars 10.8g; Fat 3.5g, of which saturates 0.9g; Cholesterol 2mg; Calcium 142mg; Fibre 10.2g; Sodium 45mg.

Italian Cavolo Nero and Bean Soup

Cavolo nero is a dark green cabbage with a nutty flavour, which comes from southern Italy. It is ideal for this traditional recipe. It is available in most large supermarkets, but if you can't get it, use Savoy cabbage instead.

Serves 4

2 × 400g/14oz cans chopped
    tomatoes with herbs
250g/9oz cavolo nero leaves,
    rinsed and drained
400g/14oz can cannellini beans
20ml/4 tsp extra virgin olive oil
salt and ground black pepper

1 Pour the chopped tomatoes into a large pan and add a can of cold water. Season with salt and pepper and bring to the boil, then reduce the heat to a simmer.

2 Roughly shred the cabbage leaves and add them to the pan. Partially cover the pan and simmer gently, stirring occasionally, for about 15 minutes, or until the cabbage is tender.

3 Drain and rinse the cannellini beans, add to the pan and warm through for a few minutes.

4 Check and adjust the seasoning, then ladle the soup into warmed bowls. Drizzle each portion with a little olive oil and serve immediately.

> **Cook's Tip**
> Canned cannellini beans are very convenient, but for added flavour and texture, use dried cannellini beans. To prepare dried beans, place in a bowl, cover with plenty of cold water and allow to soak for at least 5 hours (the beans will expand, so make sure your bowl is large enough). Drain and rinse, then place in a large pan, cover with cold water, bring to the boil, scoop off any foam, then boil for a further 10 minutes. Scoop the foam off again, then add a pinch of salt. Partially cover and simmer gently for about 1 hour, until tender. Top up the water level if necessary.

Pasta, Bean and Vegetable Soup

This is a Calabrian speciality and by tradition anything edible can go into it: use whatever beans and vegetables are to hand.

Serves 6

75g/3oz/scant 1/2 cup dried
    brown lentils
15g/1/2oz/1/4 cup dried
    mushrooms
15ml/1 tbsp olive oil
1 carrot, diced
1 celery stick, diced
1 onion, finely chopped
1 garlic clove, finely chopped
a little chopped fresh flat
    leaf parsley
a good pinch of crushed red
    chillies (optional)
1.5 litres/2 1/2 pints/6 1/4 cups
    vegetable stock
150g/5oz/1 cup each canned
    red kidney beans, cannellini
    beans and chickpeas, rinsed
    and drained
115g/4oz/1 cup dried small pasta
    shapes, such as rigatoni, penne
    or penne rigate
salt and ground black pepper
chopped flat leaf parsley, to
    garnish
freshly grated Pecorino cheese, to
    serve (optional)

1 Put the lentils in a pan, add 475ml/16fl oz/2 cups water and bring to the boil. Reduce the heat and simmer gently, stirring occasionally, for 15–20 minutes, or until tender. Soak the dried mushrooms in 175ml/6fl oz/3/4 cup warm water for 20 minutes.

2 Drain the lentils, then rinse under cold water. Drain the soaked mushrooms and reserve the soaking liquid. Finely chop the mushrooms and set aside.

3 Heat the oil in a large saucepan and add the carrot, celery, onion, garlic, chopped parsley and chillies, if using. Cook over a low heat, stirring constantly, for 5–7 minutes. Add the stock, then the mushrooms and their soaking liquid. Bring to the boil, then add the beans, chickpeas and lentils, with salt and pepper to taste. Cover, and simmer gently for 20 minutes.

4 Add the pasta and bring the soup back to the boil, stirring. Simmer, stirring frequently, for 7–8 minutes or until the pasta is al dente. Season, then serve hot in soup bowls, garnished with chopped parsley. Sprinkle with grated Pecorino, if you like.

Cabbage and Bean Soup: Energy 155kcal/655kJ; Protein 8.2g; Carbohydrate 22.3g, of which sugars 10.4g; Fat 4.2g, of which saturates 0.7g, Cholesterol 0mg; Calcium 60mg; Fibre 7.9g; Sodium 443mg.
Pasta Soup: Energy 206kcal/874kJ; Protein 10.7g; Carbohydrate 36.7g, of which sugars 5g; Fat 2.9g, of which saturates 0.4g, Cholesterol 0mg; Calcium 72mg; Fibre 6.4g; Sodium 306mg.

Spicy Red Lentil Soup

In Istanbul and Izmir, Turkish lentil soups are light and subtly spiced, and served as an appetizer or as a snack. In Anatolia, lentil and bean soups flavoured with tomato and spices are usually served as a meal on their own.

Serves 4–6
30–45ml/2–3 tbsp olive or
   sunflower oil
1 large onion, finely chopped
2 garlic cloves, finely chopped
1 fresh red chilli, seeded and
   finely chopped
5–10ml/1–2 tsp cumin seeds
5–10ml/1–2 tsp coriander seeds
1 carrot, finely chopped
scant 5ml/1 tsp ground fenugreek
5ml/1 tsp sugar
15ml/1 tbsp tomato purée
   (paste)
250g/9oz/generous 1 cup split
   red lentils
1.75 litres/3 pints/7½ cups
   vegetable stock
salt and ground black pepper

To serve
1 small red onion, finely chopped
1 large bunch of fresh flat leaf
   parsley, finely chopped
4–6 lemon wedges

1 Heat the oil in a heavy pan. Add the onion, garlic, chilli, cumin and coriander seeds and stir. When the onion begins to colour, toss in the carrot and cook for a further 2–3 minutes. Next add the fenugreek, sugar and tomato purée and stir in the lentils.

2 Pour in the stock, stir well and bring to the boil. Lower the heat, partially cover the pan and simmer for 30–40 minutes, until the lentils have broken up.

3 If the soup is too thick, thin it down with a little water. Season with salt and pepper to taste.

4 Serve the soup straight from the pan or, if you prefer a smooth texture, whizz it in a blender, then reheat if necessary.

5 Ladle the soup into individual serving bowls and sprinkle each one liberally with the chopped onion and chopped parsley. Serve with a wedge of lemon on the side to squeeze over the soup.

Cream of Courgette Soup

The colour of this soup is beautifully delicate, and really suits its rich and creamy texture and subtle taste. If you prefer a more pronounced cheese flavour, you can use Gorgonzola instead of Dolcelatte.

Serves 4–6
30ml/2 tbsp olive oil
15g/½oz/1 tbsp butter
1 medium onion, roughly chopped
900g/2lb courgettes (zucchini),
   trimmed and sliced
5ml/1tsp dried oregano
about 600ml/1 pint/2½ cups
   vegetable stock
115g/4oz Dolcelatte cheese, rind
   removed, diced
300ml/½ pint/1¼ cups single
   (light) cream
salt and freshly ground black
   pepper
fresh oregano and extra
   Dolcelatte, to garnish

1 Heat the oil and butter in a large saucepan until foaming. Add the onion and cook gently for about 5 minutes, stirring frequently, until softened but not brown.

2 Add the courgettes, oregano, and salt and pepper to taste. Cook over a medium heat for 10 minutes, stirring frequently.

3 Pour in the stock and bring to the boil, stirring. Lower the heat, half cover the pan and simmer gently, stirring occasionally, for about 30 minutes. Stir in the diced Dolcelatte until melted.

4 Process the soup in a blender or food processor until smooth, then press through a sieve into a clean pan.

5 Add two-thirds of the cream and stir over a low heat until hot, but not boiling. Check the consistency and add more stock if the soup is too thick. Taste for seasoning, then pour into heated bowls. Swirl in the remaining cream. Garnish with oregano and extra cheese and serve.

> **Cook's Tip**
> *To save time, trim off and discard the ends of the courgettes, cut them into thirds, then chop in a food processor.*

Spicy Lentil Soup: Energy 203kcal/856kJ; Protein 11.1g; Carbohydrate 31.8g, of which sugars 7.3g; Fat 4.4g, of which saturates 0.6g; Cholesterol 0mg; Calcium 45mg; Fibre 3.5g; Sodium 26mg.
Courgette Soup: Energy 248kcal/1024kJ; Protein 8.5g; Carbohydrate 5.4g, of which sugars 4.8g; Fat 21.5g, of which saturates 11.7g; Cholesterol 47mg; Calcium 181mg; Fibre 1.6g; Sodium 266mg.

Spicy Pumpkin Soup

Pumpkin is popular all over the Mediterranean and it's an important ingredient in Middle Eastern cooking. Ginger and cumin give the soup its spicy flavour.

Serves 4
900g/2lb pumpkin
10ml/2 tsp olive oil
2 leeks, trimmed and sliced
1 garlic clove, crushed
5ml/1 tsp ground ginger
5ml/1 tsp ground cumin
900ml/1½ pints/3¾ cups
    vegetable stock
salt and ground black pepper
fresh coriander (cilantro) leaves,
    to garnish
60ml/4 tbsp natural (plain)
    yogurt, to serve

1 With a sharp knife, carefully peel the pumpkin. Remove the seeds. Cut the pumpkin flesh into equally-sized chunks, about 2.5cm/1in.

2 Heat the oil in a large pan and add the leeks and garlic. Cook gently until softened.

3 Add the ginger and cumin and cook, stirring, for a further minute. Add the pumpkin chunks and the stock and season with salt and pepper.

4 Bring to the boil, then reduce the heat and simmer for about 30 minutes, or until the pumpkin is tender.

5 Allow to cool slightly, then process the soup, in batches if necessary, in a blender or food processor.

6 Gently reheat the soup in the rinsed out pan, then serve in warmed individual soup bowls, with a swirl of yogurt and a garnish of coriander leaves.

Cook's Tip
Pumpkin seeds are edible and highly nutritious. They make a delicious healthy snack, or sprinkle over soups and salads.

Sherried Onion Soup with Saffron

The Spanish combination of onions, sherry and saffron gives this soup a beguiling flavour that is perfect for the opening course of a meal. The addition of ground almonds to thicken the soup gives it a wonderful texture and flavour.

Serves 4
40g/1½ oz/3 tbsp butter
2 large yellow onions, thinly sliced
1 small garlic clove, chopped
pinch of saffron threads
50g/2oz blanched almonds,
    toasted and finely ground
750ml/1¼ pints/3 cups vegetable
    stock
45ml/3 tbsp fino sherry
2.5ml/½ tsp paprika
salt and ground black pepper

To garnish
30ml/2 tbsp flaked or slivered
    almonds, toasted
chopped fresh parsley

1 Melt the butter in a heavy pan over a low heat. Add the onions and garlic, stirring to ensure that they are thoroughly coated in the melted butter, then cover the pan and cook very gently, stirring frequently, for about 20 minutes, or until the onions are soft and golden yellow.

2 Add the saffron threads to the pan and cook, uncovered, for 3–4 minutes, then add the finely ground almonds and cook, stirring the ingredients constantly, for a further 2–3 minutes, until the almonds are golden.

3 Pour the vegetable stock and sherry into the pan and stir in 5ml/1 tsp salt and the paprika. Season with plenty of black pepper. Bring to the boil, then lower the heat and simmer gently for about 10 minutes.

4 Pour the soup into a food processor and process until smooth, then return it to the rinsed-out pan. Reheat slowly, stirring occasionally, without allowing the soup to boil. Taste for seasoning, adding more salt and pepper if required.

5 Ladle the soup into heated bowls, garnish with the toasted flaked or slivered almonds and a little chopped fresh parsley and serve immediately.

Pumpkin Soup: Energy 105kcal/441kJ; Protein 2.3g; Carbohydrate 12.5g, of which sugars 7.9g; Fat 3.6g, of which saturates 0.6g, Cholesterol 0mg; Calcium 27mg; Fibre 2.3g; Sodium 61mg.
Sherried Onion Soup: Energy 246kcal/1017kJ; Protein 5.5g; Carbohydrate 9.5g, of which sugars 6.7g; Fat 19.6g, of which saturates 6.1g; Cholesterol 21mg; Calcium 76mg; Fibre 2.9g; Sodium 68mg.

Garlic and Butternut Squash Soup

This is a richly flavoured soup, given bite by the spicy tomato salsa served with it. It makes a fabulous soup for an autumn lunch.

Serves 6

2 garlic bulbs, outer papery
  skin removed
a few fresh thyme sprigs
15ml/1 tbsp olive oil
1 large butternut squash, halved
2 onions, chopped
5ml/1 tsp ground coriander
1.2 litres/2 pints/5 cups
  vegetable stock
30–45ml/2–3 tbsp chopped fresh
  oregano or marjoram
salt and ground black pepper

For the salsa

4 large ripe tomatoes, halved
  and seeded
1 red (bell) pepper
1 large fresh red chilli, seeded
15ml/1 tbsp extra virgin olive oil
15ml/1 tbsp balsamic vinegar
pinch of caster (superfine) sugar

1 Preheat the oven to 220°C/425°F/Gas 7. Wrap the garlic bulbs in foil with the thyme and 7.5ml/1½ tsp of the oil. Put the parcel on a baking sheet with the squash and the tomatoes, pepper and fresh chilli for the salsa. Brush the squash with 10ml/2 tsp of the remaining oil.

2 Roast the vegetables for 25 minutes, then remove the tomatoes, pepper and chilli. Reduce the oven temperature to 190°C/375°F/Gas 5 and roast the squash and garlic for a further 20–25 minutes, or until tender.

3 Heat the remaining oil in a large non-stick pan and cook the onions and ground coriander gently for about 10 minutes.

4 Meanwhile, skin the pepper and chilli, then process them with the tomatoes and the oil for the salsa. Stir in the vinegar and seasoning to taste, adding a pinch of sugar if necessary.

5 Squeeze the roasted garlic out of its skin into the onions and add the squash, scooped out of its skin. Add the stock, season with salt and pepper, and simmer for 10 minutes. Stir in half the chopped fresh herbs then process or sieve (strain) the soup. Reheat and taste for seasoning. Serve in warmed bowls topped with a spoonful of salsa and sprinkled with the remaining herbs.

Roasted Pepper Soup

Grilling intensifies the flavour of sweet red and yellow peppers and helps this low-fat soup to keep its stunning colour and delicious flavour.

Serves 4

3 red (bell) peppers
1 yellow (bell) pepper
1 onion, chopped
1 garlic clove, crushed
750ml/1¼ pints/3 cups
  vegetable stock
15ml/1 tbsp plain
  (all-purpose) flour
salt and ground black pepper
red and yellow (bell) peppers,
  diced, to garnish

1 Preheat the grill (broiler) to high. Halve the peppers lengthways, then remove and discard their stalks, cores and seeds.

2 Line a grill (broiling) pan with foil and arrange the pepper halves skin side up in a single layer. Grill (broil) until the skins have blackened and blistered.

3 Transfer the peppers to a plastic bag and leave until cool, then peel away and discard the charred skins. Roughly chop the pepper flesh and set aside.

4 Put the onion, garlic clove and 150ml/¼ pint/⅔ cup stock into a large pan. Bring to the boil on a high heat and boil for about 5 minutes, or until the stock has reduced in volume. Reduce the heat and stir until the onion is softened and just beginning to colour.

5 Sprinkle the flour over the onion, then gradually stir in the remaining stock. Stir in the chopped, roasted pepper flesh and bring to the boil. Cover and simmer for a further 5 minutes.

6 Remove the pan from the heat and leave to cool slightly, then purée the mixture in a blender or food processor until smooth. Season to taste with salt and pepper. Return the soup to the pan and reheat gently until it is piping hot. Ladle into four soup bowls and garnish each with a sprinkling of diced peppers to serve.

Garlic and Squash Soup: Energy 238kcal/986kJ; Protein 2.9g; Carbohydrate 11.9g, of which sugars 10.3g; Fat 20.2g, of which saturates 3.1g; Cholesterol 0mg; Calcium 79mg; Fibre 4.1g; Sodium 11mg.
Pepper Soup: Energy 79kcal/330kJ; Protein 2.4g; Carbohydrate 16.3g, of which sugars 11.6g; Fat 0.8g, of which saturates 0.2g; Cholesterol 0mg; Calcium 25mg; Fibre 3.2g; Sodium 8mg.

Tomato and Fresh Basil Soup

This is a good soup to make in late summer, when wonderful fresh tomatoes are at their most flavoursome and abundant.

Serves 4–6
15ml/1 tbsp olive oil
25g/1oz/2 tbsp butter
1 medium onion, finely chopped
900g/2lb ripe Italian plum
  tomatoes, roughly chopped
1 garlic clove, roughly chopped

750 ml/1¼ pints/3 cups
  vegetable stock
120ml/4fl oz/½ cup dry
  white wine
30ml/2 tbsp sun-dried
  tomato paste
30ml/2 tbsp shredded fresh
  basil, plus a few whole leaves,
  to garnish
150ml/¼ pint/⅔ cup double
  (heavy) cream
salt and ground black pepper

1 Heat the oil and butter together in a large saucepan until the butter starts to foam. Add the chopped onion and cook gently for about 5 minutes, stirring frequently, until softened but not beginning to brown.

2 Stir in the chopped tomatoes and garlic, then add the stock, white wine and sun-dried tomato paste, with salt and pepper to taste. Bring to the boil, then lower the heat, half cover the pan and simmer gently for 20 minutes, stirring occasionally to stop the tomatoes sticking to the base of the pan.

3 Process the soup with the basil in a blender or food processor, then press through a sieve (strainer) into a clean pan.

4 Add the double cream and heat through, stirring. Do not allow the soup to approach boiling point. Check the consistency and add more stock if necessary and then taste for seasoning. Pour into heated bowls and garnish with a few sprigs of fresh basil.

Variation
The soup can also be served chilled. Pour it into a container after sieving and chill for at least 4 hours. Serve in chilled bowls.

Summer Tomato Soup

The success of this soup depends on having really ripe, full-flavoured tomatoes, such as the oval plum variety, so make it when the tomato season is at its peak.

Serves 4
15ml/1 tbsp olive oil
1 large onion, chopped
1 carrot, chopped
1kg/2¼lb ripe tomatoes, cored
  and quartered

2 garlic cloves, chopped
5 thyme sprigs, or 1.5ml/¼ tsp
  dried thyme
4–5 marjoram sprigs, or
  1.5ml/¼ tsp dried marjoram
1 bay leaf
45ml/3 tbsp crème fraîche, sour
  cream or yogurt, plus a little
  extra to garnish
salt and ground black pepper

1 Heat the olive oil in a large, preferably stainless-steel, pan or flameproof casserole.

2 Add the onion and carrot and cook over a medium heat for 3–4 minutes, until just softened, stirring occasionally.

3 Add the tomatoes, garlic and herbs. Reduce the heat and simmer, covered, for 30 minutes.

4 Pass the soup through a food mill or press through a sieve (strainer) into the pan. Stir in the cream or yogurt and season. Reheat gently and serve with a spoonful of cream or yogurt and a sprig of marjoram.

Variation
This soup is also delicious served cold. Make it a few hours in advance, omitting the cream or yogurt, and cool, then chill.

Cook's Tip
Plum tomatoes have relatively few seeds, firm flesh and an intense flavour, making them the best type for cooking.

Summer Tomato Soup: Energy 138kcal/576kJ; Protein 3g; Carbohydrate 13.7g, of which sugars 12.4g; Fat 8.3g, of which saturates 3.7g; Cholesterol 13mg; Calcium 61mg; Fibre 4.2g; Sodium 35mg.
Tomato and Basil Soup: Energy 97kcal/409kJ; Protein 2.4g; Carbohydrate 9.6g, of which sugars 9.2g; Fat 3.7g, of which saturates 1.4g; Cholesterol 4mg; Calcium 32mg; Fibre 2.7g; Sodium 42mg.10mg.

Wild Mushroom Soup

In France, many people pick their own wild mushrooms, taking them to a pharmacy to be checked before using them. Dried mushrooms add an earthy flavour to this soup, but use 175g/6oz fresh wild mushrooms instead when available.

Serves 6–8

25g/1oz dried wild mushrooms, such as morels, ceps or porcini
1.5 litres/2½ pints/6 cups vegetable stock
25g/1oz/2 tbsp butter
2 onions, coarsely chopped
2 garlic cloves, chopped
900g/2lb button or other cultivated mushrooms, trimmed and sliced
2.5ml/½ tsp dried thyme
1.5ml/¼ tsp freshly grated nutmeg
30–45ml/2–3 tbsp plain (all-purpose) flour
125ml/4fl oz/½ cup Madeira or dry sherry
125ml/4fl oz/½ cup crème fraîche or sour cream
salt and ground black pepper
chopped fresh chives, to garnish

1 Put the dried mushrooms in a sieve (strainer) and rinse them well under cold running water. Place them in a pan with 250ml/8fl oz/1 cup of the stock and bring to the boil. Remove the pan from the heat and set aside for 30–40 minutes to soak.

2 Meanwhile, in a large, heavy pan, melt the butter over a medium-high heat. Add the onions and cook for 5–7 minutes until they are softened and just golden. Stir in the garlic and fresh mushrooms and cook for 4–5 minutes until they begin to soften, then add the salt and pepper, thyme and nutmeg and sprinkle over the flour. Cook for 3–5 minutes, stirring frequently.

3 Add the Madeira or sherry, the remaining vegetable stock, the dried mushrooms and their soaking liquid and cook, covered, over a medium heat for 30–40 minutes until the mushrooms are very tender.

4 Purée the soup in batches in a blender or food processor. Strain it back into the pan, pressing firmly to force the purée through. Stir in the crème fraîche or soured cream and sprinkle with the chopped chives just before serving.

Spanish Potato and Garlic Soup

Served in earthenware dishes, this creamy soup is a classic Spanish dish that really is one to savour.

Serves 6

15ml/1 tbsp olive oil
1 large onion, thinly sliced
4 garlic cloves, crushed
1 large potato
5ml/1 tsp paprika
400g/14oz can chopped tomatoes, drained
5ml/1 tsp chopped fresh thyme leaves
900ml/1½ pints/3¾ cups vegetable stock
5ml/1 tsp cornflour (cornstarch)
salt and freshly ground black pepper
chopped fresh thyme leaves, to garnish

1 With a sharp knife, cut the potato in half, then into thin slices. Heat the oil in a large pan.

2 Add the sliced onions, crushed garlic, potato slices and paprika to the pan and cook gently for 5 minutes, or until the onions are softened, but not browned.

3 Add the chopped tomatoes, thyme and vegetable stock. Bring to the boil, reduce the heat and simmer for 15–20 minutes until the potatoes are tender.

4 Blend the cornflour with a little water in a small bowl to form a paste, then stir into the soup. Simmer for 5 minutes, stirring, until the soup is thickened.

5 Break the potatoes up slightly with a fork. Season to taste. Transfer to individual serving bowls. Sprinkle each bowl with the chopped thyme leaves to garnish.

Cook's Tip

Potatoes are high in complex carbohydrates and include both protein and fibre. Main crop potatoes, such as Estima and Maris Piper are good choices to use in this soup. Discard any potatoes with green patches as these indicate the presence of toxic alkaloids called solamines.

Wild Mushroom Soup: Energy 153kcal/638kJ; Protein 3.2g; Carbohydrate 9.3g, of which sugars 0.5g; Fat 11.8g, of which saturates 7.2g; Cholesterol 29mg; Calcium 26mg; Fibre 1.6g; Sodium 82mg.
Spanish Potato Soup: Energy 74kcal/313kJ; Protein 1.6g; Carbohydrate 12.8g, of which sugars 4.8g; Fat 2.2g, of which saturates 0.4g; Cholesterol 0mg; Calcium 17mg; Fibre 1.6g; Sodium 12mg.

Provençal Vegetable Soup

This satisfying soup captures all the flavours of a summer in Provence. The basil and garlic purée, *pistou*, is an essential part of the soup.

Serves 6–8

275g/10oz/1½ cups fresh broad (fava) beans, shelled, or 175g/6oz/¾ cup dried haricot (navy) beans, soaked overnight
2.5ml/½ tsp dried herbes de Provence
2 garlic cloves, finely chopped
15ml/1 tbsp olive oil
1 onion, finely chopped
2 small leeks, finely sliced
1 celery stick, finely sliced
2 carrots, finely diced
2 small potatoes, finely diced

120g/4oz green beans
1.2 litres/2 pints/5 cups water
120g/4oz/1 cup shelled garden peas, fresh or frozen
2 small courgettes (zucchini), finely chopped
3 medium tomatoes, peeled, seeded and finely chopped
handful of spinach leaves, cut into thin ribbons
sprigs of fresh basil, to garnish

For the pistou

1 or 2 garlic cloves, finely chopped
15g/½oz/½ cup (packed) basil leaves
60ml/4 tbsp grated Parmesan cheese
60 ml/4 tbsp extra virgin olive oil

1 To make the *pistou*, put the garlic, basil and Parmesan cheese in a food processor and process until smooth, scraping down the sides once. With the machine running, slowly add the olive oil through the feed tube. Or, alternatively, pound the garlic, basil and cheese in a mortar and pestle and stir in the oil.

2 To make the soup, if using dried haricot beans, place them in a pan and cover with water. Boil vigorously for 10 minutes and drain. Place the parboiled beans, or fresh beans if using, in a pan with the *herbes de Provence* and one of the garlic cloves. Add water to cover by 2.5cm/1in. Bring to the boil, reduce the heat and simmer over a medium-low heat until tender, about 10 minutes for fresh beans and about 1 hour for dried beans. Set aside in the cooking liquid.

3 Heat the oil in a large pan or flameproof casserole. Add the onion and leeks, and cook for 5 minutes, stirring occasionally, until the onion just softens.

4 Add the celery, carrots and the other garlic clove and cook, covered, for 10 minutes, stirring. Add the potatoes, green beans and water, then season lightly with salt and pepper. Bring to the boil, skimming any foam that rises to the surface, then reduce the heat, cover and simmer gently for 10 minutes.

5 Add the courgettes, tomatoes and peas together with the reserved beans and their cooking liquid and simmer for 25–30 minutes, or until all the vegetables are tender. Add the spinach and simmer for 5 minutes. Season the soup and swirl a spoonful of *pistou* into each bowl. Garnish with basil and serve.

Summer Minestrone

This brightly coloured, fresh-tasting soup is low in fat and makes the most of intensely flavoured summer vegetables.

Serves 4

10ml/2 tsp olive oil
1 large onion, finely chopped
15ml/1 tbsp sun-dried tomato purée (paste)
450g/1lb ripe Italian plum tomatoes, peeled and finely chopped

225g/8oz green courgettes (zucchini), trimmed and roughly chopped
225g/8oz yellow courgettes (zucchini), trimmed and roughly chopped
3 waxy new potatoes, diced
2 garlic cloves, crushed
about 1.2 litres/2 pints/5 cups vegetable stock or water
60ml/4 tbsp shredded fresh basil
25g/1oz/¼ cup finely grated fresh Parmesan cheese
salt and ground black pepper

1 Heat the olive oil in a large saucepan, add the chopped onion and cook gently, stirring constantly, for about 5 minutes, or until softened.

2 Stir in the sun-dried tomato purée, chopped tomatoes, courgettes, potatoes and garlic. Mix well and cook gently for 10 minutes, uncovered, shaking the pan frequently to stop the vegetables sticking to the base.

3 Add the stock or water. Bring to the boil, reduce the heat, partially cover the pan and simmer gently for 15 minutes, or until the vegetables are just tender. Add a little more stock or water if necessary.

4 Remove the pan from the heat and stir in the basil and half the cheese. Taste for seasoning. Serve hot, sprinkled with the remaining cheese.

Cook's Tip

Both the pistou and the soup can be made one or two days in advance and chilled. To serve, reheat the soup gently, stirring occasionally.

Cook's Tip

Classic recipes for minestrone usually include either pasta or rice to make a thick, substantial soup, but this is a lighter summer version.

Vegetable Soup: Energy 126kcal/525kJ; Protein 6.1g; Carbohydrate 8.7g, of which sugars 3.3g; Fat 7.6g, of which saturates 2g; Cholesterol 6mg; Calcium 102mg; Fibre 3.6g; Sodium 72mg.
Minestrone: Energy 228kcal/951kJ; Protein 9.2g; Carbohydrate 18.8g, of which sugars 7.2g; Fat 13.4g, of which saturates 4.1g; Cholesterol 13mg; Calcium 194mg; Fibre 3.1g; Sodium 156mg.

Vegetable Moussaka with Tofu

This Greek dish, traditionally made with lamb, has been ingeniously adapted for vegetarians and vegans. It contains no animal products, but is as rich-tasting and full of flavour as the original.

Serves 8
600g/1lb 5oz aubergines (eggplant), thickly sliced
30ml/2 tbsp olive oil
50ml/3½ tbsp water
paprika and fresh basil leaves, to garnish

For the sauce
30ml/2 tbsp olive oil
2 large onions, coarsely chopped
2 garlic cloves, crushed
2 large carrots, finely chopped
4 courgettes (zucchini), sliced
200g/7oz mushrooms, sliced
2 × 400g/14oz cans chopped tomatoes
30ml/2 tbsp balsamic vinegar
5ml/1 tsp Tabasco sauce
15ml/1 tbsp clear honey
salt and ground black pepper

For the tofu topping
200g/7oz/1¾ cups ground almonds
350g/12oz silken tofu, drained
15ml/1 tbsp soy sauce
15ml/1 tbsp lemon juice
2.5ml/½ tsp English (hot) mustard powder

1 Preheat the grill (broiler) to high and place the aubergine slices in one layer on the grill rack. Drizzle with olive oil and grill (broil) for 2–3 minutes on each side until lightly browned.

2 To make the sauce, heat the oil in a large pan and sauté the onion, garlic and carrots for 5–7 minutes, until softened. Add the remaining ingredients, bring to the boil, then simmer for 20 minutes, stirring occasionally. Season.

3 Meanwhile make the topping. Dry-fry the almonds in a heavy pan for 1–2 minutes, tossing occasionally, until golden. Reserve 75g/3oz/¾ cup. Tip the remainder into a food processor and add the remaining ingredients. Process until smooth.

4 Preheat the oven to 180°C/350°F/Gas 4. Spread half the sauce in the base of a 35 × 23cm/14 × 9in deep-sided ovenproof dish. Arrange the aubergines on top and spread over the remaining sauce. Add the topping, sprinkle with the almonds and bake for 20 minutes. Garnish with paprika and basil.

Roasted Ratatouille Moussaka

Roasting brings out the deep rich flavours of the vegetables, which contrast with the light egg-and-cheese topping.

Serves 4–6
2 red (bell) peppers, cut into large chunks
2 yellow (bell) peppers, cut into large chunks
2 aubergines (eggplant), cut into large chunks
3 courgettes (zucchini), thickly sliced
45ml/3 tbsp olive oil
3 garlic cloves, crushed
400g/14oz can chopped tomatoes
30ml/2 tbsp sun-dried tomato paste
45ml/3 tbsp chopped fresh basil
15ml/1 tbsp balsamic vinegar
1.5ml/¼ tsp soft brown sugar
salt and ground black pepper
basil leaves, to garnish

For the topping
25g/1oz/2 tbsp butter
25g/1oz/¼ cup plain (all-purpose) flour
300ml/½ pint/1¼ cups milk
1.5ml/¼ tsp freshly grated nutmeg
250g/9oz ricotta cheese
3 eggs, beaten
25g/1oz/⅓ cup freshly grated Parmesan cheese

1 Preheat the oven to 230°C/450°F/Gas 8. Arrange the chunks of aubergines and courgettes in an even layer in a large roasting pan. Season well with salt and ground black pepper.

2 Mix together the oil and crushed garlic cloves and pour them over the vegetables. Shake the pan to coat the vegetables thoroughly in the garlic mixture.

3 Roast in the oven for 15–20 minutes, until slightly charred, tossing once during cooking. Remove the pan from the oven and set aside. Reduce the temperature to 200°C/400°F/Gas 6.

4 Put the chopped tomatoes, sun-dried tomato paste, basil, balsamic vinegar and brown sugar in a large, heavy pan and heat gently to boiling point. Reduce the heat and simmer, uncovered, for about 10–15 minutes, until reduced, stirring occasionally. Season with salt and pepper to taste.

5 Carefully tip the roasted vegetables out of their pan and into the tomato sauce. Mix well, coating the vegetables thoroughly. Spoon into an ovenproof dish.

6 To make the topping, melt the butter in a large, heavy pan over a gentle heat. Stir in the flour and cook for 1 minute. Pour in the milk, stirring constantly, then whisk until blended. Add the nutmeg and continue whisking over a gentle heat until thickened. Cook for a further 2 minutes, then remove from the heat and leave to cool slightly.

7 Mix the ricotta cheese and beaten eggs thoroughly into the sauce. Season with salt and plenty of freshly ground black pepper to taste.

8 Level the surface of the roasted vegetable mixture with the back of a spoon. Spoon the moussaka topping over the vegetables and sprinkle with the Parmesan cheese. Bake for 30–35 minutes, until the topping is golden brown. Serve immediately, garnished with basil leaves.

Moussaka: Energy 768kcal/3255kJ; Protein 60.3g; Carbohydrate 109.6g, of which sugars 10.3g; Fat 13.1g, of which saturates 2.9g; Cholesterol 99mg; Calcium 357mg; Fibre 21.8g; Sodium 320mg.
Ratatouille Moussaka: Energy 570kcal/2367kJ; Protein 22.1g; Carbohydrate 27.5g, of which sugars 21.7g; Fat 42.1g, of which saturates 20.3g; Cholesterol 223mg; Calcium 339mg; Fibre 7.1g; Sodium 447mg.

Polenta with Mushroom Sauce

This is a fine example of just how absolutely delicious soft polenta can be. Polenta is a staple of northern Italian cuisine, and is served as an accompaniment to many savoury dishes. Topped with a robust mushroom and tomato sauce, it tastes quite sublime.

Serves 4
1.2 litres/2 pints/5 cups
  vegetable stock
350g/12oz/3 cups fine
  polenta or cornmeal
50g/2oz/ ²⁄₃ cup freshly grated
  Parmesan cheese
salt and ground black pepper

For the sauce
15g/ ½ oz/ ¼ cup dried
  porcini mushrooms
150ml/ ¼ pint/ ²⁄₃ cup hot water
15ml/1 tbsp olive oil
50g/2oz/¼ cup butter
1 onion, finely chopped
1 carrot, finely chopped
1 celery stick, finely chopped
2 garlic cloves, crushed
450g/1lb/6 cups mixed brown
  cap (cremini) and large flat
  mushrooms, roughly chopped
120ml/4fl oz/ ½ cup red wine
400g/14oz can
  chopped tomatoes
5ml/1 tsp tomato purée (paste)
15ml/1 tbsp chopped fresh thyme

1 To make the sauce, soak the mushrooms in the hot water for 20 minutes. Drain, reserving the liquid, and chop roughly.

2 Heat the oil and butter in a saucepan and fry the onion, carrot, celery and garlic for 5 minutes, until beginning to soften. Raise the heat and add the both mushrooms. Cook for another 10 minutes. Pour in the wine and cook rapidly for 2–3 minutes, then add the tomatoes and strained, reserved soaking liquid. Stir in the tomato purée and thyme and season with salt and pepper. Lower the heat and simmer for 20 minutes.

3 Meanwhile, heat the stock in a large heavy-based saucepan. Add a pinch of salt. As soon as it simmers, tip in the polenta in a fine stream, whisking until the mixture is smooth. Cook for 30 minutes, stirring constantly, until the polenta comes away from the pan. Stir in half the Parmesan and some pepper.

4 Divide among four heated bowls and top each with sauce. Sprinkle with the remaining Parmesan.

Baked Vegetables with Thyme

Crunchy golden batter surrounds this attractive combination of bright summer vegetables. Flavoured with thyme, the combination is both delicious and filling, and, served with salad, this dish makes an excellent light lunch or supper.

Serves 6
1 small aubergine (eggplant),
  halved and thickly sliced
1 egg

115g/4oz/1 cup plain
  (all-purpose) flour
300ml/½ pint/1 ¼ cups milk
30ml/2 tbsp fresh thyme leaves,
  or 10ml/2 tsp dried
1 red onion
2 large courgettes (zucchini)
1 red (bell) pepper
1 yellow (bell) pepper
60–75ml/4–5 tbsp sunflower oil
30ml/2 tbsp freshly grated
  Parmesan cheese
salt and ground black pepper
fresh herbs, to garnish

1 Place the aubergine in a colander or sieve (strainer), sprinkle generously with salt, and leave for 10 minutes. Drain, rinse well and pat dry on kitchen paper.

2 Meanwhile, beat the egg in a bowl, then gradually beat in the flour and a little milk to make a smooth, thick paste. Gradually blend in the rest of the milk, add the thyme and seasoning to taste, and stir to make a smooth batter. Leave in a cool place until required.

3 Preheat the oven to 220°C/425°F/Gas 7. Quarter the onion, slice the courgettes and quarter the peppers, removing the seeds. Put the oil in a roasting pan and heat in the oven. Add the vegetables, including the aubergines, and toss them in the oil to coat thoroughly. Return the pan to the oven for 20 minutes.

4 When the fat in the pan is really hot, whisk the batter and pour it over the vegetables – it should sizzle as it hits the hot fat. Return the pan to the oven for 30 minutes.

5 When the batter is puffed up and golden, reduce the heat to 190°C/375°F/Gas 5 for 10–15 minutes, or until crisp around the edges. Sprinkle with Parmesan and herbs, and serve.

Polenta with Mushroom Sauce: Energy 572kcal/2384kJ; Protein 17.2g; Carbohydrate 72.2g, of which sugars 6.1g; Fat 21g, of which saturates 9.7g; Cholesterol 39mg; Calcium 185mg; Fibre 5.4g; Sodium 242mg.
Baked Vegetables: Energy 231kcal/966kJ; Protein 8.9g; Carbohydrate 24.1g, of which sugars 8.9g; Fat 11.7g, of which saturates 2.9g; Cholesterol 40mg; Calcium 181mg; Fibre 3.3g; Sodium 93mg.

Spicy Chickpea and Aubergine Stew

This is a Lebanese dish, but similar recipes are found all over the Mediterranean. The vegetables have a warm, smoky flavour, subtly enriched with spices. Crunchy fried onion rings provide a contrast of taste and texture. Serve the stew on a bed of rice.

Serves 4
3 large aubergines
 (eggplants), cubed
200g/7oz/1 cup chickpeas,
 soaked overnight
60ml/4 tbsp olive oil
3 garlic cloves, chopped
2 large onions, chopped
2.5ml/½ tsp ground cumin
2.5ml/½ tsp ground cinnamon
2.5ml/½ tsp ground coriander
3 × 400g/14oz cans
 chopped tomatoes
salt and ground black pepper
cooked rice, to serve

For the garnish
30ml/2 tbsp olive oil
1 onion, sliced
1 garlic clove, sliced
sprigs of coriander (cilantro)

1 Place the aubergines in a colander and sprinkle them with salt. Sit the colander in a bowl and leave for 30 minutes, to allow the bitter juices to escape. Rinse with cold water and dry on kitchen paper.

2 Drain the chickpeas and put in a pan with enough water to cover. Bring to the boil and simmer for 30 minutes, or until tender. Drain.

3 Heat the oil in a large pan. Add the garlic and onion and cook gently until soft. Add the spices and cook, stirring, for a few seconds. Add the aubergine and stir to coat with the spices and onion. Cook for 5 minutes. Add the tomatoes and chickpeas and season with salt and pepper. Cover and simmer for 20 minutes.

4 To make the garnish, heat the oil in a frying pan and, when very hot, add the sliced onion and garlic. Fry until golden and crisp. Serve the stew with rice, topped with the onion and garlic and garnished with coriander.

Mediterranean Vegetables with Chickpeas

The flavours of the Mediterranean are captured in this delicious, healthy vegetable dish, ideal for a light lunch, served with crusty bread.

Serves 6
1 onion, sliced
2 leeks, sliced
2 garlic cloves, crushed
1 red (bell) pepper, sliced
1 green (bell) pepper, sliced
1 yellow (bell) pepper, sliced
350g/12oz courgettes
 (zucchini), sliced
225g/8oz/3 cups
 mushrooms, sliced
400g/14oz can
 chopped tomatoes
30ml/2 tbsp ruby port or
 red wine
30ml/2 tbsp tomato purée (paste)
15ml/1 tbsp tomato
 ketchup (optional)
400g/14oz can chickpeas
115g/4oz/1 cup stoned (pitted)
 black olives
45ml/3 tbsp chopped fresh
 mixed herbs, including oregano
 and basil
salt and ground black pepper
chopped fresh mixed herbs,
 to garnish

1 Put the onion, leeks, garlic, red, yellow and green peppers, courgettes and mushrooms into a large, heavy pan.

2 Add the tomatoes, port or red wine, tomato purée and tomato ketchup, if using, to the pan and mix all the ingredients together well.

3 Rinse and drain the chickpeas and add to the pan. Stir, cover, bring to the boil then reduce the heat and simmer the mixture gently for 20–30 minutes, until the vegetables are cooked and tender but not overcooked, stirring occasionally.

4 Remove the lid of the saucepan and increase the heat slightly for the last 10 minutes of the cooking time, to thicken the sauce, if you like.

5 Stir in the olives, herbs and seasoning. Serve either hot or cold, garnished with chopped mixed herbs.

Spicy Chickpea Stew: Energy 201kcal/843kJ; Protein 7.1g; Carbohydrate 22.3g, of which sugars 10.4g; Fat 10g, of which saturates 1.4g; Cholesterol 0mg; Calcium 57mg; Fibre 5.9g; Sodium 175mg.
Mediterranean Vegetables: Energy 161kcal/678kJ; Protein 7.9g; Carbohydrate 21.7g, of which sugars 13.4g; Fat 4.7g, of which saturates 0.8g; Cholesterol 0mg; Calcium 78mg; Fibre 7g; Sodium 639mg.

Spiced Turnips with Spinach and Tomatoes

Delicate baby turnips, tender spinach and ripe tomatoes make tempting partners in this simple Eastern Mediterranean vegetable stew, which makes a lovely dish for spring or summer, served warm or cold. Adding a pinch of sugar to the mixture during cooking brings out the natural sweetness of the vegetables.

Serves 6

450g/1lb plum or other
  well-flavoured tomatoes
60ml/4 tbsp olive oil
2 onions, sliced
450g/1lb baby turnips, peeled
5ml/1 tsp paprika
2.5ml/½ tsp caster
  (superfine) sugar
60ml/4 tbsp chopped fresh
  coriander (cilantro)
450g/1lb fresh young spinach
salt and ground black pepper

1 Plunge the tomatoes into a large bowl of boiling water for 30 seconds, then refresh in a bowl of cold water. Peel away the tomato skins and chop the flesh roughly.

2 Heat the olive oil in a large frying pan or sauté pan and fry the onion slices for about 5 minutes until they are golden.

3 Add the baby turnips, tomatoes and paprika to the pan with 60ml/4 tbsp water and cook until the tomatoes are pulpy. Cover the pan with a lid and continue cooking until the baby turnips have softened.

4 Add the sugar and coriander to the pan, stir well to mix, then add the spinach and a little salt and pepper and cook for a further 2–3 minutes until all the spinach has wilted. This dish can either be served immediately, warm or allowed to cool.

Variation
For a spicier version of the stew, double the amount of paprika and add a pinch of cayenne.

Aubergine Parmigiana

This is a classic Italian dish, in which blissfully tender sliced aubergines (eggplants) are layered with melting creamy mozzarella, fresh Parmesan and a good home-made tomato sauce, then baked in a hot oven until appetizingly golden brown.

Serves 4–6

3 medium aubergines (eggplants),
  thinly sliced
olive oil, for brushing
300g/11oz mozzarella
  cheese, sliced
115g/4oz/1⅓ cups freshly grated
  Parmesan cheese
30–45ml/2–3 tbsp dry
  breadcrumbs
salt and ground black pepper
fresh basil sprigs, to garnish

For the sauce
30ml/2 tbsp olive oil
1 onion, finely chopped
2 garlic cloves, crushed
400g/14oz can
  chopped tomatoes
5ml/1 tsp granulated sugar
about 6 fresh basil leaves

1 Layer the aubergine slices in a colander, sprinkling each layer with a little salt. Leave to drain over a bowl for about 20 minutes, then rinse thoroughly under cold running water and pat dry with kitchen paper.

2 Preheat the oven to 200°C/400°F/Gas 6. Lay the aubergine slices on non-stick baking sheets, brush the tops with olive oil and bake for 10–15 minutes until softened.

3 Meanwhile, make the sauce. Heat the oil in a pan. Add the onion and garlic and fry over a low heat, stirring occasionally, for 5 minutes. Add the canned tomatoes and sugar and season with salt and pepper to taste. Bring to the boil, then lower the heat and simmer for about 10 minutes, until reduced and thickened. Tear the basil leaves and stir them into the sauce.

4 Layer the aubergines in a greased shallow ovenproof dish with the sliced mozzarella, the tomato sauce and the grated Parmesan, ending with a layer of Parmesan mixed with the breadcrumbs. Bake for 20–25 minutes, until golden brown and bubbling. Allow to stand for 5 minutes before cutting. Serve garnished with basil.

Spiced Turnips: Energy 363kcal/1519kJ; Protein 326g; Carbohydrate 80g, of which sugars 37g; Fat 2.62g, of which saturates 0.2g; Cholesterol 0mg; Calcium 891mg; Fibre 12.5g; Sodium 1520mg.
Aubergine Parmigiana: Energy 819kcal/3417kJ; Protein 51.2g; Carbohydrate 30.9g, of which sugars 14.7g; Fat 55.6g, of which saturates 30.7g; Cholesterol 128mg; Calcium 1169mg; Fibre 7.9g; Sodium 1258mg.

Stuffed Aubergine

This dish from the Ligurian region of Italy is spiked with paprika and allspice, a legacy of the days when spices came into northern Italy via the port of Genoa.

Serves 4
2 medium aubergines (eggplants), stalks removed
275g/10oz potatoes, peeled and diced
15ml/1 tbsp olive oil

1 small onion, finely chopped
1 garlic clove, finely chopped
good pinch of ground allspice and paprika
30ml/2 tbsp skimmed milk
25g/1oz grated fresh Parmesan cheese
15ml/1 tbsp fresh white breadcrumbs
salt and freshly ground black pepper
fresh mint sprigs, to garnish
salad leaves, to serve

1 Bring a large saucepan of lightly salted water to the boil. Add the whole aubergines and cook for 5 minutes. Remove with a slotted spoon and set aside. Add the diced potatoes to the pan and boil for about 15 minutes or until cooked.

2 Meanwhile, cut the aubergines in half lengthways and scoop out the flesh, leaving 5mm/¼in of the shell intact. Select a baking dish that will hold the aubergine shells snugly in a single layer. Brush it lightly with oil. Put the shells in the dish and chop the aubergine flesh roughly. Set aside.

3 Heat the oil in a frying pan, add the onion and cook gently, stirring, until softened. Add the chopped aubergine flesh and the garlic. Cook, stirring frequently, for 6–8 minutes. Tip into a bowl and set aside. Preheat the oven to 190°C/375°F/Gas 5.

4 Drain and mash the potatoes. Add to the aubergine mixture with the spices and milk. Set aside 15ml/1 tbsp of the Parmesan and add the rest to the aubergine mixture, adding salt and pepper to taste. Spoon the mixture into the aubergine shells.

5 Mix the breadcrumbs with the reserved Parmesan cheese and sprinkle the mixture evenly over the aubergines. Bake in the oven for 30–40 minutes until the topping is crisp. Garnish with mint sprigs and serve with salad leaves.

Onions Stuffed with Goat's Cheese and Sun-dried Tomatoes

Roasted onions and goat's cheese are a winning combination. These stuffed onions make an excellent main course served with a rice or cracked wheat pilaff.

Serves 4
4 large onions
150g/5oz goat's cheese, crumbled or cubed
50g/2oz fresh breadcrumbs

8 sun-dried tomatoes in olive oil, drained and chopped
1–2 garlic cloves, finely chopped
2.5ml/½ tsp chopped fresh thyme
30ml/2 tbsp chopped fresh parsley
1 small egg, beaten
45ml/3 tbsp pine nuts, toasted
30ml/2 tbsp olive oil (use oil from the tomatoes)
salt and ground black pepper

1 Bring a large pan of lightly salted water to the boil. Add the whole onions in their skins and boil for 10 minutes. Drain and cool, then cut each onion in half horizontally and peel. Using a teaspoon, remove the centre of each onion, leaving a thick shell. Reserve the flesh and place the shells in an oiled baking dish. Preheat the oven to 190°C/375°F/Gas 5.

2 Chop the scooped-out onion flesh and place in a bowl. Add the goat's cheese, breadcrumbs, sun-dried tomatoes, garlic, thyme, parsley and egg. Mix well, then season with salt and pepper and add the toasted pine nuts.

3 Divide the stuffing among the onions and cover with foil. Bake for about 25 minutes. Uncover, drizzle with the oil and cook for another 30–40 minutes, until bubbling and well cooked. Baste occasionally during cooking.

Variations
• Stuff the onions with spinach and rice mixed with some smoked mozzarella and toasted almonds instead of the goat's cheese and sun-dried tomato mixture.
• Use peppers preserved in olive oil instead of tomatoes.

Stuffed Aubergine: Energy 88kcal/369kJ; Protein 3.3g; Carbohydrate 11.2g, of which sugars 2.2g; Fat 3.6g, of which saturates 1.3g; Cholesterol 4mg; Calcium 68mg; Fibre 1.4g; Sodium 73mg.
Onions with Goat's Cheese: Energy 402kcal/1669kJ; Protein 14.8g; Carbohydrate 25.1g, of which sugars 11.7g; Fat 27.7g, of which saturates 8.8g; Cholesterol 82mg; Calcium 120mg; Fibre 3.2g; Sodium 346mg.

Roasted Peppers with Sweet Cicely and Fennel

The aniseed flavours of sweet cicely and fennel combine beautifully with succulent peppers and tomatoes and piquant capers. Sweet cicely leaves make an excellent garnish and they taste just like the flowers.

Serves 4
4 red (bell) peppers, halved
8 small or 4 medium tomatoes

15ml/1 tbsp semi-ripe sweet
cicely seeds
15ml/1 tbsp fennel seeds
15ml/1 tbsp capers
8 sweet cicely flowers, newly
opened, stems removed
60ml/4 tbsp olive oil

For the garnish
a few small sweet cicely leaves
8 more sweet cicely flowers,
newly opened

1 Preheat the oven to 180°C/350°F/Gas 4. Place the red pepper halves in a large ovenproof dish and set aside.

2 To skin the tomatoes, cut a cross at the base, then pour over boiling water and leave them to stand for 30 seconds to 1 minute. Cut them in half if they are of medium size.

3 Place a whole small or half a medium tomato in each half of a pepper cavity. Cover with a scattering of semi-ripe sweet cicely seeds, fennel seeds and capers and about half the sweet cicely flowers. Drizzle the olive oil all over.

4 Bake in the top of the oven for 1 hour. Remove from the oven and add the rest of the flowers. Garnish with fresh sweet cicely leaves and flowers, and serve with lots of crusty bread to soak up the juices.

> **Cook's Tip**
> Try adding the stems from the sweet cicely to the water in which fruit is stewed. They will add a delightful flavour and reduce the need for sugar.

Pepper Gratin

Serve this simple but delicious Italian dish as a starter or snack with a mixed leaf salad and plenty of good crusty bread to mop up the juices from the peppers.

Serves 4
2 red (bell) peppers
15ml/1 tbsp extra virgin olive oil
1 garlic clove, finely chopped
5ml/1 tsp capers, drained
and rinsed

8 stoned (pitted) black olives,
roughly chopped
15ml/1 tbsp chopped fresh
oregano
15ml/1 tbsp chopped fresh flat
leaf parsley
60ml/4 tbsp fresh white
breadcrumbs
salt and ground black pepper
fresh herbs, to garnish

1 Preheat the oven to 200°C/400°F/Gas 6. Place the peppers on a grill rack and cook under a hot grill. Turn occasionally until the skins are blackened and blistered all over.

2 Remove the peppers from the heat and place them in a plastic bag. Seal and leave to cool.

3 When they are cool, carefully peel the peppers. (Don't skin them under the tap as the water will wash away some of the delicious smoky flavour.)

4 Cut the peppers in half, remove and discard the seeds, then cut the flesh into large strips. Use a little of the olive oil to grease a small baking dish. Arrange the pepper strips in the dish.

5 Sprinkle the garlic, capers, olives and chopped herbs on top of the peppers. Season with salt and pepper. Scatter over the fresh white breadcrumbs and drizzle with the remaining olive oil.

6 Bake in the oven for about 20 minutes until the breadcrumbs are a golden-brown colour. Garnish with fresh herbs and serve immediately.

Roasted Peppers with Cicely: Energy 172kcal/714kJ; Protein 2.5g; Carbohydrate 14.3g, of which sugars 13.8g; Fat 12g, of which saturates 1.9g; Cholesterol 0mg; Calcium 21mg; Fibre 3.8g; Sodium 16mg.
Pepper Gratin: Energy 110kcal/460kJ; Protein 2.7g; Carbohydrate 15.5g, of which sugars 5.8g; Fat 4.5g, of which saturates 0.7g; Cholesterol 0mg; Calcium 44mg; Fibre 2.4g; Sodium 326mg.

Middle Eastern Stuffed Peppers

Couscous is a form of semolina, and is used extensively in the Middle East – a major influence on Mediterranean cuisine. Choose ripe red peppers for the fullest flavour.

Serves 4
6 red (bell) peppers
25g/1oz/2 tbsp butter
1 medium onion, finely chopped

5ml/1 tsp olive oil
2.5ml/½ tsp salt
175g/6oz/1 cup couscous
25g/1oz/2 tbsp raisins
30ml/2 tbsp chopped
   fresh mint
1 egg yolk
salt and ground black pepper
mint leaves, to garnish

1 Preheat the oven to 200°C/400°F/Gas 6. Carefully slit each pepper and remove the core and seeds. Melt the butter in a small pan and add the onion. Cook until softened and golden, stirring frequently.

2 To cook the couscous, bring 250ml/8fl oz/1 cup water to the boil. Add the oil and the salt, then remove the pan from the heat and add the couscous. Stir and leave to stand, covered, for 5 minutes.

3 Stir in the cooked onion, raisins and mint, then season well with salt and pepper. Stir in the egg yolk.

4 Using a teaspoon, fill the peppers with the couscous mixture to only about three-quarters full, as the couscous will swell when cooked further.

5 Place in a lightly oiled ovenproof dish and bake, uncovered, for about 20 minutes until tender. Serve hot or cold, garnished with the mint leaves.

Cook's Tip
The couscous sold in supermarkets is pre-cooked and only needs soaking for a brief time and fluffing up with a fork.

Italian Stuffed Peppers

These flavourful Italian stuffed peppers are quick and easy to make for a light, healthy lunch or supper.

Serves 4
10ml/2 tsp olive oil
1 red onion, sliced
1 courgette (zucchini),
   diced
115g/4oz mushrooms, sliced
1 garlic clove, crushed

400g/14oz can
   chopped tomatoes
15ml/1 tbsp tomato purée (paste)
25g/1oz pine nuts
30ml/2 tbsp chopped fresh basil
4 large yellow (bell) peppers
25g/1oz/¼ cup finely
   grated fresh Parmesan or
   Fontina cheese
salt and freshly ground
   black pepper
fresh basil leaves, to garnish

1 Preheat the oven to 180°C/350°F/Gas 4. Heat the oil in a saucepan, add the onion, courgette, mushrooms and garlic and cook gently for 3 minutes, stirring the mixture occasionally.

2 Stir in the tomatoes and tomato purée, then bring to the boil and simmer, uncovered, for 10–15 minutes, stirring occasionally, until thickened slightly. Remove the pan from the heat and stir in the pine nuts, if using, chopped basil and seasoning. Set aside.

3 Cut the peppers in half lengthways and deseed them. Blanch the pepper halves in boiling water for about 3 minutes. Drain.

4 Place the peppers cut side-up in a shallow ovenproof dish and fill with the vegetable mixture.

5 Cover the dish with foil and bake in the oven for 20 minutes. Uncover, sprinkle each pepper half with a little grated cheese, if using, and bake, uncovered, for a further 5–10 minutes. Garnish with fresh basil leaves and serve.

Cook's Tip
Red (bell) peppers could be used, but yellow ones look particularly beautiful filled with the vivid red and green stuffing.

Stuffed Peppers: Energy 392kcal/1630kJ; Protein 9.2g; Carbohydrate 25.4g, of which sugars 17.9g; Fat 28.8g, of which saturates 3.2g; Cholesterol 0mg; Calcium 110mg; Fibre 5.5g; Sodium 19mg.
Italian Stuffed Peppers: Energy 108kcal/450kJ; Protein 4.2g; Carbohydrate 17g, of which sugars 16.1g; Fat 2.9g, of which saturates 0.6g; Cholesterol 0mg; Calcium 40mg; Fibre 4.9g; Sodium 28mg.

Leek, Pepper and Spinach Frittata

Garlic and Goat's Cheese Soufflé

Unlike Spanish tortilla, Italian frittata does not usually contain potato and is generally slightly softer in texture. The combination of leek, red pepper and spinach is delicious with egg.

Serves 3–4
30ml/2 tbsp olive oil
1 large red (bell) pepper, diced
2.5–5ml/½–1 tsp ground
   toasted cumin
3 leeks (about 450g/1lb),
   thinly sliced
150g/5oz small spinach leaves
45ml/3 tbsp pine nuts, toasted
5 large eggs
15ml/1 tbsp chopped fresh basil
15ml/1 tbsp chopped fresh flat
   leaf parsley
salt and ground black pepper
watercress, to garnish
50g/2oz Parmesan cheese, grated,
   to serve (optional)

1 Heat a frying pan and add the oil. Add the red pepper and cook over a medium heat, stirring occasionally, for 6–8 minutes, until soft and beginning to brown at the edges. Add 2.5ml/½ tsp of the cumin and cook for another 1–2 minutes, stirring to prevent it burning.

2 Stir in the leeks, then part-cover the pan and cook gently for about 5 minutes, until the leeks have softened and collapsed. Season with salt and ground black pepper.

3 Add the spinach and cover. Allow the spinach to wilt in the steam for 3–4 minutes, then stir to mix it into the vegetables, adding the pine nuts.

4 Beat the eggs with salt, pepper, the remaining cumin, basil and parsley. Add to the pan and cook over a gentle heat until the bottom of the omelette sets and turns golden brown. Pull the edges of the frittata away from the sides of the pan as it cooks and tilt the pan so that the uncooked egg runs underneath and sets.

5 Preheat the grill (broiler). Flash the frittata under the hot grill to set the egg on top, but do not let it become too brown. Cut the frittata into wedges and serve warm, garnished with watercress and sprinkled with Parmesan, if using.

Balance this rich soufflé with a crisp green salad, including peppery leaves, such as mizuna and watercress.

Serves 3–4
2 large, plump heads of garlic
3 fresh thyme sprigs
15ml/1 tbsp olive oil
250ml/8fl oz/1 cup milk
1 fresh bay leaf
2 × 1cm/½in thick onion slices
2 cloves
50g/2oz/¼ cup butter
40g/1½oz/⅓ cup plain
   (all-purpose) flour, sifted
cayenne pepper
3 eggs, separated, plus 1 egg white
150g/5oz goat's cheese, crumbled
50g/2oz/⅔ cup freshly grated
   Parmesan cheese
2.5–5ml/½–1 tsp chopped
   fresh thyme
2.5ml/½ tsp cream of tartar
salt and freshly ground black
   pepper

1 Preheat the oven to 180°C/350°F/Gas 4. Place the garlic and thyme sprigs on a piece of foil. Sprinkle with the oil and close the foil around the garlic, then bake for about 1 hour. Leave to cool. Discard the thyme and squeeze the garlic out of its skin and purée the flesh with the oil.

2 Meanwhile, bring the milk to the boil with the bay leaf, onion and cloves, then remove from the heat. Cover and leave to stand for 30 minutes. Melt 40g/1½oz/3 tbsp of the butter in another pan. Stir in the flour and cook gently for 2 minutes, stirring. Reheat and strain the milk, then stir it into the roux. Cook very gently for 10 minutes, stirring frequently. Season with salt, pepper and cayenne. Cool slightly. Preheat the oven to 200°C/400°F/Gas 6.

3 Beat in the egg yolks, one at a time, the goat's cheese, all but 15ml/1 tbsp of the Parmesan and the chopped thyme. Use the remaining butter to grease four 250ml/8fl oz/1 cup ramekins.

4 Whisk the egg whites and cream of tartar until firm but not dry. Stir 45ml/3 tbsp of the whites into the sauce, then fold in the remainder. Pour the mixture into the prepared dishes and scatter with the reserved Parmesan. Place on a baking sheet and cook for 20 minutes until risen and firm to a light touch in the centre. Serve immediately.

Frittata: Energy 267kcal/1107kJ; Protein 12.7g; Carbohydrate 7.1g, of which sugars 6.2g; Fat 21.2g, of which saturates 3.4g; Cholesterol 238mg; Calcium 131mg; Fibre 4.2g; Sodium 144mg.
Goat's Cheese Soufflé: Energy 563kcal/2338kJ; Protein 28.8g; Carbohydrate 16.5g, of which sugars 5.8g; Fat 42.9g, of which saturates 24.1g; Cholesterol 294mg; Calcium 422mg; Fibre 0.7g; Sodium 710mg.

Moroccan Pancakes

An unusual dish that makes a good main course for an informal dinner party.

Serves 4–6

15ml/1 tbsp olive oil
1 large onion, chopped
250g/9oz fresh spinach
400g/14oz can chickpeas
2 courgettes, grated
30ml/2 tbsp chopped
   fresh coriander (cilantro)
2 eggs, beaten
salt and ground black pepper
fresh coriander (cilantro) leaves,
   to garnish

For the pancakes

150g/5oz/1¼ cups plain
   (all-purpose) flour
1 egg
about 350ml/12fl oz/
   1½ cups milk
75ml/5 tbsp water
15ml/1 tbsp sunflower oil, plus
   extra for greasing

For the sauce

25g/1oz/2 tbsp butter
30ml/2 tbsp plain
   (all-purpose) flour
about 300ml/ ½ pint/
   1¼ cups milk

1 Make the batter by blending the flour, egg, milk and water until smooth in a blender. Stir in the oil and a pinch of salt. Heat a lightly greased frying pan and ladle in one-eighth of the batter. Cook for 2–3 minutes, without turning, then slide the pancake out of the pan. Make seven more pancakes.

2 Heat the olive oil in a small pan and fry the onion until soft. Set aside. Wash the spinach, place it in a pan and cook until wilted, shaking the pan occasionally. Chop the spinach roughly.

3 Drain the chickpeas, place in a bowl of cold water and rub them until the skins float to the surface. Drain the chickpeas and mash roughly with a fork. Add the onion, courgettes, spinach and coriander. Stir in the eggs, season and mix well.

4 Preheat the oven to 180°C/350°F/Gas 4. Arrange the pancakes cooked side up and spoon the filling down the centres. Roll up and place in a large oiled ovenproof dish. To make the sauce, melt the butter in a pan, stir in the flour and cook for 1 minute. Gradually whisk in the milk until the mixture boils. Season and pour over the pancakes. Bake for 15 minutes, until golden. Serve garnished with the coriander leaves.

Baked Herb Crêpes

Add fresh herbs to make crêpes something special, then fill them with spinach, pine nuts and ricotta cheese and serve with a garlicky tomato sauce.

Serves 4

25g/1oz/½ cup chopped
   fresh herbs
15ml/1 tbsp sunflower oil, plus
   extra for frying
120ml/4fl oz/½ cup milk
3 eggs
25g/1oz/¼ cup plain
   (all-purpose) flour
pinch of salt
oil, for greasing

For the sauce

30ml/2 tbsp olive oil
1 small onion, chopped
2 garlic cloves, crushed
400g/14oz can
   chopped tomatoes
pinch of soft light brown sugar

For the filling

450g/1lb fresh spinach, cooked
175g/6oz/¾ cup ricotta cheese
25g/1oz/¼ cup pine nuts, toasted
5 sun-dried tomatoes in olive oil,
   drained and chopped
30ml/2 tbsp chopped fresh basil
salt, nutmeg and ground
   black pepper
4 egg whites

1 To make the crêpes, place the herbs and oil in a food processor and blend until smooth. Add the milk, eggs, flour and salt and process again. Leave to rest for 30 minutes. Heat a small frying pan and add a little oil. Add a ladleful of batter. Swirl around to cover the base. Cook for 2 minutes, turn and cook for 2 minutes. Make seven more crêpes.

2 To make the sauce, heat the oil in a pan, add the onion and garlic and cook gently for 5 minutes. Add the tomatoes and sugar and cook for about 10 minutes, or until thickened. Purée in a blender, then sieve and set aside.

3 Preheat the oven to 190°C/375°F/Gas 5. To make the filling, mix the spinach with the ricotta, pine nuts, tomatoes and basil. Season with salt, nutmeg and pepper. Whisk the egg whites until stiff. Fold one-third into the mixture, then gently fold in the rest.

4 Place one crêpe at a time on a lightly oiled baking sheet, add a spoonful of filling and fold into quarters. Bake for 12 minutes until set. Reheat the sauce and serve with the crêpes.

Moroccan Pancakes: Energy 284kcal/1192kJ; Protein 12.1g; Carbohydrate 32.6g, of which sugars 8.9g; Fat 12.7g, of which saturates 4.7g; Cholesterol 110mg; Calcium 279mg; Fibre 2.7g; Sodium 168mg.
Herb Crêpes: Energy 434kcal/1800kJ; Protein 14.9g; Carbohydrate 15.1g, of which sugars 9.8g; Fat 35.4g, of which saturates 8.3g; Cholesterol 161mg; Calcium 251mg; Fibre 5g; Sodium 229mg.

Spinach and Filo Pie

This popular spinach and filo pastry pie comes from Greece. There are several ways of making it, but feta or Kefalotiri cheese is inevitably included. It is at its best served warm rather than straight from the oven.

Serves 6
1kg/2¼lb fresh spinach
4 spring onions (scallions), chopped
300g/11oz feta or Kefalotiri cheese, crumbled or coarsely grated
2 large eggs, beaten
30ml/2 tbsp chopped fresh parsley
15ml/1 tbsp chopped fresh dill
about 8 filo pastry sheets, each about 30 × 18cm/12 × 7in, thawed if frozen
150ml/ ¼ pint/ ⅔ cup olive oil
freshly ground black pepper

1 Preheat the oven to 190°C/375°F/Gas 5. Break off any thick stalks from the spinach, then wash the leaves and cook them in just the water that clings to the leaves in a heavy-based pan. As soon as they have wilted, drain them, refresh under cold water and drain again. Squeeze dry and chop roughly.

2 Place the spinach in a bowl. Add the spring onions and cheese, then pour in the eggs. Mix in the herbs and season the filling with pepper.

3 Brush a filo sheet with oil and fit it into a 23cm/9in pie dish, allowing it to hang over the edge. (Keep the other filo sheets covered with a damp cloth to stop them drying out.) Top with three or four more sheets, placing each one at a different angle and brushing each one with oil.

4 Spoon in the spinach filling, then top the pie with all but one of the remaining filo sheets. Brush each sheet with oil. Fold in the overhanging filo to seal in the filling. Brush the reserved sheet with oil and scrunch it over the top of the pie.

5 Brush the pie with oil. Sprinkle with a little water to stop the filo edges from curling, then place on a baking sheet. Bake for about 40 minutes, until golden and crisp. Cool the pie for 15 minutes before serving.

Vegetable Tarte Tatin

This savoury upside-down tart combines Mediterranean vegetables with a medley of rice, garlic, onions and olives.

Serves 2–3
30ml/2 tbsp sunflower oil
25ml/1½ tbsp olive oil
1 aubergine (eggplant), sliced lengthways
1 large red (bell) pepper, cut into long strips
10 tomatoes
2 red shallots, finely chopped
1–2 garlic cloves, crushed
150ml/¼ pint/⅔ cup white wine
10ml/2 tsp chopped fresh basil
225g/8oz/2 cups cooked white or brown long grain rice
40g/1½oz/scant ½ cup stoned (pitted) black olives, chopped
350g/12oz puff pastry, thawed if frozen
ground black pepper
salad leaves, to serve

1 Preheat the oven to 190°C/375°F/ Gas 5. Heat the sunflower oil with 15ml/1 tbsp of the olive oil in a frying pan and fry the aubergine slices for 4–5 minutes on each side until golden brown. Drain on several sheets of kitchen paper.

2 Add the pepper strips to the pan, turning them to coat in the oil. Cover and sweat the peppers over a medium high heat for 5–6 minutes, stirring occasionally, until soft and browned.

3 Slice two of the tomatoes and set them aside. Plunge the remaining tomatoes into boiling water for 30 seconds, then drain and peel. Remove the core and seeds and chop roughly.

4 Heat the remaining oil and fry the shallots and garlic for 3–4 minutes. Add the tomatoes and cook for a few minutes. Stir in the wine and basil, with black pepper to taste. Bring to the boil, then remove from the heat. Add the rice and olives.

5 Arrange the tomatoes, aubergines and peppers in a single layer in a 30cm/12in shallow ovenproof dish. Spread the rice mixture on top. Roll out the pastry slightly larger than the dish and place it on top of the rice, tucking the overlap down inside the dish. Bake for 25–30 minutes, until golden and risen. Cool slightly, then invert the tart on to a large, warmed serving plate. Serve in slices, with a leafy green salad.

Spinach and Filo Pie: Energy 402kcal/1668kJ; Protein 16.5g; Carbohydrate 16.8g, of which sugars 3.9g; Fat 30.3g, of which saturates 10g; Cholesterol 98mg; Calcium 516mg; Fibre 4.5g; Sodium 980mg.
Vegetable Tarte Tatin: Energy 536kcal/2242kJ; Protein 8.3g; Carbohydrate 59.1g, of which sugars 8.8g; Fat 29.5g, of which saturates 1.2g; Cholesterol 0mg; Calcium 89mg; Fibre 2.6g; Sodium 522mg.

Onion, Fennel and Lavender Tarts

Fragrant lavender combines perfectly with the aromatic flavour of fennel and mild Spanish onion. These unusual tartlets make an appealing light summer meal.

Serves 4
75g/3oz/6 tbsp butter
1 large Spanish onion, finely sliced
1 fennel bulb, trimmed and sliced
30ml/2 tbsp fresh lavender florets
    or 15ml/1 tbsp chopped dried
    culinary lavender
2 egg yolks
150ml/¼ pint/⅔ cup
    crème fraîche
salt and ground black pepper
fresh lavender florets, to garnish

For the pastry
115g/4oz/1 cup plain
    (all-purpose) flour
pinch of salt
50g/2oz/¼ cup chilled butter, cut
    into cubes
10ml/2 tsp cold water

1 To make the pastry, sift the flour and salt together. Rub the butter into the flour until the mixture resembles breadcrumbs. Stir in the water and bring the dough together to form a ball.

2 Roll the pastry out on a lightly floured surface to line four 7.5cm/3in round, loose-based flan tins (quiche pans). Prick the bases and chill. Preheat the oven to 200°C/400°F/Gas 6.

3 Melt the butter in a shallow pan and add the sliced onion, fennel and lavender. Reduce the heat, cover the pan and cook gently for 15 minutes, or until golden.

4 Line the pastry cases with greaseproof (waxed) paper and bake blind for 5 minutes. Remove the paper, return to the oven and bake for a further 4 minutes.

5 Reduce the oven temperature to 180°C/350°F/Gas 4. Mix the egg yolks, crème fraîche and seasoning together.

6 Spoon the onion mixture into the pastry cases. Spoon the crème fraîche mixture on top and bake for 10–15 minutes, or until the mixture has set and the filling is puffed up and golden.

7 Sprinkle with a little extra lavender and serve warm or cold.

Tomato and Basil Tart

This is a very simple yet extremely tasty tart made with rich shortcrust pastry, topped with mozzarella cheese and tomatoes, drizzled with olive oil and dotted with fresh basil leaves. It tastes best served while it is hot.

Serves 4
150g/5oz mozzarella cheese,
    thinly sliced
4 large tomatoes, thickly sliced
about 10 fresh basil leaves
30ml/2 tbsp olive oil
2 garlic cloves, thinly sliced
salt and ground black pepper

For the pastry
115g/4oz/1 cup plain
    (all-purpose) flour, plus extra
    for dusting
pinch of salt
50g/2oz/¼ cup butter, at
    room temperature
1 egg yolk

1 To prepare the pastry, sift the flour and salt into a bowl. Rub in the butter until the mixture resembles fine breadcrumbs. Beat the egg yolk and add to the mixture. Add a little water at a time, and mix together until the dough is smooth. Knead lightly on a floured work surface for a few minutes. Place in a plastic bag and chill for about 1 hour.

2 Preheat the oven to 190°C/375°F/Gas 5. Remove the pastry from the refrigerator, allow about 10 minutes for it to return to room temperature and then roll out into a 20cm/8in round. The pastry should be an even thickness all over.

3 Press the pastry into a 20cm/8in flan tin (quiche pan). Bake in the oven for 10 minutes. Allow to cool. Reduce the oven temperature to 180°C/350°F/Gas 4.

4 Lay the mozzarella slices over the pastry. On top, arrange the sliced tomatoes. Dip the basil leaves in olive oil and scatter them over the tomatoes.

5 Sprinkle the slices of garlic on top, drizzle the surface with the remaining oil and season. Bake the tart for 45 minutes, or until the pastry case is golden brown and the tomatoes are well cooked. Serve hot.

Lavender Tarts: Energy 539kcal/2233kJ; Protein 6.8g; Carbohydrate 30.7g, of which sugars 6.9g; Fat 44.1g, of which saturates 27.3g; Cholesterol 210mg; Calcium 116mg; Fibre 3.8g; Sodium 214mg.
Tomato and Basil Tart: Energy 307kcal/1280kJ; Protein 9.6g; Carbohydrate 19.1g, of which sugars 2.4g; Fat 22g, of which saturates 12.6g; Cholesterol 51mg; Calcium 207mg; Fibre 1.3g; Sodium 262mg.

Pissaladière

A Provençal classic, this is a delicious and colourful tart full of punchy flavour.

Serves 6
225g/8oz/2 cups plain
    (all-purpose) flour
115g/4oz/ ½ cup butter, chilled
    and cut into dice
5ml/1 tsp dried mixed herbs
pinch of salt

For the filling
45ml/3 tbsp olive oil
2 large onions, thinly sliced
2 garlic cloves, crushed
400g/14oz can
    chopped tomatoes
5ml/1 tsp granulated sugar
leaves from small sprig of thyme
freshly grated nutmeg
75g/3oz/ ¾ cup stoned (pitted)
    black olives, sliced
30ml/2 tbsp capers, rinsed
salt and ground black pepper
chopped fresh parsley, to garnish

1 Preheat the oven to 190°C/375°F/Gas 5. Put the flour in a bowl and rub in the butter until the mixture resembles fine breadcrumbs, then stir in the herbs and salt. Mix to a firm dough with cold water.

2 Roll out the pastry on a lightly floured surface and line a 23cm/9in round flan dish. Line the pastry case with baking parchment and add baking beans. Bake for 20 minutes, then lift out the paper and beans and bake the empty case for 5–7 minutes more. Leave to cool.

3 To make the filling, heat the oil in a frying pan and fry the onions and garlic gently for about 10 minutes, until quite soft. Stir in the tomatoes, sugar, thyme and nutmeg. Season and simmer for 10 minutes.

4 Leave the filling to cool. Mix in the olives and capers, then spoon into the flan case. Sprinkle with parsley and serve.

> **Variation**
> To serve Pissaladière hot, top with grated cheese and grill until the cheese is golden and bubbling.

Greek Picnic Pie

Aubergines layered with spinach, feta and rice make a marvellous filling for a pie. It is equally delicious served warm or cool.

Serves 6
375g/13oz shortcrust pastry,
    thawed if frozen
45–60ml/3–4 tbsp olive oil
1 large aubergine (eggplant),
    sliced into rounds
1 onion, chopped
1 garlic clove, crushed
175g/6oz spinach
4 eggs
75g/3oz feta cheese
40g/1½oz/ ½ cup freshly grated
    Parmesan cheese
60ml/4 tbsp natural (plain) yogurt
90ml/6 tbsp creamy milk
225g/8oz/2 cups cooked
    long grain rice
salt and ground black pepper

1 Preheat the oven to 180°C/350°F/Gas 4. Roll out the pastry thinly and line a 25cm/10in flan ring. Prick the pastry all over and bake the unfilled case in the oven for 10–12 minutes, until the pastry is pale golden.

2 Heat 30–45ml/2–3 tbsp of the oil in a frying pan and fry the aubergine slices for 6–8 minutes on each side, until golden. Lift out and drain on kitchen paper.

3 Add the onion and garlic to the oil remaining in the pan and fry gently until soft, adding a little extra oil if necessary.

4 Chop the spinach finely, by hand or in a food processor. Beat the eggs in a large mixing bowl, then add the spinach, feta, Parmesan, yogurt, milk and the onion mixture. Season well with salt and pepper and stir thoroughly.

5 Spread the rice in an even layer over the base of the partially cooked pastry case. Reserve a few aubergine slices for the top, and arrange the rest in an even layer over the rice.

6 Spoon the spinach and feta mixture over the aubergines and place the remaining aubergine slices on top. Bake for 30–40 minutes, until lightly browned. Serve the pie warm, or cool completely before transferring to a serving plate or wrapping and packing for a picnic.

Pissaladière: Energy 431kcal/1797kJ; Protein 9.9g; Carbohydrate 51.6g, of which sugars 10g; Fat 21.7g, of which saturates 3.1g; Cholesterol 8mg; Calcium 138mg; Fibre 3.8g; Sodium 825mg.
Greek Picnic Pie: Energy 554kcal/2309kJ; Protein 16.6g; Carbohydrate 53.3g, of which sugars 4.3g; Fat 31.4g, of which saturates 15.5g; Cholesterol 185mg; Calcium 299mg; Fibre 2.7g; Sodium 473mg.

Potato, Rosemary and Garlic Pizza

New potatoes, smoked mozzarella, rosemary and garlic make the flavour of this pizza unique. For a delicious variation, use sage instead of rosemary.

Serves 2–3
350g/12oz new potatoes
45ml/3 tbsp olive oil
2 garlic cloves, crushed
1 pizza base, 25–30cm/10–12in
   in diameter
1 red onion, thinly sliced
150g/5oz smoked mozzarella,
   grated
10ml/2 tsp chopped fresh
   rosemary
salt and freshly ground black
   pepper
30ml/2 tbsp freshly grated
   Parmesan cheese, to garnish

1 Preheat the oven to 200°C/425°F/ Gas 7. Cook the potatoes in boiling salted water for 5 minutes. Drain well. When cool, peel and slice thinly.

2 Heat 30 ml/2 tbsp of the oil in a frying pan. Add the sliced potatoes and garlic and fry for 5–8 minutes until tender.

3 Brush the pizza base with the remaining oil. Scatter over the onion, then arrange the potatoes on top.

4 Sprinkle over the mozzarella and rosemary. Grind over plenty of black pepper and bake for 15–20 minutes until crisp and golden. Remove from the oven and sprinkle over the Parmesan to serve.

Cook's Tip
Rosemary is a common wild shrub in the Mediterranean region. As a flavouring it is particularly popular in Italy, where it appears in both savoury and sweet dishes, and in the South of France. It is most often used to flavour meat, especially lamb, and the woody stems are sometimes burned when smoking cured meat and sausages. It goes very well with garlic and potatoes, as in this pizza topping.

Shallot and Garlic Tarte Tatin

Savoury versions of the famous apple tarte tatin have been popular for some years. Here, shallots are caramelized in butter, sugar and vinegar before being baked beneath a layer of Parmesan pastry.

Serves 4–6
300g/11oz puff pastry, thawed
   if frozen
50g/2oz/¼ cup butter
75g/3oz/1 cup freshly grated
   Parmesan cheese

For the topping
40g/1½oz/3 tbsp butter
500g/1¼lb shallots
12–16 large garlic cloves, peeled
   but left whole
15ml/1 tbsp golden caster
   (superfine) sugar
15ml/1 tbsp balsamic or
   sherry vinegar
45ml/3 tbsp water
5ml/1 tsp chopped fresh thyme,
   plus a few extra sprigs
   (optional)
salt and ground black pepper

1 Roll out the pastry into a rectangle. Spread the butter over it, leaving a 2.5cm/1in border. Scatter the Parmesan on top. Fold the bottom third of the pastry up to cover the middle and the top third down. Seal the edges, give a quarter turn and roll out to a rectangle, then fold as before. Chill for 30 minutes.

2 Melt the butter in a 23–25cm/9–10in round heavy pan that will go in the oven. Add the shallots and garlic, and cook until lightly browned. Scatter the sugar over the top and increase the heat a little. Cook until the sugar begins to caramelize, then turn the shallots and garlic in the buttery juices.

3 Add the vinegar, water, thyme and seasoning. Cook, part-covered, for 5–8 minutes, until the garlic is just tender. Cool.

4 Preheat the oven to 190°C/375°F/Gas 5. Roll out the pastry to the diameter of the pan and lay it over the shallots and garlic. Prick the pastry with a sharp knife, then bake for 25–35 minutes, or until the pastry is risen and golden.

5 Set aside to cool for 5–10 minutes, then invert the tart on to a serving platter. Scatter with a few thyme sprigs, if you like, and serve.

Pizza: Energy 690kcal/2899kJ; Protein 24.8g; Carbohydrate 85.2g, of which sugars 6.4g; Fat 30.1g, of which saturates 10.6g; Cholesterol 39mg; Calcium 410mg; Fibre 4.2g; Sodium 620mg.
Tarte Tatin: Energy 618kcal/2567kJ; Protein 12.8g; Carbohydrate 35.5g, of which sugars 9.6g; Fat 48.2g, of which saturates 22.8g; Cholesterol 79mg; Calcium 313mg; Fibre 3g; Sodium 605mg.

Golden Vegetable Paella

Hearty enough for the hungriest guests, this simple vegetarian version of a classic dish takes very little time to prepare and cook.

Serves 4

pinch of saffron strands
750ml/1¼ pints/3 cups hot
  vegetable stock
90ml/6 tbsp olive oil
2 large onions, sliced
3 garlic cloves, chopped
275g/10oz/1½ cups long
  grain rice
50g/2oz/⅓ cup wild rice
175g/6oz pumpkin, chopped
1 large carrot, cut into
  matchstick strips
1 yellow (bell) pepper, sliced
4 tomatoes, peeled, seeded
  and chopped
115g/4oz/1½ cups oyster
  mushrooms, quartered
salt and ground black pepper
strips of red, yellow and green
  pepper, to garnish

1 Place the saffron in a bowl with 60ml/4 tbsp of the hot stock. Leave to stand for 5 minutes.

2 Meanwhile, heat the oil in a paella pan or large, heavy-based frying pan. Add the onions and garlic and fry over a low heat, stirring occasionally, for 3 minutes, until just beginning to soften.

3 Add the long grain rice and wild rice to the pan and toss for 2–3 minutes, until coated in oil. Add the stock to the pan, together with the pumpkin and the saffron strands and liquid. Stir the mixture as it comes to the boil, then reduce the heat to the lowest setting.

4 Cover and cook very gently for 15 minutes, without lifting the lid. Add the carrot strips, yellow pepper and chopped tomatoes and season to taste with salt and pepper. Replace the lid and cook very gently for a further 5 minutes, or until the rice is almost tender.

5 Add the oyster mushrooms, check the seasoning and cook, uncovered, for just enough time to soften the mushrooms without letting the paella stick to the pan. Garnish with the peppers and serve.

Red Pepper Risotto

Several different types of risotto rice are available, and it is worth experimenting to find the one your family prefers. Look out for Arborio, Carnaroli and Vialone Nano.

Serves 6

3 large red (bell) peppers
30ml/2 tbsp olive oil
3 large garlic cloves,
  thinly sliced
1½ × 400g/14oz cans
  chopped tomatoes
2 bay leaves
450g/1lb/2½ cups risotto rice
about 1.5 litres/2½ pints/6 cups
  hot vegetable stock
6 fresh basil leaves, snipped
salt and ground black pepper

1 Put the peppers in a grill (broiler) pan and grill (broil) until the skins are charred and blistered all over. Put them in a bowl, cover with crumpled kitchen paper and leave to steam for 10 minutes to loosen the skin. Peel off the skins, then slice the flesh, discarding the cores and seeds.

2 Heat the oil in a wide, shallow pan. Add the garlic and tomatoes and cook over a low heat, stirring occasionally, for 5 minutes. Stir in the pepper slices and bay leaves and cook for 15 minutes more.

3 Stir the rice into the vegetable mixture and cook, stirring constantly, for 2 minutes, then add a ladleful of the hot stock. Cook, stirring constantly, until it has been absorbed. (Keep the stock simmering in a pan next to the risotto.)

4 Continue to add stock in this way, making sure that each addition has been absorbed before ladling in the next. When the rice is tender, season with salt and pepper to taste. Remove from the heat, cover and leave to stand for 10 minutes before stirring in the basil and serving.

> **Variation**
> Both yellow and orange (bell) peppers are also suitable for this recipe, but green peppers are too acerbic.

Vegetable Paella: Energy 388kcal/1646kJ; Protein 13.5g; Carbohydrate 78.8g, of which sugars 7.5g; Fat 3.6g, of which saturates 0.9g; Cholesterol 0mg; Calcium 57mg; Fibre 8.5g; Sodium 299mg.
Red Pepper Risotto: Energy 501kcal/2099kJ; Protein 10.9g; Carbohydrate 103.8g, of which sugars 13.6g; Fat 4.4g, of which saturates 0.7g; Cholesterol 0mg; Calcium 44mg; Fibre 3.9g; Sodium 20mg.

Tofu Balls with Spaghetti

This dish makes a great family supper, as children and adults alike really love the little tofu balls and the rich vegetable sauce, while pasta never fails to please.

Serves 4

250g/9oz firm tofu, drained
1 onion, coarsely grated
2 garlic cloves, crushed
5ml/1 tsp Dijon mustard
15ml/1 tbsp ground cumin
1 small bunch of parsley,
   finely chopped
15ml/1 tbsp soy sauce
50g/2oz/½ cup ground almonds
30ml/2 tbsp olive oil

350g/12oz spaghetti
sea salt and ground black pepper

For the sauce

15ml/1 tbsp olive oil
1 large onion, finely chopped
2 garlic cloves, chopped
1 large aubergine
   (eggplant), diced
2 courgettes (zucchini), diced
1 red (bell) pepper, finely chopped
pinch of sugar
400g/14oz can
   chopped tomatoes
200ml/7fl oz/scant 1 cup
   vegetable stock
1 bunch of fresh basil

1 Place the tofu, onion, garlic, mustard, cumin, parsley, soy sauce and ground almonds in a bowl. Season with salt and pepper and mix thoroughly. Roll into about 20 walnut-sized balls.

2 Heat the olive oil in a large frying pan, then cook the balls, turning them gently until brown all over. Remove from the pan and set aside on a plate. Heat the oil for the sauce in the same pan, add the onion and garlic and cook for 5 minutes, until soft.

3 Add the aubergine, courgette, pepper, sugar and seasoning and stir-fry for 10 minutes until the vegetables are beginning to soften and brown. Stir in the tomatoes and stock. Cover and simmer for 20–30 minutes, or until the sauce is thick. Place the tofu balls gently on top of the sauce, replace the lid and heat through for 2–3 minutes.

4 Meanwhile, cook the pasta in a large pan of salted, boiling water according to the manufacturer's instructions, then drain. Sprinkle the sauce with the basil and check the seasoning before serving with the spaghetti.

Spaghetti with Mixed Bean Sauce

Mixed beans are flavoured with fresh chilli and garlic and cooked in a tomato sauce in this quick and easy pasta dish, which makes a warming and substantial winter meal.

Serves 6

1 onion, finely chopped
1–2 garlic cloves, crushed
1 large green chilli, seeded and
   finely chopped
150ml/¼ pint/⅔ cup
   vegetable stock

400g/14oz can
   chopped tomatoes
30ml/2 tbsp tomato purée (paste)
120ml/4fl oz/½ cup red wine
5ml/1 tsp dried oregano
200g/7oz French beans, sliced
400g/14oz can red kidney
   beans, drained
400g/14oz can cannellini
   beans, drained
400g/14oz can
   chickpeas, drained
450g/1lb dried spaghetti
salt and ground black pepper

1 Put the onion, garlic and chilli in a pan with the stock. Bring to the boil and cook for 5 minutes, stirring occasionally.

2 Stir in the tomatoes, tomato purée, wine, oregano and seasoning. Bring to the boil, cover, then reduce the heat and simmer for 20 minutes, stirring the mixture occasionally.

3 Meanwhile, cook the French beans in a saucepan of boiling, salted water for about 5–6 minutes until tender. Drain the beans thoroughly. Add all the beans and the chickpeas to the sauce, stir to mix and simmer for a further 10 minutes.

4 Meanwhile, cook the spaghetti in a large saucepan of boiling salted water, according to the packet instructions, until al dente. Drain thoroughly. Transfer the pasta to a serving dish and top with the bean sauce. Serve immediately.

Cook's Tip
Use whatever varieties of canned beans you have in your storecupboard (pantry) for this quick standby recipe.

Tofu Balls with Spaghetti: Energy 576kcal/2422kJ; Protein 22.5g; Carbohydrate 79.4g, of which sugars 15.6g; Fat 21g, of which saturates 2.6g; Cholesterol 0mg; Calcium 425mg; Fibre 8g; Sodium 288mg.
Spaghetti with Bean Sauce: Energy 507kcal/2154kJ; Protein 24.6g; Carbohydrate 94.7g, of which sugars 11.7g; Fat 4.5g, of which saturates 0.6g; Cholesterol 0mg; Calcium 165mg; Fibre 14.9g; Sodium 689mg.

Spinach & Hazelnut Lasagne

Using fromage frais instead of a white sauce makes this a lighter, healthier version of a popular vegetarian dish, and spinach and hazelnuts add wonderful colour and crunch to the dish.

Serves 4

900g/2lb fresh spinach
300ml/ 1/2 pint/1 1/4 cups
   vegetable stock
1 medium onion, finely chopped
1 garlic clove, crushed
75g/3oz/ 3/4 cup hazelnuts
30ml/2 tbsp chopped fresh basil
6 sheets no pre-cook lasagne
400g/14oz can chopped tomatoes
200g/7oz/scant 1 cup low-fat
   fromage frais or ricotta cheese
salt and ground black pepper
flaked hazelnuts and chopped
   fresh parsley, to garnish

1 Preheat the oven to 200°C/400°F/Gas 6. Wash the spinach and place it in a pan with just the water that is still clinging to the leaves. Cover and cook over a fairly high heat for about 2 minutes, until the spinach has wilted. Drain well and set aside until required.

2 Heat 30ml/2 tbsp of the stock in a large pan. Add the onion and garlic, bring to the boil, then simmer until softened. Stir in the spinach, hazelnuts and basil.

3 In a large ovenproof dish, make layers of the spinach, lasagne and tomatoes. Season each layer with salt and pepper to taste. Pour over the remaining stock. Spread the fromage frais evenly over the top.

4 Bake the lasagne for about 45 minutes, or until golden brown. Serve hot, garnished with lines of flaked hazelnuts and chopped fresh parsley.

> **Cook's Tip**
> The flavour of hazelnuts is greatly improved if they are roasted. Place them on a baking sheet and bake in a moderate oven or under a hot grill until light golden. Rub off the brown skins, if necessary, in a clean dish towel.

Pappardelle and Summer Vegetable Sauce

A delicious, vibrantly colourful sauce of tomatoes and crisp fresh vegetables, chunkily cut, adds colour and robust flavour to ribbon pasta in this rustic and extremely simple Italian-style supper dish.

Serves 4

2 small red onions, peeled, root
   left intact
150ml/1/4 pint/2/3 cup
   vegetable stock
1–2 garlic cloves, crushed
60ml/4 tbsp red wine
2 courgettes (zucchini), cut
   into fingers
1 yellow (bell) pepper, sliced
400g/14oz can tomatoes
10ml/2 tsp chopped fresh thyme
5ml/1 tsp caster
   (superfine) sugar
350g/12oz dried pappardelle
salt and ground black pepper
fresh thyme and 6 black olives,
   stoned (pitted) and roughly
   chopped, to garnish

1 Cut each onion into eight wedges, cutting through the root end so that the layers will hold together during cooking. Put the pieces into a saucepan with the stock and garlic. Bring to the boil, cover then reduce the heat and simmer for 5 minutes, until tender.

2 Add the wine, courgettes, yellow pepper, tomatoes, chopped thyme and sugar. Season with salt and pepper and stir to mix.

3 Bring to the boil and cook gently for 5–7 minutes, shaking the pan occasionally to coat the vegetables with the sauce. (Do not overcook the vegetables as they are much nicer if they are still slightly crunchy.)

4 Meanwhile, cook the pasta in a large saucepan of boiling salted water, according to the packet instructions, until *al dente*. Drain thoroughly.

5 Transfer the pasta to a warmed serving dish and top with the vegetables. Garnish with fresh thyme and chopped black olives and serve immediately.

Spinach Lasagne: Energy 442kcal/1853kJ; Protein 19.6g; Carbohydrate 48.8g, of which sugars 12.3g; Fat 20g, of which saturates 4.8g; Cholesterol 5mg; Calcium 501mg; Fibre 8.6g; Sodium 350mg.
Pappardelle: Energy 424kcal/1792kJ; Protein 15.3g; Carbohydrate 83.6g, of which sugars 18.5g; Fat 4.3g, of which saturates 0.6g; Cholesterol 0mg; Calcium 99mg; Fibre 7.3g; Sodium 511mg.

Turkish Salad

This classic salad is a wonderful combination of textures and flavours. The saltiness of the feta cheese is perfectly balanced by the refreshing sweetness and crunch of the salad vegetables.

Serves 4
1 cos lettuce heart
1 green (bell) pepper
1 red (bell) pepper
1/2 cucumber
4 tomatoes
1 red onion

225g/8oz/2 cups feta
    cheese, crumbled
black olives, to garnish

For the dressing
45ml/3 tbsp olive oil
45ml/3 tbsp lemon juice
1 garlic clove, crushed
15ml/1 tbsp chopped fresh
    parsley
15ml/1 tbsp chopped
    fresh mint
salt and ground black pepper

1 Chop the lettuce into bitesize pieces. Seed the peppers, remove the cores and cut the flesh into thin strips. Chop the cucumber and slice or chop the tomatoes. Cut the onion in half, then slice finely.

2 Place the chopped lettuce, peppers, cucumber, tomatoes and onion in a large bowl. Scatter the feta over the top and toss together lightly.

3 To make the dressing, blend together the olive oil, lemon juice and garlic. Stir in the chopped parsley and mint and season with salt and pepper to taste.

4 Pour the dressing over the salad and toss lightly. Garnish with a handful of black olives and serve immediately.

Spanish Salad

Make this refreshing and substantial salad in the summer when tomatoes are at their sweetest and full of flavour. The distinctively flavoured dressing is spiced with paprika and cumin.

Serves 4
4 tomatoes
1/2 cucumber
1 bunch spring onions (scallions),
    trimmed and chopped
1 bunch watercress

8 stuffed olives
30ml/2 tbsp drained capers

For the dressing
30ml/2 tbsp red wine vinegar
5ml/1 tsp paprika
2.5 ml/1/2 tsp ground cumin
1 garlic clove, crushed
75ml/5 tbsp olive oil
salt and freshly ground black
    pepper

1 Plunge the tomatoes into a saucepan of boiling water for a minute, then transfer them to a bowl of cold water. Drain, then slip off and discard their skins.

2 Halve the tomatoes, remove and discard the seeds and cores and finely dice the flesh. Put them in a salad bowl.

3 Peel the cucumber, dice it finely and add it to the tomatoes. Then add half the spring onions to the salad bowl and mix lightly. Break the watercress into sprigs. Add this to the tomato mixture, followed by the olives and capers. Mix well.

4 To make the dressing, mix the wine vinegar, paprika, cumin and garlic in a bowl. Whisk in the oil and add salt and pepper to taste. Pour over the salad and toss lightly. Serve immediately with the remaining spring onions.

> **Variation**
> *Early in the year when tomatoes have yet to reach perfection, add extra flavour to this salad by tossing in the peeled segments of a large, juicy orange.*

> **Cook's Tip**
> *Most of the ingredients of this salad will happily sit for a short time in the dressing without deteriorating, so if you need to prepare it a little while before a meal, omit the lettuce.*

Spanish Salad: *Energy 172kcal/712kJ; Protein 2.5g; Carbohydrate 5g, of which sugars 4.3g; Fat 16g, of which saturates 2.4g; Cholesterol 0mg; Calcium 71mg; Fibre 2.2g; Sodium 305mg.*
Turkish Salad: *Energy 273kcal/1133kJ; Protein 11.1g; Carbohydrate 11.2g, of which sugars 10.9g; Fat 20.7g, of which saturates 9.2g; Cholesterol 39mg; Calcium 242mg; Fibre 3.2g; Sodium 826mg.*

Sun-ripened Tomato and Feta Salad

This tasty salad is a version of a traditional Greek salad, with plenty of purslane added to the usual combination of tomato, pepper, onion, cucumber, feta and olives. This recipe is popular in the rural communities of Greece as purslane is a common grassland plant and grows wild in many Greek gardens and meadows.

Serves 4
225g/8oz tomatoes
1 red onion, thinly sliced
1 green (bell) pepper, cored and
    sliced in thin ribbons
1 piece of cucumber, about
    15cm/6in in length, peeled and
    sliced in rounds
150g/5oz feta cheese, cubed
a large handful of fresh purslane,
    trimmed of thick stalks
8–10 black olives
90–105ml/6–7 tbsp extra virgin
    olive oil
15ml/1 tbsp lemon juice
1.5ml/¼ tsp dried oregano
salt and ground black pepper

1 Cut the tomatoes into quarters and place them in a large salad bowl. Add the onion, green pepper, cucumber, feta, purslane and olives.

2 Sprinkle the extra virgin olive oil, lemon juice and oregano on top of the salad. Add salt and ground black pepper to taste.

3 Toss well to coat everything in the olive oil and lemon, and to amalgamate the flavours.

4 If possible, let the salad stand for 10–15 minutes at room temperature before serving.

> **Cook's Tip**
> *Purslane is a succulent plant whose paddle-shaped leaves have a mild sweet-sour flavour. It grows wild in many parts of Europe, Asia and America and is easy to grow in the vegetable garden. If it is not available, you can use rocket (arugula) in this salad instead.*

Tomato, Mozzarella and Onion Salad

Sweet tomatoes and the heady scent of basil make a perfect marriage, and between them capture the essence of summer in this simple but delicious salad. Choose vine-ripened tomatoes as they usually have the best flavour.

Serves 4
5 large ripe tomatoes, peeled
2 buffalo mozzarella cheeses,
    drained and sliced
1 small red onion, chopped

For the dressing
½ small garlic clove, peeled
15g/½oz fresh basil
30ml/2 tbsp chopped fresh flat
    leaf parsley
25ml/5 tsp small salted
    capers, rinsed
2.5ml/½ tsp mustard
75–90ml/5–6 tbsp extra virgin
    olive oil
5–10ml/1–2 tsp balsamic vinegar
salt and ground black pepper

For the garnish
fresh basil leaves
fresh parsley sprigs

1 First make the dressing. Put the garlic, basil, parsley, half the capers and the mustard in a food processor or blender and process briefly to chop.

2 With the motor of the processor or blender running, gradually pour in the olive oil through the feeder tube until you have a smooth purée with a dressing consistency.

3 Add the balsamic vinegar to taste and season with plenty of freshly ground black pepper.

4 Slice the tomatoes. Carefully arrange the tomatoes with the mozzarella slices on a plate. Scatter the chopped red onion over the top and season to taste with a little ground black pepper.

5 Drizzle the dressing over the salad, then scatter a few whole or roughly torn basil leaves, parsley sprigs and the remaining capers on top as a garnish.

6 Leave the salad for 10–15 minutes before serving to allow the flavours to blend.

Mozzarella Salad: Energy 232kcal/960kJ; Protein 10.3g; Carbohydrate 3.6g, of which sugars 3.3g; Fat 19.7g, of which saturates 8.3g; Cholesterol 29mg; Calcium 206mg; Fibre 1.4g; Sodium 208mg.
Tomato and Feta Salad: Energy 283kcal/1168kJ; Protein 7.2g; Carbohydrate 6.8g, of which sugars 6.3g; Fat 25.4g, of which saturates 7.7g; Cholesterol 26mg; Calcium 158mg; Fibre 1.9g; Sodium 717mg.

Sour Cucumber with Fresh Dill

This is half pickle, half salad, and totally delicious served with rye or other coarse, dark, full-flavoured breads. Cucumbers are widely used for salads in hot regions as they are so refreshing. In summer you may be able to find the small cucumbers that are normally used for pickling, which are ideal for this treatment.

Serves 4

2 small cucumbers
3 onions
75–90ml/5–6 tbsp cider vinegar
30–45ml/2–3 tbsp chopped
    fresh dill
salt, to taste

1 Slice the cucumbers and the onions thinly and put them into a large mixing bowl. Season the vegetables with salt and toss together until they are thoroughly combined.

2 Leave the mixture to stand in a cool place for 5–10 minutes.

3 Add the cider vinegar, 30–45ml/2–3 tbsp cold water and the chopped dill to the cucumber and onion mixture.

4 Toss all the ingredients together until they are well combined, then chill in the refrigerator for a few hours, or until ready to serve.

> **Variation**
> *For a sweet and sour mixture, add 45ml/3 tbsp caster (superfine) sugar to the cucumber and onions with the cider vinegar in step 2.*

> **Cook's Tip**
> *Choose smooth-skinned, smallish cucumbers for this salad, as larger ones tend to be less tender. If you can only buy a large cucumber, peel it before slicing..*

Wild Rocket and Cos Lettuce Salad with Herbs

Salads in Greece are clean-tasting and often quite lemony in flavour. There is a national preference for strong-tasting leaves – sometimes quite bitter ones – that is also reflected in fresh salads, especially those that make use of the native cos lettuce. Rocket is another favourite ingredient, added to give salads a sharp edge.

Serves 4

a large handful of rocket
    (arugula) leaves
2 cos or romaine lettuce hearts
3 or 4 fresh flat leaf parsley
    sprigs, coarsely chopped
30–45ml/2–3 tbsp finely chopped
    fresh dill
75ml/5 tbsp extra virgin olive oil
15–30ml/1–2 tbsp lemon juice
salt

1 If the rocket leaves are young and tender they can be left whole, but older ones should be trimmed of thick stalks and then sliced coarsely. Discard any tough stalks.

2 Slice the cos or romaine lettuce hearts into thin ribbons and place these in a bowl, then add the rocket and the chopped fresh parsley and dill.

3 Make a dressing by whisking the extra virgin olive oil and lemon juice with salt to taste in a bowl until the mixture emulsifies and thickens.

4 Just before serving, pour over the dressing and toss lightly to coat everything in the glistening oil. Serve with crusty bread and a cheese or fish dish.

> **Cook's Tip**
> *It is important to mix the salad leaves in the right proportions to balance the bitterness of the rocket and the sweetness of the cos or romaine lettuce, and the best way to find this out is by taste.*

Sour Cucumber: Energy 59kcal/243kJ; Protein 2.5g; Carbohydrate 11.7g, of which sugars 8.7g; Fat 0.5g, of which saturates 0g; Cholesterol 0mg; Calcium 72mg; Fibre 2.9g; Sodium 11mg.
Rocket and Cos Salad: Energy 134kcal/554kJ; Protein 0.6g; Carbohydrate 1.3g, of which sugars 1.3g; Fat 14.1g, of which saturates 2.1g; Cholesterol 0mg; Calcium 21mg; Fibre 0.7g; Sodium 2mg.

Cucumber and Tomato Salad

This salad has been adopted from Bulgaria, where it was traditionally made with the local yogurt. Luxurious Greek yogurt, olive oil and sweet tomatoes lend themselves to this recipe.

Serves 4
450g/1lb firm ripe tomatoes
1/2 cucumber
1 onion
1 small fresh red or green chilli, seeded and chopped, or fresh chives, chopped into 2.5cm/1in lengths, to garnish
crusty bread or pitta breads, to serve

For the dressing
60ml/4 tbsp olive or vegetable oil
90ml/6 tbsp Greek (US strained plain) yogurt
30ml/2 tbsp chopped fresh parsley or chives
2.5ml/1/2 tsp vinegar
salt and freshly ground black pepper

1 Plunge the tomatoes into a saucepan of boiling water for 1 minute, then transfer them to a bowl of cold water. Drain, then slip off and discard their skins. Halve the tomatoes, remove and discard the seeds and cores and chop the flesh into even-sized pieces. Put them into a salad bowl.

2 Chop the cucumber and onion into pieces of similar size to the tomatoes and put them in the bowl.

3 Mix all the dressing ingredients together and season to taste. Pour the dressing over the salad and toss all the ingredients together thoroughly.

4 Sprinkle over black pepper and garnish with the chopped chilli or chives. Serve with chunks of crusty bread or pile into pitta pockets.

> **Cook's Tip**
> If you have time, before assembling the salad salt the chopped cucumber lightly and leave it in a colander for about 30 minutes to drain. This will avoid making the salad watery.

Moroccan Orange, Onion and Olive Salad

This is a refreshing salad, full of sweet, interesting flavours, to follow a rich main dish, such as a Moroccan tagine, or to lighten any spicy meal. It is also a very good salad to serve as part of a cold buffet.

Serves 6
5 large oranges
90g/3 1/2 oz/scant 1 cup black olives
1 red onion, thinly sliced
1 large fennel bulb, thinly sliced, feathery tops reserved
15ml/1 tbsp chopped fresh mint, plus a few extra sprigs
15ml/1 tbsp chopped fresh coriander (cilantro), plus a few extra sprigs
2.5ml/1/2 tsp orange flower water

For the dressing
60ml/4 tbsp olive oil
10ml/2 tsp lemon juice
2.5ml/1/2 tsp ground toasted coriander seeds
salt and freshly ground black pepper

1 Peel the oranges with a knife, removing all the white pith, and cut them into 5mm/1/2in slices. Remove any pips and work over a bowl to catch all the orange juice. Set the juice aside.

2 Stone (pit) the olives, if you wish. In a bowl, toss the orange slices, onion and fennel together with the olives, chopped mint and fresh coriander.

3 Make the dressing. In a bowl or jug (pitcher), whisk together the olive oil, 15ml/1 tbsp of the reserved fresh orange juice and the lemon juice. Add the ground toasted coriander seeds and season to taste with a little salt and pepper. Whisk thoroughly to emulsify the dressing.

4 Toss the dressing into the salad and leave to stand for 30–60 minutes for the flavours to mingle.

5 Drain off any excess dressing and place the salad on a serving dish. Scatter with the herbs and fennel tops, and sprinkle with the orange flower water.

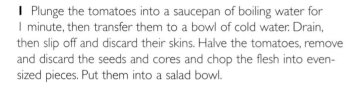

Cucumber & Tomato Salad: Energy 156kcal/646kJ; Protein 3g; Carbohydrate 5.8g, of which sugars 5.4g; Fat 13.9g, of which saturates 2.9g; Cholesterol 0mg; Calcium 75mg; Fibre 2.1g; Sodium 32mg.
Moroccan Salad: Energy 150kcal/629kJ; Protein 3g; Carbohydrate 18.9g, of which sugars 16.4g; Fat 7.6g, of which saturates 1.1g; Cholesterol 0mg; Calcium 102mg; Fibre 3.8g; Sodium 292mg.

Cabbage Salad with Lemon and Olive

Mushroom Salad

In winter, *lahano salata* frequently appears on the Greek table. It is made with compact creamy-coloured "white" cabbage. In more northern climates, this type of tight-headed cabbage can sometimes be a little woody, but in Greece, it always produces a rather sweet-tasting, unusual salad, which has a crisp and refreshing texture.

Serves 4
1 white cabbage
12 black olives

For the dressing
75–90ml/5–6 tbsp extra virgin olive oil
30ml/2 tbsp lemon juice
1 garlic clove, crushed
30ml/2 tbsp finely chopped fresh flat leaf parsley
salt

1 Cut the cabbage in quarters, discard the outer leaves and trim off any thick, hard stems, as well as the hard base.

2 Lay each cabbage quarter in turn on its side and cut long, very thin slices until you reach the central core, which should be discarded.

3 Place the shredded cabbage in a large bowl and stir in all the black olives.

4 Make the dressing by whisking the extra virgin olive oil, lemon juice, garlic, chopped parsley and salt together in a bowl until well blended.

5 Pour the dressing over the cabbage and olives, and toss the salad until everything is evenly coated.

Cook's Tip
The key to a perfect cabbage salad is to shred the cabbage as finely as possible. If you have a slicing blade on your food processor you can use it for cabbage, but be scrupulous about trimming away any woody or fibrous parts before feeding the leaves into the machine.

Thanks to their rich earthiness, mushrooms add substance and flavour to all sorts of dishes. This refreshing mushroom salad is often served as part of a selection of vegetable salads, or crudités, or it could be eaten as a simple first course. Leaving it to stand before serving brings out the inherent sweetness of the mushrooms.

Serves 4
175g/6oz white mushrooms, trimmed
grated rind and juice of ¹/₂ lemon
about 30–45ml/2–3 tbsp crème fraîche or sour cream
salt and white pepper
15ml/1 tbsp chopped fresh chives, to garnish

1 Wipe the mushrooms clean. Slice them thinly with a sharp knife. Place in a large salad bowl.

2 Add the lemon rind and juice and the cream to the mushrooms, adding a little more cream if needed. Stir gently to mix, then season with salt and pepper.

3 Leave the salad to stand for at least 1 hour, stirring occasionally to mix.

4 Sprinkle the salad with chopped chives before serving.

Cook's Tip
When preparing mushrooms do not wash them or some of the flavour will disappear. Instead, gently wipe them clean with a cloth or brush.

Variation
If you prefer, toss the mushrooms in a little vinaigrette – made by whisking 60ml/4 tbsp walnut oil or extra virgin olive oil into the lemon juice.

Cabbage Salad: Energy 208Kcal/861kJ; Protein 4g; Carbohydrate 12.9g, of which sugars 12.5g; Fat 15.8g, of which saturates 2.2g; Cholesterol 0mg; Calcium 155mg; Fibre 6.2g; Sodium 303mg.
Mushroom Salad: Energy 22kcal/93kJ; Protein 1.1g; Carbohydrate 0.6g, of which sugars 0.5g; Fat 1.8g, of which saturates 1g; Cholesterol 5mg; Calcium 17mg; Fibre 0.7g; Sodium 7mg.

Lemon and Carrot Salad

Lamb's Lettuce and Beetroot Salad

This tangy, colourful and refreshing salad has a wonderfully clear, sweet flavour that balances rich cheese or egg-based dishes. The smaller the carrots you use, the sweeter they will be.

Serves 6
450g/1lb small, young carrots
finely grated rind and juice of
  ½ lemon
15ml/1 tbsp soft light
  brown sugar
30ml/2 tbsp sunflower oil
5ml/1 tsp hazelnut or
  sesame oil
5ml/1 tsp chopped fresh oregano
salt and freshly ground
  black pepper

1 Finely grate the carrots and place them in a large bowl. Stir in the lemon rind and 15–30ml/1–2 tbsp of the lemon juice.

2 Add the sugar, sunflower and hazelnut or sesame oils, and mix well. Add more lemon juice and seasoning to taste, then sprinkle on the oregano and toss lightly to mix.

3 Leave the salad for 1 hour before serving, garnished with a sprig of oregano.

> **Cook's Tip**
> *Carrots are a wonderfully versatile vegetable and are available all year round. They are a great source of beta carotine, an antioxidant which helps to enhance the immune system. A single carrot will supply enough vitamin A for an entire day, and is reputed to cut the risk of lung cancer by half.*

> **Variation**
> *Experiment with using different fresh herbs in this salad. Tarragon goes very well with carrots, or use a few sprigs of lemon thyme or rosemary.*

The delicate flavour of the lamb's lettuce in this salad is perfect with the tangy beetroot. If you like, sprinkle the salad with chopped walnuts before serving.

Serves 4
150–175g/5–6 oz/3–4 cups
  lamb's lettuce (corn salad),
  washed and roots trimmed
250g/½ lb/3 or 4 small beetroot
  (beets), cooked, peeled
  and diced
30ml/2 tbsp chopped
  fresh parsley

For the vinaigrette
30–45ml/2–3 tbsp white wine
  vinegar or lemon juice
20ml/1 heaped tbsp
  Dijon mustard
2 garlic cloves, finely chopped
2.5ml/½ tsp sugar
125ml/4fl oz/½ cup sunflower or
  grapeseed oil
125ml/4fl oz/½ cup crème
  fraîche or double (heavy) cream
salt and ground black pepper

1 First make the vinaigrette. Mix the vinegar or lemon juice, mustard, garlic, sugar, salt and pepper in a small bowl, then slowly whisk in the oil until the sauce thickens.

2 Lightly beat the crème fraîche or double cream to lighten it slightly, then whisk it into the dressing.

3 Toss the lamb's lettuce with a little of the vinaigrette and arrange on a serving plate or in a bowl.

4 Spoon the beetroot into the centre of the lamb's lettuce and drizzle over the remaining vinaigrette. Sprinkle with chopped parsley and serve immediately.

> **Cook's Tip**
> *Lamb's lettuce has a mild flavour and a delicate texture. It is known as mâche in France, where it has always been very popular. It is a fairly hardy plant, often found growing wild, so has traditionally been used in winter salads, and can also be steamed and served as a vegetable.*

Carrot Salad Energy 90kcal/372kJ; Protein 1.1g; Carbohydrate 11.8g, of which sugars 8.4g; Fat 4.5g, of which saturates 2.7g; Cholesterol 11mg; Calcium 34mg; Fibre 2.8g; Sodium 59mg.
Lamb's Lettuce Salad: Energy 348kcal/1447kJ; Protein 8.7g; Carbohydrate 22.1g, of which sugars 3.4g; Fat 25.7g, of which saturates 7.3g; Cholesterol 20mg; Calcium 199mg; Fibre 3.2g; Sodium 764mg.

Radicchio, Artichoke and Walnut Salad

The distinctive, earthy taste of Jerusalem artichokes makes a lovely contrast to the slightly bitter edge of the radicchio and the sharp freshness of the lemony dressing. Serve this unusual grilled salad warm or cold – it is perfect for a winter meal.

Serves 4
1 large radicchio or 150g/5oz
   radicchio leaves
40g/1½oz/⅓ cup walnut pieces
45ml/3 tbsp walnut oil
500g/1¼lb Jerusalem artichokes
   thinly pared rind and juice of
   1 lemon
coarse sea salt and freshly ground
   black pepper
fresh flat leaf parsley, to garnish

1 If using a whole radicchio, cut it into 8–10 wedges. Put the wedges or leaves in a flameproof dish. Scatter over the walnuts, then spoon over the oil and season.

2 Peel the Jerusalem artichokes and cut up any large ones so that the pieces are all roughly the same size.

3 Add the artichokes to a pan of boiling salted water with half the lemon juice and cook for 5–7 minutes, until just tender. Drain. Preheat the grill to high.

4 Toss the artichokes into the salad with the remaining lemon juice and the pared rind. Season with coarse salt and pepper. Grill for 2–3 minutes, until beginning to brown. Serve at once garnished with torn pieces of parsley.

Rocket and Pear Salad

For a sophisticated start to an elaborate meal, try this simple Italian salad of honey-rich pears, fresh Parmesan shavings and aromatic leaves of rocket. Williams or Packhams pears have the right texture for this dish, and should be ripe but not soft. Their slightly gritty texture is perfectly reflected in the shavings of Parmesan cheese.

Serves 4
3 ripe pears
10ml/2 tsp lemon juice
45ml/3 tbsp hazelnut or
   walnut oil
115g/4oz rocket (arugula),
   washed and dried
75g/3oz Parmesan
   cheese,
   shaved
ground black pepperopen-
   textured bread, to serve

1 Peel and core the pears and slice thickly lengthways. Moisten the flesh with lemon juice to keep it white.

2 Combine the nut oil with the pears. Add the rocket leaves and toss.

3 Turn the salad out on to four small plates and top with shavings of Parmesan cheese. Season with pepper and serve with the bread.

Cook's Tip
Rocket is fairly easy to find in supermarkets, but if you have a garden you can grow your own from early spring to late summer. The flowers are also edible and tasty.

Variations
• *Crumble a little blue cheese, such as Gorgonzola or Dolcelatte, over the salad instead of the Parmesan.*
• *Scatter a small handful of roasted, roughly chopped hazelnuts into the salad.*
• *Instead of the hazelnuts, try toasted pumpkin seeds.*

Cook's Tip
Jerusalem artichokes, which are not related to globe artichokes but are relatives of the sunflower, are popular in France and are sometimes used raw, grated, in salads. They can be difficult to peel, so choose the least knobbly tubers you can find. Drop them into water with lemon juice as you peel them to stop them discolouring.

Celery and Coconut Salad with Lime

Chicory, Carrot and Rocket Salad

This bright and colourful salad combines two of France's most popular vegetables, rocket and chicory. If you don't like rocket, baby spinach leaves or watercress can be used instead, as they have a similarly peppery quality. Use very fresh, juicy carrots to attain the attractive colour and sweetness that will make this salad a firm favourite.

Serves 4–6

3 carrots, coarsely grated
about 50g/2oz fresh rocket (arugula), roughly chopped
1 large head of chicory, separated into leaves

For the dressing

45ml/3 tbsp sunflower oil
15ml/1 tbsp hazelnut or walnut oil
30ml/2 tbsp cider or white wine vinegar
10ml/2 tsp clear honey
5ml/1 tsp grated lemon rind
15ml/1 tbsp poppy seeds
salt and ground black pepper

1 Mix together the carrots and rocket in a bowl and season.

2 Shake the dressing ingredients together in a screw-top jar then pour on to the carrot mixture. Toss the salad thoroughly.

3 Line shallow salad bowls with the chicory leaves and spoon the salad into the centre. Serve lightly chilled.

Cook's Tip
- Chicory has white, yellow-tipped leaves with a mildly bitter flavour. It is grown in the dark to prevent the leaves from turning green and opening up.
- Once you have cut the chicory head, brush the leaves with lemon juice to prevent discolouration.

Variation
- If you can't find chicory, use raddichio, which comes from the same family and has a similar bitter taste.

This Turkish salad is unusual in its use of grated coconut, which is mainly reserved in Turkey as a garnish for sweet dishes, or served with shelled pomegranate seeds as a medieval meze. Juicy and refreshing, it is welcome on a hot sunny day as part of a buffet spread outdoors, or as an accompaniment to spicy dishes. It looks especially appealing served in coconut shell halves.

Serves 3–4

45–60ml/3–4 tbsp thick natural (plain) yogurt
2 garlic cloves, crushed
5ml/1 tsp grated lime rind
juice of 1 lime
8 long celery sticks, leaves reserved for the garnish
flesh of ½ fresh coconut
salt and ground black pepper
sprigs of fresh flat leaf parsley, to garnish

1 Mix the yogurt and garlic in a bowl, add the lime rind and juice and season with salt and pepper. Set aside.

2 Coarsely grate the celery sticks and the fresh coconut flesh.

3 Fold the grated celery and coconut into the dressing, then leave to sit for 15–20 minutes to let the celery juices mingle with the dressing. Don't leave it for too long or the salad will become watery.

4 To serve, spoon the salad into a bowl and garnish with celery leaves and parsley sprigs.

Cook's Tip
To prepare fresh coconut, pierce the eye at the base of the nut with a nail and drain out the coconut milk. Crack the nut open with a hammer and remove the flesh. The thin brown inner skin can be peeled off using a vegetable peeler or a sharp knife. Grate the flesh coarsely.

Chicory, Carrot and Rocket Salad: Energy 90kcal/374kJ; Protein 1.2g; Carbohydrate 5.2g, of which sugars 5g; Fat 7.3g, of which saturates 1g; Cholesterol 0mg; Calcium 51mg; Fibre 1.6g; Sodium 16mg
Celery and Coconut Salad: Energy 126kcal/521kJ; Protein 2.1g; Carbohydrate 2.9g, of which sugars 2.9g; Fat 11.9g, of which saturates 10.1g; Cholesterol 0mg; Calcium 63mg; Fibre 3.6g; Sodium 69mg.

Simple Cooked Salad

A version of a North African favourite, this cooked salad is usually served as a side dish with a main course. Make this delicious salad one day in advance to improve the flavours.

Serves 4
2 well-flavoured tomatoes, quartered
2 onions, chopped
1/2 cucumber, halved lengthways, seeded and sliced
1 green (bell) pepper, chopped
30ml/2 tbsp lemon juice
45ml/3 tbsp olive oil
2 garlic cloves, crushed
30ml/2 tbsp chopped fresh coriander (cilantro)
salt and ground black pepper
sprigs of fresh coriander (cilantro) leaves, to garnish

1 Put the tomatoes, onions, cucumber and green pepper into a pan and add 60ml/4 tbsp water. Heat gently and allow to simmer for about 5 minutes. Leave to cool.

2 In a small jug (pitcher), mix together the lemon juice, olive oil and crushed garlic.

3 Carefully strain the cooked vegetables, then transfer to a large salad bowl.

4 Pour the dressing over the vegetables, season with salt and pepper and stir in the chopped coriander.

5 Serve at once or chill overnight so that the flavours develop. Garnish with fresh coriander leaves, if you like.

> **Variation**
> To add a fiery kick to this salad, try adding one green chilli (deseeded and finely chopped) to the vegetables before cooking them. You could also use chilli oil instead of olive oil to make the dressing.

Halloumi and Grape Salad

In the east Mediterranean, firm salty halloumi cheese is often served fried for breakfast or supper. In this recipe the fried slices of cheese are tossed with sweet, juicy grapes, which really complement the distinctive flavour of halloumi.

Serves 4
For the dressing
60ml/4 tbsp olive oil
2.5ml/1/2 tsp caster (superfine) sugar

15ml/1 tbsp lemon juice
salt and ground black pepper
15ml/1 tbsp chopped fresh thyme or dill

For the salad
150g/5oz mixed salad leaves
75g/3oz seedless green grapes
75g/3oz seedless black grapes
250g/9oz halloumi cheese
45ml/3 tbsp olive oil
fresh young thyme leaves or dill, to garnish

1 To make the dressing, mix together the olive oil, lemon juice and caster sugar. Season to taste with salt and pepper. Stir in the thyme or dill and set aside.

2 Toss together the salad leaves and the green and black grapes, then transfer to a large serving plate.

3 Thinly slice the halloumi cheese. Heat the oil in a large frying pan. Add the cheese slices and fry briefly until they are turning golden on the underside. Turn the cheese with a fish slice and cook the other side.

4 Arrange the cheese over the salad. Pour over the dressing and garnish with thyme or dill.

> **Cook's Tip**
> Halloumi is a sheep's milk cheese that originates in Cyprus and is eaten all over the eastern Mediterranean. It cooks extremely well, without losing its shape, and is often grilled on skewers with vegetables.

Halloumi and Grape Salad: Energy 434Kcal/1811kJ; Protein 16.6g; Carbohydrate 31.4g, of which sugars 2.7g; Fat 27.8g, of which saturates 4g; Cholesterol 0mg; Calcium 149mg; Fibre 12.5g; Sodium 334mg.
Cooked Salad: Energy 131kcal/540kJ; Protein 2.2g; Carbohydrate 11g, of which sugars 9.1g; Fat 8.9g, of which saturates 1.3g; Cholesterol 0mg; Calcium 55mg; Fibre 3g; Sodium 13mg.

Moroccan Braised Chickpeas

This sweet and spicy
chickpea salad is a real treat.
Serve it cold with couscous
to make a perfect barbecue
side dish.

Serves 6
250g/9oz/1½ cups dried
    chickpeas, soaked overnight in
    cold water
15ml/1 tbsp olive oil
2 onions, cut into wedges
10ml/2 tsp ground cumin
1.5ml/¼ tsp ground turmeric
1.5ml/¼ tsp cayenne pepper
15ml/1 tbsp ground coriander
5ml/1 tsp ground cinnamon
300ml/½ pint/1¼ cups
    vegetable stock
2 carrots, sliced
115g/4oz/½ cup ready-to-eat
    dried apricots, halved
50g/2oz/scant ½ cup raisins
25g/1oz/¼ cup flaked
    (sliced) almonds
30ml/2 tbsp chopped fresh
    coriander (cilantro)
30ml/2 tbsp chopped fresh flat
    leaf parsley
salt and ground black pepper

1 Soak a clay pot in cold water for 20 minutes, then drain.
Alternatively use a standard casserole dish. Place the chickpeas
in a pan with plenty of cold water. Bring to the boil and boil
rapidly for 10 minutes, then drain and place the chickpeas in
the pot, cover with lukewarm water and cover with the lid.

2 Place in a cold oven and set the temperature to
200°C/400°F/Gas 6. Cook for 1 hour, then reduce the oven
temperature to 160°C/325°F/Gas 3. Cook for a further 1 hour,
or until the chickpeas are tender.

3 Meanwhile, heat the olive oil in a frying pan, add the onions
and cook for about 6 minutes, or until softened. Add the cumin,
turmeric, cayenne pepper, coriander and cinnamon and cook
for 2–3 minutes. Stir in the stock, carrots, apricots, raisins and
almonds and bring to the boil.

4 Drain the chickpeas and return them to the clay pot, add the
spicy vegetable mixture and stir to mix. Cover and return to the
oven for 30 minutes. Remove from the oven and allow to cool.

5 Season with salt and pepper, lightly stir in half the chopped
coriander and parsley and serve sprinkled with the remainder.

Grilled Aubergine and Couscous Salad

Packets of flavoured
couscous are available in
most supermarkets – you
can use whichever you like,
but garlic and coriander is
particularly good for this
recipe. Together with a crisp
green salad, this dish makes
a wonderful accompaniment
for fish or poultry.

Serves 2
1 large aubergine (eggplant)
30ml/2 tbsp olive oil
115g/4oz packet garlic-and-
    coriander (cilantro)
    flavoured couscous
30ml/2 tbsp chopped fresh mint
salt and ground black pepper
fresh mint leaves, to garnish

1 Preheat the grill (broiler) to high. Cut the aubergine into
large chunky pieces and toss them with the olive oil.

2 Season with salt and pepper to taste and spread the
aubergine pieces on a non-stick baking sheet. Grill (broil)
for 5–6 minutes, turning occasionally, until golden brown.
Remove from the heat.

3 Meanwhile, in a large bowl, prepare the couscous in boiling
water, according to the instructions on the packet.

4 Stir the grilled aubergine and chopped fresh mint into the
couscous, toss the salad thoroughly to spread the flavours, and
serve immediately, garnished with mint leaves.

Variations
- A similar dish, which is also popular around Greece, uses
grilled (broiled) courgettes (zucchini) instead of, or as well as,
the aubergine. Slice the courgettes into thin rounds or ovals,
brush with olive oil, and place under a hot grill (broiler) for a
few minutes on each side.
- Make the salad using 115g/4oz/⅔ cup plain couscous,
soaked in 175ml/6fl oz/¾ cup boiling water for 5–10
minutes. Add a generous squeeze of lemon juice and a
handful of chopped fresh herbs of your choice before tossing
the couscous with the aubergine.

Braised Chickpeas: Energy 630kcal/2639kJ; Protein 51.4g; Carbohydrate 64.1g, of which sugars 16.5g; Fat 20.2g, of which saturates 4.2g; Cholesterol 170mg; Calcium 91mg; Fibre 2.5g; Sodium 169mg.
Aubergines and Couscous: Energy 248Kcal/1,033kJ; Protein 4.4g; Carbohydrate 32.3g, of which sugars 2.5g; Fat 12.1g, of which saturates 1.7g; Cholesterol 0mg; Calcium 24mg; Fibre 2.5g; Sodium 3mg.

Spanish Rice Salad

Rice and a choice of chopped crunchy salad vegetables are served in a well-flavoured dressing. This is a universally popular salad that lends itself to endless variations and is a staple of summer buffet tables.

Serves 6
275g/10oz/1½ cups white long
    grain rice
1 bunch spring onions (scallions),
    finely sliced
1 green (bell) pepper, finely diced
1 yellow (bell) pepper, finely diced
225g/8oz tomatoes, peeled,
    seeded and chopped
30ml/2 tbsp chopped fresh
    coriander (cilantro)

For the dressing
75ml/5 tbsp mixed sunflower and
    olive oil
15ml/1 tbsp rice vinegar
5ml/1 tsp Dijon mustard
salt and ground black pepper

1 Cook the rice in plenty of boiling water for 10–12 minutes until it is tender but still *al dente*. Be careful not to overcook it. Drain in a colander, rinse under cold water and drain again. Leave to cool.

2 Place the rice in a large serving bowl. Add the spring onions, peppers, tomatoes and coriander.

3 To make the salad dressing, mix all the ingredients in a jar with a tight-fitting lid and shake vigorously until well mixed. Stir 60–75ml/4–5 tbsp of the dressing into the rice and adjust the seasoning to taste.

4 Cover and chill for about 1 hour before serving. Offer the remaining dressing separately.

> **Cook's Tips**
> • Cooked garden peas, cooked diced carrot and drained, canned sweetcorn can be added to this versatile salad.
> • Leftover plain boiled rice, either long grain or basmati, can be turned into a salad in this way, provided it is perfectly cooked and not sticky.

Brown Bean Salad

Brown beans, which are dried broad beans, are widely used in Egyptian cookery, principally to make *ful medames*, which is something of a national dish and is generally eaten for breakfast. The beans can increasingly be found in wholefood shops and supermarkets in other countries outside Egypt.

Serves 6
350g/12oz/1½ cups dried
    brown beans
3 thyme sprigs
2 bay leaves
1 onion, halved
4 garlic cloves, crushed
7.5ml/1½ tsp cumin
    seeds, crushed
3 spring onions (scallions),
    finely chopped
90ml/6 tbsp chopped
    fresh parsley
20ml/4 tsp lemon juice
90ml/6 tbsp olive oil
3 hard-boiled eggs, shelled and
    roughly chopped
1 pickled cucumber, roughly
    chopped
salt and ground black pepper

1 Put the beans in a bowl with plenty of cold water and leave to soak overnight. Drain, transfer to a saucepan and cover with fresh water. Bring to the boil and boil rapidly for 10 minutes.

2 Reduce the heat and add the thyme, bay leaves and onion. Simmer very gently for about 1 hour until tender. Drain and discard the herbs and onion.

3 Mix together the garlic, cumin, spring onions, parsley, lemon juice, oil and add a little salt and pepper. Pour over the beans and toss the ingredients lightly together.

4 Gently stir in the eggs and cucumber and serve immediately.

> **Cook's Tips**
> • The cooking time for dried beans can vary considerably. They may need only 45 minutes, or a lot longer.
> • If brown beans are not available, dried black or red kidney beans make good substitutes.

Spanish Rice Salad: Energy 246kcal/1028kJ; Protein 4.7g; Carbohydrate 42.4g, of which sugars 5.6g; Fat 6.3g, of which saturates 0.8g; Cholesterol 0mg; Calcium 24mg; Fibre 1.7g; Sodium 33mg.
Brown Bean Salad: Energy 300kcal/1258kJ; Protein 16.6g Carbohydrate 27.1g, of which sugars 2.5g; Fat 14.8g, of which saturates 2.5g; Cholesterol 95mg; Calcium 99mg; Fibre 9.9g; Sodium 50mg

Artichokes with Beans and Aioli

Broad Bean and Feta Salad

As with the French aioli, there are many recipes for the Spanish equivalent. The one used here is exceptionally garlicky, a perfect partner to freshly cooked vegetables.

Serves 4
For the aioli
6 large garlic cloves, sliced
10ml/2 tsp white wine vinegar

250ml/8fl oz/1 cup olive oil
salt and ground black pepper

For the salad
225g/8oz French beans
3 small globe artichokes
15ml/1 tbsp olive oil
pared rind of 1 lemon
coarse salt and ground black pepper, to sprinkle
lemon wedges, to garnish

1 To make the aioli, put the garlic and vinegar in a blender or mini food processor. With the machine running, gradually pour in the olive oil until the mixture is thickened and very smooth. (Alternatively, crush the garlic to a paste with the vinegar and gradually beat in the oil using a hand whisk.) Season to taste.

2 To make the salad, cook the beans in boiling water for 1–2 minutes until slightly softened. Drain.

3 Trim the artichoke stalks close to the base. Cook the artichokes in a large pan of boiling salted water for about 30 minutes or until you can easily pull away a leaf from the base. Drain well.

4 Halve the cooked artichokes lengthways with a sharp knife and carefully pull out the choke using a teaspoon.

5 Arrange the artichokes and beans on serving plates and drizzle with the oil. Scatter with pared lemon rind and season with coarse salt and pepper. Spoon the aioli into the artichoke hearts and serve warm, garnished with lemon wedges.

Variation
Mediterranean baby artichokes are sometimes available and, unlike the larger ones, can be eaten whole.

This recipe is loosely based on a typical medley of fresh-tasting Greek salad ingredients – broad beans, tomatoes and feta cheese. It is lovely served warm or cold as an appetizer or main course accompaniment.

Serves 4–6
900g/2lb broad (fava) beans, shelled, or 350g/12oz shelled frozen beans
60ml/4 tbsp olive oil
175g/6oz plum tomatoes, halved, or quartered if large
4 garlic cloves, crushed
115g/4oz/1 cup firm feta cheese, cut into chunks
45ml/3 tbsp chopped fresh dill
12 black olives
salt and ground black pepper
chopped fresh dill, to garnish

1 Cook the fresh or frozen broad beans in boiling, salted water until just tender. Drain and set aside.

2 Meanwhile, heat the olive oil in a heavy frying pan and add the tomatoes and garlic. Cook until the tomatoes are beginning to colour.

3 Add the feta cheese to the pan and toss the ingredients together for 1 minute. Remove the pan from the heat.

4 Add the drained beans, dill, olives and salt and pepper to the pan and mix well.

5 Turn into a large salad bowl and serve immediately, garnished with chopped dill.

Cook's Tip
Feta is a creamy soft white cheese traditionally made in Greece. It was first made by shepherds who needed to preserve the milk of their flocks. It is usually made with sheep's milk and goat's milk, and is produced in blocks. Feta is widely used in salads, pastries and in baking.

Artichokes with Beans & Aioli: Energy 540kcal/2221kJ; Protein 2.1g; Carbohydrate 3.6g, of which sugars 2.9g; Fat 57.6g, of which saturates 8.2g; Cholesterol 0mg; Calcium 82mg; Fibre 3.1g; Sodium 80mg.
Broad Bean & Feta Salad: Energy 175kcal/727kJ; Protein 8.3g; Carbohydrate 8.8g, of which sugars 2.2g; Fat 12g, of which saturates 3.8g; Cholesterol 13mg; Calcium 121mg; Fibre 4.7g; Sodium 342mg.

Warm Black-Eyed Bean Salad

This is an easy dish to make without too much forward planning, as black-eyed beans do not need to be soaked overnight. Adding spring onions and loads of aromatic dill transforms them into a refreshing and healthy meal. The dish can be served hot or at room temperature.

Serves 4

275g/10oz/1½ cups black-eyed
   beans (peas)
5 spring onions (scallions), sliced
   into rounds
a large handful of fresh rocket
   (arugula) leaves, chopped
   if large
45–60ml/3–4 tbsp chopped
   fresh dill
150ml/¼ pint/⅔ cup extra virgin
   olive oil
juice of 1 lemon, or to taste
10–12 black olives
salt and ground black pepper
small cos or romaine lettuce
   leaves, to serve

1 Thoroughly rinse the beans and drain them well. Transfer them to a pan and pour in enough cold water to just about cover them. Slowly bring them to the boil over a low heat. As soon as the water is boiling, remove the pan from the heat and drain the water off immediately.

2 Put the beans back in the pan with fresh cold water to cover and add a pinch of salt – this will make their skins harder and stop them from disintegrating when they are cooked.

3 Bring the beans to the boil over a medium heat, then lower the heat and cook them until they are soft but not mushy. They will take only 20–30 minutes, so keep an eye on them.

4 Drain the beans, reserving 75–90ml/5–6 tbsp of the cooking liquid. Transfer the beans to a large salad bowl. Immediately add the remaining ingredients, including the reserved cooking liquid, and mix well.

5 Serve immediately, piled on the lettuce leaves, or leave to cool slightly before serving.

Baked Vegetables with Rosemary

The Spanish love to scoop up cooked vegetables with bread, and the local name of this dish, mojete, is derived from the word meaning "to dip". Peppers, tomatoes and onions are baked together to make a colourful, soft cooked salad.

Serves 8

2 red (bell) peppers
2 yellow (bell) peppers
1 red onion, sliced
2 garlic cloves, halved
50g/2oz/⅓ cup black olives
6 large ripe tomatoes,
   quartered
5ml/1 tsp soft light brown sugar
45ml/3 tbsp Amontillado sherry
3–4 fresh rosemary sprigs
25ml/1½ tbsp olive oil
salt and ground black pepper
fresh bread, to serve

1 Halve the peppers lengthways and remove and discard the stalks, cores and seeds. Cut each pepper lengthways into 12 even strips. Preheat the oven to 200°C/400°F/Gas 6.

2 Place the peppers, onion, garlic, olives and tomatoes in a large non-stick roasting pan. Sprinkle the vegetables with the sugar, then pour in the sherry. Season well with salt and pepper, cover with foil and bake in the oven for 45 minutes.

3 Remove the foil from the pan and stir the mixture well. Add the rosemary sprigs and drizzle with the olive oil. Return the pan to the oven and bake, uncovered, for a further 30 minutes, or until the vegetables are very tender.

4 Serve hot or cold with plenty of fresh crusty bread.

Cook's Tip
Spain is the world's chief olive producer, with over 300 million trees. Much of the crop goes into the production of olive oil, and about half the olives sold as fruit are exported. Try to use good quality Spanish olives for this recipe. Choose unpitted ones as they have a better flavour.

Black-eyed Bean Salad: Energy 238kcal/1007kJ; Protein 16.1g; Carbohydrate 31g, of which sugars 2.4g; Fat 6.4g, of which saturates 0.9g; Cholesterol 0mg; Calcium 114mg; Fibre 12.3g; Sodium 580mg.
Baked Vegetables: Energy 75kcal/313kJ; Protein 1.3g; Carbohydrate 7.5g, of which sugars 7.2g; Fat 3.9g, of which saturates 0.6g; Cholesterol 0mg; Calcium 17mg; Fibre 2g; Sodium 151mg.

Grilled Pepper Salad

Ideally this salad should be made with a combination of red and yellow peppers for the most jewel-like, colourful effect and the sweetest flavour.

Serves 6

4 large (bell) peppers, red or
  yellow or a combination of
  the two

30 ml/2 tbsp capers, rinsed
18–20 black or green olives

For the dressing
90 ml/6 tbsp extra-virgin olive oil
2 garlic cloves, finely chopped
30 ml/2 tbsp balsamic or
  wine vinegar
salt and ground black pepper

1 Place the peppers under a hot grill (broiler) and turn occasionally until they are black and blistered on all sides. Remove from the heat, place in a plastic food bag and close the top loosely to trap the steam and loosen the skins. Set aside until they are cool enough to handle.

2 Carefully peel the peppers, then cut them into quarters. Remove the stems and seeds.

3 Cut the peppers into strips, and arrange them on a serving dish. Distribute the capers and olives evenly over the peppers.

4 To make the dressing, mix the oil and garlic in a small bowl, crushing the garlic with a spoon to release the flavour. Mix in the vinegar and season with salt and pepper. Pour over the salad, mix well and leave to stand for at least 30 minutes before serving to allow the flavours of the dressing to permeate the peppers. Serve at room temperature.

Cook's Tip
- *Grilling (broiling) the peppers until they start to char not only softens and loosens the skins but intensifies their flavour and imparts a lovely smoky flavour to the flesh.*
- *Use any colour (bell) pepper for this salad except green, as green peppers are unripe and their flavour is too sour.*

Rich Red Salad

This delectable and colourful recipe perfectly combines several red ingredients. Eat the dish at room temperature, accompanied by a leafy green salad and some good, crusty bread.

Serves 4

3 red (bell) peppers
6 large plum tomatoes

2.5 ml/½ tsp dried red
  chilli flakes
1 red onion, finely sliced
3 garlic cloves, finely chopped
grated rind and juice of 1 lemon
45 ml/3 tbsp chopped fresh flat
  leaf parsley
30 ml/2 tbsp extra-virgin olive oil
salt and ground black pepper
black and green olives and extra
  chopped flat leaf parsley,
  to garnish

1 Preheat the oven to 220°C/425°F/Gas 7. Place the peppers on a baking sheet and roast, turning occasionally, for 10 minutes or until the skins are almost blackened.

2 Add the tomatoes to the baking sheet and return to the oven for a further 5 minutes.

3 Place the peppers in a plastic bag and close the top loosely, trapping in the steam, to loosen the skins. Set aside, with the tomatoes, until they are cool enough to handle.

4 Carefully pull the skins off the peppers. Remove the core and seeds, then chop the peppers roughly and place in a mixing bowl. Chop the tomatoes roughly and add them to the bowl with the peppers.

5 Add the chilli flakes, onion, garlic, lemon rind and juice. Sprinkle over the parsley. Mix well, then transfer to a serving dish. Sprinkle with a little salt and black pepper, drizzle over the olive oil and scatter the olives and extra parsley over the top. Serve at room temperature.

Cook's Tip
Peel the tomatoes as well as the peppers, if you prefer.

Grilled Pepper Salad: Energy 411kcal/1724kJ; Protein 10.8g; Carbohydrate 52.8g, of which sugars 8.2g; Fat 18.8g, of which saturates 2.8g; Cholesterol 3mg; Calcium 103mg; Fibre 4.6g; Sodium 41mg.
Rich Red Salad: Energy 122kcal/510kJ; Protein 2.5g; Carbohydrate 14.3g, of which sugars 13.5g; Fat 6.5g, of which saturates 1.1g; Cholesterol 0mg; Calcium 24mg; Fibre 3.8g; Sodium 18mg.

Roasted Peppers with Tomatoes

This is a Sicilian-style salad, that uses some typical ingredients from the Italian island. The flavour improves if the salad is made about two hours before you plan to eat it.

Serves 4

1 red (bell) pepper
1 yellow (bell) pepper
1 green (bell) pepper
4 sun-dried tomatoes in oil, drained
4 ripe plum tomatoes, sliced
15ml/1 tbsp capers, drained
15ml/1 tbsp pine nuts
1 garlic clove, very thinly sliced
fresh basil sprigs, to garnish

For the dressing

75ml/5 tbsp extra virgin olive oil
15ml/1 tbsp balsamic vinegar
5ml/1 tsp lemon juice
chopped fresh mixed herbs, such as oregano, basil and flat leaf parsley
salt and ground black pepper

1 Preheat the grill (broiler). Cut the peppers in half and remove the seeds and stalks. Cut into quarters and cook, skin-side up, under the hot grill until the skin chars.

2 Put the peppers into a plastic bag and seal loosely to trap the steam and loosen the skin. Leave until cool enough to handle, then peel the pepper halves and cut into strips.

3 Thinly slice the sun-dried tomatoes. Arrange the peppers and fresh tomatoes on a serving dish and scatter over the sun-dried tomatoes, capers, pine nuts and garlic.

4 To make the dressing, mix together the olive oil, balsamic vinegar, lemon juice and chopped fresh herbs and season with salt and pepper to taste. Pour over the salad and leave the bowl in a cool place for the flavours to infuse. Scatter with fresh basil leaves before serving.

> **Cook's Tip**
> A little of the flavoured oil from the jar of sun-dried tomatoes can be added to the dressing if you like.

Roasted Peppers with Tomatoes and Artichokes

If you have time, make and dress this salad an hour or two before serving, as this will allow the juices to mingle and create the most mouthwatering salad.

Serves 4

1 red (bell) pepper
1 yellow (bell) pepper
1 green (bell) pepper
4 ripe plum tomatoes, sliced
2 canned or bottled artichokes, drained and quartered
4 sun-dried tomatoes in oil, drained and thinly sliced
15ml/1 tbsp capers, drained
15ml/1 tbsp pine nuts
1 garlic clove, sliced thinly

For the dressing

15ml/1 tbsp balsamic vinegar
5ml/1 tsp lemon juice
75ml/5 tbsp extra virgin olive oil
chopped fresh mixed herbs
salt and freshly ground black pepper

1 Preheat the grill (broiler) to high. Cut the peppers in half, and remove the seeds and stalks. Cut into quarters and place on a grill pan covered with foil. Grill (broil), skin-side up until the skin chars.

2 Put the peppers into a plastic bag and seal loosely to trap the steam and loosen the skin. Leave until cool enough to handle, then peel the peppers and cut into strips.

3 Arrange the peppers, fresh tomatoes and artichokes on a serving dish. Sprinkle over the sun-dried tomatoes, the capers, pine nuts and the garlic.

4 To make the dressing, put the balsamic vinegar and lemon juice in a bowl and whisk in the olive oil, then the chopped herbs. Season with salt and pepper. Pour the dressing over the salad an hour or two before it is served, if possible.

> **Variation**
> The flavour of the salad can be varied by using different herbs in the salad dressing.

Roasted Peppers with Tomatoes: Energy 216kcal/890kJ; Protein 1.5g; Carbohydrate 8.1g, of which sugars 7.9g; Fat 19.9g, of which saturates 2.9g; Cholesterol 0mg; Calcium 22mg; Fibre 2.4g; Sodium 24mg.
Peppers with Tomatoes and Artichokes: Energy 218kcal/902kJ; Protein 3.2g; Carbohydrate 12.7g, of which sugars 12.2g; Fat 17.4g, of which saturates 2.4g; Cholesterol 0mg; Calcium 73mg; Fibre 4.6g; Sodium 62mg.

Spiced Aubergine Salad

The delicate flavours of aubergine, tomatoes and cucumber are lightly spiced with cumin and coriander in this fresh-tasting salad, which is topped with yogurt. It is lovely with grilled vegetable kebabs or a rice dish.

Serves 4

2 small aubergines (eggplants), sliced
75ml/5 tbsp extra virgin olive oil
50ml/2fl oz/¼ cup red wine vinegar
2 garlic cloves, crushed
15ml/1 tbsp lemon juice
2.5ml/½ tsp ground cumin
2.5ml/½ tsp ground coriander
½ cucumber, thinly sliced
2 well-flavoured tomatoes, thinly sliced
30ml/2 tbsp natural (plain) yogurt
salt and ground black pepper
chopped fresh flat leaf parsley, to garnish

1 Preheat the grill. Lightly brush the aubergine slices with olive oil and cook under a high heat, turning once, until golden and tender. Alternatively, cook them on a griddle pan.

2 When they are done, remove the aubergine slices to a chopping board and cut them into quarters.

3 Mix together the remaining oil, the vinegar, garlic, lemon juice, cumin and coriander. Season with salt and pepper and mix thoroughly. Add the warm aubergines, stir well and chill for at least 2 hours.

4 Add the cucumber and tomatoes to the aubergines. Transfer to a serving dish and spoon the yogurt on top. Sprinkle with parsley and serve.

Cook's Tips
The advice is often given to sprinkle sliced aubergines with salt and leave them to disgorge their bitter juices. Most modern varieties of aubergine are not bitter, but this technique is also useful in breaking down the cell walls of the fruit to reduce their capacity to absorb oil.

Marinated Courgettes

This is a simple summer dish served all over Italy when courgettes are in season. It has a light and fresh flavour and can be eaten hot or cold. It is a delicious accompaniment to many meals and would be an excellent addition to a cold buffet.

Serves 6

4 courgettes (zucchini), sliced
30ml/2 tbsp extra virgin olive oil
30ml/2 tbsp chopped fresh mint, plus whole leaves, to garnish
30ml/2 tbsp white wine vinegar
salt and ground black pepper

1 Fry the courgette slices in 15ml/1 tbsp of the oil in batches, for 4–6 minutes, or until tender and brown around the edges. Transfer to a bowl. Season well with salt and pepper.

2 Heat the remaining oil in the pan, then add the chopped mint and vinegar and let it bubble for a few seconds. Stir into the courgettes. Set aside to marinate for 1 hour, then serve garnished with mint leaves.

Aubergine, Lemon and Caper Salad

Ensure you cook the aubergine until it is meltingly soft and luscious.

Serves 6

1 aubergine (eggplant), about 675g/1½lb, cut into 2.5cm/1in cubes
60ml/4 tbsp olive oil
grated rind and juice of 1 lemon
30ml/2 tbsp capers, rinsed
12 pitted green olives
30ml/2 tbsp chopped fresh flat leaf parsley
salt and ground black pepper

1 Shallow fry the aubergine cubes for about 10 minutes until soft and golden. Drain on kitchen paper, sprinkled with salt.

2 In a large bowl, toss the aubergine with the rest of the ingredients and season well. Serve at room temperature.

Spiced Aubergine Salad: Energy 161kcal/669kJ; Protein 2.3g; Carbohydrate 5.8g, of which sugars 5.5g; Fat 14.6g, of which saturates 2.2g; Cholesterol 0mg; Calcium 37mg; Fibre 3.7g; Sodium 15mg.
Marinated Courgettes: Energy 60kcal/248kJ; Protein 2.7g; Carbohydrate 2.8g, of which sugars 2.3g; Fat 4.3g, of which saturates 0.7g; Cholesterol 0mg; Calcium 49mg; Fibre 1.2g; Sodium 3mg.
Aubergine, Lemon & Caper: Energy 141kcal/585kJ; Protein 2g; Carbohydrate 4.1g, of which sugars 3.7g; Fat 13.2g, of which saturates 2g; Cholesterol 0mg; Calcium 50mg; Fibre 4.4g; Sodium 289mg.

Potatoes Baked with Fennel, Onions, Garlic and Saffron

Potatoes, fennel and onions infused with garlic, saffron and spices and baked in the oven make a sophisticated and attractive accompaniment for an egg-based main-course dish.

Serves 4–6
500g/1¼lb small waxy potatoes, cut into chunks or wedges
good pinch of saffron strands (12–15 strands)
1 head of garlic, separated into cloves
12 small red or yellow onions, peeled but left whole
3 fennel bulbs, cut into wedges, feathery tops reserved
4–6 fresh bay leaves
6–9 fresh thyme sprigs
175ml/6fl oz/¾ cup vegetable stock
30ml/2 tbsp sherry vinegar
2.5ml/½ tsp sugar
5ml/1 tsp fennel seeds, lightly crushed
2.5ml/½ tsp paprika
45ml/3 tbsp olive oil
salt and ground black pepper

1 Boil the potatoes in salted water for 8–10 minutes. Drain. Preheat the oven to 190°C/375°F/Gas 5. Soak the saffron in 30ml/2 tbsp warm water for 10 minutes.

2 Peel and finely chop 2 garlic cloves. Place the potatoes, onions, unpeeled garlic cloves, fennel wedges, bay leaves and thyme sprigs in a roasting dish.

3 Mix together the stock, saffron and its soaking liquid, vinegar and sugar, then pour over the vegetables. Stir in the fennel seeds, paprika, garlic and oil, and season with salt and pepper.

4 Cook in the oven for 1–1¼ hours, stirring occasionally, until the vegetables are tender. Chop the reserved fennel tops, sprinkle over the vegetables and serve.

> **Cook's Tip**
> *Saffron gives this dish its distinctive colour and flavour, but it is still delicious if made without saffron.*

Greek Potato and Tomato Bake

This is an adaptation of a classic Greek dish, which is usually cooked in a pot on the stove. This recipe has a richer flavour as it is stove-cooked first and then baked in the oven, so that the potatoes have time to absorb the flavours of the onion, tomatoes and garlic. The tomatoes provide all the liquid needed in the casserole. It makes a lovely accompaniment to many different dishes.

Serves 4
120ml/4fl oz/½ cup extra virgin olive oil
1 large onion, finely chopped
3 garlic cloves, crushed
4 large ripe tomatoes, peeled, seeded and chopped
1kg/2¼lb even-size main-crop waxy potatoes
salt and ground black pepper
a few sprigs of fresh flat leaf parsley, to garnish

1 Preheat the oven to 180°C/350°F/Gas 4.

2 Heat the oil in a flameproof casserole. Fry the chopped onion and garlic for 5 minutes, or until softened and just starting to brown.

3 Add the tomatoes to the pan, season and cook for 1 minute.

4 Cut the potatoes into wedges. Add to the pan, stirring well. Cook for 10 minutes. Season again with salt and pepper, and cover with a tight-fitting lid.

5 Place the covered casserole on the middle shelf of the oven and cook for 45 minutes–1 hour. Garnish with a few sprigs of fresh flat leaf parsley.

> **Cook's Tips**
> • *Make sure that the potatoes are evenly sized and completely coated in the olive oil otherwise they will not cook evenly.*
> • *Replace the fresh tomatoes with a 400g/14oz can of plum tomatoes.*

Greek Potato Bake: Energy 399kcal/1670kJ; Protein 5.9g; Carbohydrate 49.3g, of which sugars 10.6g; Fat 21.2g, of which saturates 3.2g; Cholesterol 0mg; Calcium 41mg; Fibre 4.6g; Sodium 39mg.
Potatoes Baked with Fennel: Energy 162kcal/676kJ; Protein 4.4g; Carbohydrate 23.6g, of which sugars 7.1g; Fat 6.2g, of which saturates 0.9g; Cholesterol 0mg; Calcium 49mg; Fibre 4.9g; Sodium 23mg.

French Scalloped Potatoes

These potatoes taste rich even though only a little cream is used.

Serves 6
1kg/2¼lb potatoes
900ml/1½ pints/3⅔ cups milk
pinch of freshly grated nutmeg

1 bay leaf
15–30ml/1–2 tbsp butter,
   softened
2 or 3 garlic cloves, very
   finely chopped
45–60ml/3–4 tbsp crème fraîche
   or whipping cream
salt and ground black pepper

1 Preheat the oven to 180°C/350°F/Gas 4. Cut the potatoes into fairly thin slices. Put them in a large pan and pour over the milk, adding more to cover if needed.

2 Add the salt and pepper, nutmeg and the bay leaf to the potatoes. Bring slowly to the boil over a medium heat and simmer for about 15 minutes until the potatoes just start to soften, but are not completely cooked, and the milk has thickened.

3 Generously butter a 36cm/14in oval gratin dish and sprinkle the garlic over the base.

4 Using a slotted spoon, transfer the potatoes to the gratin or baking dish. Taste the milk and adjust the seasoning, then pour over enough of the milk to come just to the surface of the potatoes, but not cover them.

5 Spoon a thin layer of cream over the top, or, if you prefer, add more of the thickened milk to cover.

6 Bake the potatoes for about 1 hour until the milk is absorbed and the top is a deep golden brown.

Cook's Tip
If cooked ahead, this dish will keep hot in a low oven for an hour or so without suffering. Moisten the top with a little extra cream, if you like.

Wilted Spinach with Onion, Rice and Dill

Spinach is a characterful vegetable that plays a starring role in many recipes and this is a delicious dish that can be made in very little time. In Greece it is particularly popular during periods of fasting, when meat is avoided for religious reasons.

Serves 6
675g/1½lb fresh spinach,
   trimmed of any hard stalks
105ml/7 tbsp extra virgin olive oil
1 large onion, chopped
juice of ½ lemon
150ml/¼ pint/⅔ cup water
115g/4oz/generous ½ cup long
   grain rice
45ml/3 tbsp chopped fresh dill,
   plus extra sprigs to garnish
salt and ground black pepper

1 Wash the spinach in cold water and drain. Repeat up to four or five times, until the spinach is completely clean and free of grit, then drain it completely in a colander. Brush off the excess water with kitchen paper and coarsely shred the spinach leaves.

2 Heat the olive oil in a large pan and sauté the onion until translucent. Add the spinach and stir for a few minutes to coat it with the oil.

3 As soon as the spinach looks wilted, add the lemon juice and the measured water and bring to the boil. Add the rice and half of the dill, then cover and cook gently for about 10 minutes or until the rice is cooked to your taste. If it looks too dry, add a little hot water.

4 Spoon the spinach and rice into a serving dish and sprinkle the sprigs of dill over the top. Serve the dish hot or at room temperature.

Cook's Tip
This dish is ideal to accompany fried chickpea rissoles. It can also be eaten as a first course.

Scalloped Potatoes: Energy 204kcal/866kJ; Protein 8g; Carbohydrate 33.9g, of which sugars 9.2g; Fat 5.1g, of which saturates 3.1g; Cholesterol 14mg; Calcium 191mg; Fibre 1.7g; Sodium 98mg.
Spinach with Rice: Energy 325kcal/1344kJ; Protein 7.8g; Carbohydrate 29.9g, of which sugars 5.6g; Fat 19.2g, of which saturates 2.7g; Cholesterol 0mg; Calcium 328mg; Fibre 4.8g; Sodium 242mg.

Rice with Onions and Lentils

Lentils are a favourite staple in Greece, especially during periods of fasting in the Orthodox tradition, when meat is not eaten, as they are a nourishing source of protein. In this dish, which is also eaten all over the Middle East, they are combined with rice and spices, making a satisfying side dish or a main course to eat with salad.

Serves 6

350g/12oz/1½ cups large
   brown lentils, soaked overnight
   in water
2 large onions
45ml/3 tbsp olive oil
15ml/1 tbsp ground cumin
2.5ml/½ tsp ground cinnamon
225g/8oz/generous 1 cup long
   grain rice
salt and freshly ground
   black pepper
a few sprigs of fresh flat leaf
   parsley, to garnish

1 Drain the lentils and put them in a large pan. Add enough cold water to cover the lentils by 5cm/2in.

2 Bring the lentils to the boil, cover and simmer for 40 minutes to 1½ hours, or until tender. Drain thoroughly.

3 Finely chop one of the large onions, and finely slice the other. Heat 15ml/1 tbsp olive oil in a large saucepan, add the finely chopped onion and fry until soft. Do not allow to brown.

4 Add the drained lentils and gently stir them in so that they are thoroughly coated in the oil. Then add the cumin and coriander and stir in. Season to taste with salt and freshly ground black pepper.

5 Measure the volume of rice and add it, with the same volume of water, to the lentil mixture. Cover and simmer for about 20 minutes, until the rice is tender.

6 Heat the remaining olive oil in a frying pan, and cook the sliced onion over a medium heat until it has softened and caramelized to a very dark brown. Tip the rice mixture into a serving bowl, sprinkle with the onion rings and serve hot or cold, garnished with flat leaf parsley.

Spicy Roasted Vegetables

Oven roasting brings out and intensifies all the flavours of cherry tomatoes, courgettes (zucchini), onion and red peppers. Serve hot with couscous or rice for a main meal, or on its own as a delicious side dish.

Serves 4

2–3 courgettes (zucchini)
1 Spanish onion
2 red (bell) peppers
16 cherry tomatoes
2 garlic cloves, chopped
pinch of cumin seeds
5ml/1 tsp fresh thyme
   or 4–5 torn fresh basil leaves
60ml/4 tbsp olive oil
juice of ½ lemon
5–10ml/1–2 tsp harissa or
   Tabasco sauce
2–3 fresh thyme sprigs,
   to garnish

1 Preheat the oven to 220°C/425°F/ Gas 7. Trim the courgettes and cut them into long strips. Cut the onion into thin wedges. Cut the peppers into chunks, discarding the seeds and core.

2 Mix these vegetables together and spread them out in a cast-iron dish or roasting pan.

3 Add the cherry tomatoes, chopped garlic, cumin seeds and thyme or torn basil leaves.

4 Sprinkle the vegetables with the olive oil and toss to coat them evenly. Cook the mixture in the oven for 25–30 minutes until the vegetables are very soft and have begun to char slightly at the edges.

5 Meanwhile, mix the lemon juice with the harissa or Tabasco sauce. Stir into the vegetables when they are cooked, garnish with the thyme and serve immediately.

> **Cook's Tip**
> *Harissa is a chilli paste, popular in North Africa. It can be bought in cans or jars and contains pounded chillies, garlic, coriander, olive oil and seasoning.*

Rice with Lentils: Energy 394Kcal/1,656kJ; Protein 17.5g; Carbohydrate 68g, of which sugars 5.1g; Fat 6.6g, of which saturates 0.9g; Cholesterol 0mg; Calcium 54mg; Fibre 3.8g; Sodium 23mg.
Spicy Roasted Vegetables: Energy 117kcal/484kJ; Protein 4.1g; Carbohydrate 14g, of which sugars 11.2g; Fat 5.2g, of which saturates 0.8g; Cholesterol 0mg; Calcium 77mg; Fibre 3.4g; Sodium 9mg.

Baked Tomatoes with Orange Zest

This recipe for baked tomatoes is given a fruity edge with a hint of orange. For the best results, use fresh Italian plum tomatoes, which have a warm, slightly sweet flavour. They are also fleshier and have fewer seeds than other varieties. Serve this tasty dish with fresh crusty Italian bread or crispbreads.

Serves 4
25g/1oz/2 tbsp unsalted butter
1 large garlic clove, crushed
5ml/1 tsp finely grated
   orange rind
4 firm plum tomatoes, or 2 large
   beef tomatoes
salt and ground black pepper
fresh basil leaves, to garnish

1 Soften the butter in a small bowl and blend with the crushed garlic, orange rind, and seasoning. Chill for a few minutes.

2 Preheat the oven to 200°C/400°F/Gas 6. Halve the tomatoes crossways and trim the bases so they stand upright.

3 Place the tomatoes in an ovenproof dish and spread the butter equally over each.

4 Bake the tomatoes in the oven for 15–25 minutes, depending on the size of the tomato halves, until just tender. Serve sprinkled with the fresh basil leaves.

> **Cook's Tip**
> Choose a dish in which the tomato halves will fit snugly, without too much space between them. Serve them straight from the dish if possible.

> **Variation**
> Sprinkle a few black olives among the tomatoes in the dish or sprinkle the tomatoes with a little Parmesan cheese.

Roasted Garlic with Plum Tomatoes

These are so simple to prepare yet taste absolutely wonderful. Use a large, shallow earthenware dish that will allow the tomatoes to sear and char in a hot oven. The recipe includes a lot of garlic, but the cloves are left whole and the flavour is subtle. Garlic lovers can squeeze the softened cloves out of their skins and eat the sweet flesh with the tomatoes.

Serves 4
8 plum tomatoes
12 garlic cloves
20ml/4 tsp extra virgin olive oil
3 bay leaves
salt and ground black pepper
45ml/3 tbsp fresh oregano leaves,
   to garnish

1 Preheat the oven to 230°C/450°F/Gas 8. Cut all the plum tomatoes in half, lengthways. Select an ovenproof dish that will hold all the tomato halves snugly in a single layer. Place the tomatoes in the dish and push the whole, unpeeled garlic cloves between them.

2 Lightly brush the tomatoes with the oil, add the bay leaves and sprinkle freshly ground black pepper over the top.

3 Bake the tomatoes and garlic in the oven for about 45 minutes, until the tomatoes have softened and are sizzling in the dish. They should be charred around the edges.

4 Season with salt and a little more black pepper, if needed. Garnish with fresh oregano leaves and serve immediately.

> **Cook's Tip**
> Tomatoes are an essential ingredient in Mediterranean cooking, and are used in many different dishes, both raw and cooked. There are thousands of tomato varieties, from small cherry tomatoes to larger beefsteak ones. Plum tomatoes have fewer seed compartments than round ones, and more solid flesh.

Baked Tomatoes: Energy 65kcal/269kJ; Protein 0.8g; Carbohydrate 3.4g, of which sugars 3.2g; Fat 5.5g, of which saturates 3.4g; Cholesterol 13mg; Calcium 8mg; Fibre 1.1g; Sodium 47mg.
Roasted Garlic: Energy 70kcal/294kJ; Protein 1.8g; Carbohydrate 7.8g, of which sugars 7.8g; Fat 3.8g, of which saturates 0.7g; Cholesterol 0mg; Calcium 18mg; Fibre 2.5g; Sodium 23mg.

Courgette and Asparagus Parcels

To appreciate their delicate aromas, it's best if these Italian-style vegetable-filled paper parcels are brought to the table sealed, to be broken open by the diners. They are a lovely way to celebrate the unique flavours of early summer vegetables, and make a tasty and low-fat accompaniment to many main courses.

Serves 4

2 courgettes (zucchini)
1 leek
225g/8oz young
  asparagus, trimmed
4 tarragon sprigs
4 whole garlic cloves,
  unpeeled
1 egg, beaten, to glaze
salt and ground black pepper

1 Preheat the oven to 200°C/400°F/Gas 6. Using a potato peeler, carefully slice the courgettes lengthways into thin strips. (Discard the first and last strips of skin.)

2 Cut the leek into very fine julienne strips and cut the asparagus evenly into 5cm/2in lengths.

3 Cut out four sheets of greaseproof (waxed) paper measuring 30 × 38cm/12 × 15in and fold each one in half. Draw a large curve to make a oval when unfolded. Cut along the inside of the line and open out.

4 Divide the courgettes, leek and asparagus evenly between each sheet of paper, positioning the filling on one side of the fold line, then top each portion with a sprig of tarragon and an unpeeled garlic clove. Season to taste.

5 Brush the edges of the paper lightly with the beaten egg and fold over.

6 Twist the edges of the paper together tightly and firmly so that each parcel is completely sealed. Lay the parcels on a baking sheet.

7 Bake in the preheated oven for 10 minutes. Serve the parcels immediately.

Courgette and Tomato Bake

This dish has been made for centuries in Provence. Its French name is Tian Provençal, from the shallow earthenware casserole, known as a *tian*, in which it is traditionally cooked. In the days before home kitchens had ovens, this kind of dish would have been assembled at home and then carried to the baker's to make use of the heat remaining in the oven after the bread was baked.

Serves 4

15ml/1 tbsp olive oil, plus more
  for drizzling
1 large onion (about 225g/8oz),
  finely sliced
1 garlic clove, finely chopped
450g/1lb tomatoes
450g/1lb courgettes (zucchini)
5ml/1 tsp dried herbes de
  Provence
30ml/2 tbsp grated
  Parmesan cheese
salt and ground black pepper

1 Preheat the oven to 180°C/350°F/Gas 4. Heat the oil in a heavy pan over a low heat and cook the sliced onion with the garlic very gently for about 20 minutes until they are soft and golden. Spread the mixture over the base of a 30cm/12in shallow baking dish.

2 Cut the tomatoes crossways into 6mm/¼in thick slices. (If the tomatoes are very large, cut the slices in half.)

3 Trim the courgettes and cut them diagonally into slices about 1cm/½in thick.

4 Arrange alternating rows of courgettes and tomatoes over the onion mixture and sprinkle with the dried herbs and cheese. Season with salt and pepper. Drizzle with olive oil, then bake for 25 minutes until the vegetables are tender. Serve the dish hot or warm.

> **Cook's Tip**
> Choose large, ripe tomatoes that have plenty of flavour and slim, evenly sized courgettes for this dish.

Courgette Parcels: Energy 51kcal/211kJ; Protein 4.9g; Carbohydrate 4.2g, of which sugars 3.7g; Fat 1.7g, of which saturates 0.4g; Cholesterol 24mg; Calcium 54mg; Fibre 2.8g; Sodium 11mg.
Courgette and Tomato Bake: Energy 302kcal/1255kJ; Protein 16.4g; Carbohydrate 14.6g, of which sugars 5.2g; Fat 20.2g, of which saturates 6.5g; Cholesterol 120mg; Calcium 249mg; Fibre 2.1g; Sodium 495mg.

Courgettes and Tofu with Tomato

This dish is great hot or cold, and its flavour improves if it is kept for a day or two, covered, in the refrigerator. It makes the perfect accompaniment to a nut roast.

Serves 4
30ml/2 tbsp olive oil
2 garlic cloves, finely chopped
4 large courgettes (zucchini), thinly sliced on the diagonal
250g/9oz firm tofu, drained and cubed
1 lemon
sea salt and ground black pepper

For the tomato sauce
10ml/2 tsp balsamic vinegar
5ml/1 tsp sugar
300ml/½ pint/1¼ cups passata (bottled strained tomatoes)
small bunch of fresh mint or parsley, chopped

1 First, make the tomato sauce, Place all the ingredients in a small pan and heat through gently, stirring occasionally.

2 Meanwhile, heat the olive oil in a large non-stick wok or frying pan until very hot, then add the garlic and stir-fry for 30 seconds, until golden.

3 Add the courgettes and stir-fry over a high heat for about 5–6 minutes, or until golden around the edges. Remove from the pan.

4 Add the tofu to the pan and brown on one side for a few minutes. Turn gently, then brown again. Grate the rind from half the lemon and reserve for the garnish. Squeeze the lemon juice over the tofu.

5 Season to taste with sea salt and pepper, then leave to sizzle until all the lemon juice has evaporated. Gently stir the courgettes into the tofu until well combined, then remove the wok or pan from the heat.

6 Transfer the courgettes and tofu to a warm serving dish and pour the tomato sauce over the top. Sprinkle with the grated lemon rind, taste and season with more salt and pepper, if necessary, and serve immediately.

Fennel Gratin

With its delicate aniseed flavour, fennel is a popular ingredient in Mediterranean cooking, both as a herb and as a vegetable. The plant grows wild but in 17th-century Italy a cultivated variety was developed with a bulbous, edible root. It is known as Florence fennel, or finocchio, and is often braised or steamed. This gratin is one of the best ways to eat it.

Serves 6
2 fennel bulbs, about 675g/1½lb total
300ml/½ pint/1¼ cups semi-skimmed milk
15g/½oz/1 tbsp butter
15ml/1 tbsp plain (all-purpose) flour
25g/1oz/scant ½ cup dry white breadcrumbs
40g/1½oz Gruyère cheese, grated
salt and ground black pepper

1 Preheat the oven to 240°C/475°F/Gas 9. Discard the stalks and root ends from the fennel. Slice the fennel into quarters and place in a large saucepan.

2 Pour the milk over the fennel, bring to the boil, then simmer for 10–15 minutes until tender.

3 Grease a small baking dish. Remove the fennel pieces with a slotted spoon, reserving the milk, and arrange in the dish.

4 Melt the butter in a small saucepan and add the flour. Stir well, then gradually whisk in the reserved milk. Cook the sauce until thickened, stirring.

5 Pour the sauce over the fennel pieces, sprinkle with the breadcrumbs and Gruyère cheese. Season with salt and black pepper and bake in the oven for about 20 minutes until browned. Serve immediately.

Variation
Instead of the Gruyère, Parmesan, Pecorino, mature Cheddar or another similar strong cheese would work perfectly.

Courgettes and Tofu: :Energy 141kcal/585kJ; Protein 8.8g; Carbohydrate 6.8g, of which sugars 6.3g; Fat 8.9g, of which saturates 1.3g; Cholesterol 0mg; Calcium 389mg; Fibre 2.4g; Sodium 181mg.
Fennel Gratin: Energy 101kcal/423kJ; Protein 5.4g; Carbohydrate 9.6g, of which sugars 4.4g; Fat 4.9g, of which saturates 2.9g; Cholesterol 13mg; Calcium 156mg; Fibre 2.9g; Sodium 135mg.

Baked Fennel

Fennel is widely eaten all over Italy, both raw in salads and cooked in hot vegetable dishes. It is delicious married with the sharpness of Parmesan cheese in this simple recipe.

Serves 4–6

1kg/2¼lb fennel bulbs
50g/2oz/4 tbsp butter
40g/1½oz/⅓ cup freshly grated
  Parmesan cheese

1 Preheat the oven to 200°C/400°F/Gas 6. Wash the fennel bulbs thoroughly in cold water and cut each one in half.

2 Bring a large pan of water to the boil. Add the halved fennel bulbs and cook until they are soft but not mushy. Drain thoroughly.

3 Cut each of the cooked fennel bulbs lengthways into four or six pieces. Choose a baking dish that will hold all the fennel bulbs in a single layer, and butter the dish. Place the fennel bulbs in the dish.

4 Dot with butter, then sprinkle with the grated Parmesan. Bake for 20 minutes until golden brown. Remove from the oven and serve at once.

Cook's Tip
Fennel is considered to be indigenous to the Mediterranean region, but is now found growing all over the world. Fennel bulbs are used widely in traditional Mediterranean cooking, in salads, pasta dishes and risottos. Fennel can be eaten raw, and has an aniseed-like flavour. It is more mellow when cooked.

Variation
For a more substantial dish, add 240ml/8fl oz/1 cup crème fraîche to the fennel and mix well before sprinkling over the Parmesan and baking.

Italian Sweet and Sour Onions

Although raw onions are strongly flavoured, like all vegetables they are high in natural sugars, and when they are cooked at a high temperature their sweetness intensifies. Serve these delicious onions as an accompaniment to cooked fresh vegetables.

Serves 6

25g/1oz/2 tbsp butter
75ml/5 tbsp sugar
120ml/4fl oz/½ cup white
  wine vinegar
30ml/2 tbsp balsamic vinegar
675g/1½lb small pickling onions,
  peeled
salt and ground black pepper

1 Melt the butter in a large saucepan over a gentle heat. Add the sugar and cook until it begins to dissolve, stirring constantly.

2 Add the vinegars to the pan with the onions and heat gently. Season, cover and cook over a moderate heat for 20–25 minutes, stirring occasionally, until the onions are soft when pierced with a knife. Keep an eye on the pan all the time to make sure that the sugar caramelizes but does not burn. Serve hot.

Variation
This recipe also looks good and tastes delicious when made with either yellow or red onions, cut into slices. Cooking times vary, depending on the size of the pieces.

Cook's Tips
•Balsamic vinegar is a speciality of Modena, in northern Italy, where it has been produced for centuries. It is made from late-harvested grapes with a high sugar content, and is very dark brown, sweet and viscous, with a complex flavour.
•Small pickling onions are in season only in the autumn, as they are maincrop onions picked while still small and do not store well. Trim only a very small slice off the root end when preparing them to help them stay intact during cooking.

Baked Fennel: Energy 149kcal/616kJ; Protein 6.3g; Carbohydrate 2.8g, of which sugars 2.6g; Fat 12.6g, of which saturates 7.8g; Cholesterol 34mg; Calcium 188mg; Fibre 3.6g; Sodium 213mg.
Sweet and Sour Onions: Energy 121kcal/506kJ; Protein 1.4g; Carbohydrate 22g, of which sugars 19.4g; Fat 3.7g, of which saturates 2.2g; Cholesterol 9mg; Calcium 36mg; Fibre 1.6g; Sodium 29mg.

Marinated Mushrooms

Cauliflower with Egg and Lemon

The Spanish are very keen on mushrooms, and wild fungus collecting is a popular pastime. This dish, known as *champiñones en escabeche*, is a good way to serve mushrooms in summer, and makes a refreshing low-fat alternative to the ever-popular mushrooms fried in garlic. Cultivated button mushrooms work well. You could serve it as a tapas dish or a first course, with crusty bread to mop up the delicious juices.

Serves 4

10ml/2 tsp olive oil
1 small onion, very finely chopped
1 garlic clove, finely chopped
15ml/1 tbsp tomato
   purée (paste)
50ml/2fl oz/¼ cup
   amontillado sherry
50ml/2fl oz/¼ cup water
2 cloves
225g/8oz/3 cups button (white)
   mushrooms, trimmed
salt and ground black pepper
chopped fresh parsley,
   to garnish

1 Heat the oil in a non-stick pan. Add the onion and garlic and cook until soft.

2 Stir in the tomato purée, sherry, water and cloves and season with salt and black pepper. Bring to the boil, cover and simmer gently for 45 minutes, adding more water if it becomes too dry.

3 Add the mushrooms, then cover and simmer for 5 minutes. Remove from the heat and allow to cool, still covered.

4 Chill in the refrigerator overnight. Serve the mushrooms cold, sprinkled with the chopped parsley, to garnish.

Cook's Tip
A marinade is also a good way to add extra flavour to mushrooms before grilling (broiling) or baking them. Toss them in a little olive oil to which you have added some chopped garlic, crushed chillies or some chopped fresh herbs, and leave to marinate for a couple of hours before cooking.

Cauliflower is a delicate vegetable, delicious when carefully cooked or crunched raw, but easily ruined by overcooking. In the Mediterranean it is used in many different ways, and is sometimes braised or dipped in batter and fried. In this Greek recipe it is teamed with a tangy lemon sauce.

Serves 6

75–90ml/5–6 tbsp extra virgin
   olive oil
1 medium cauliflower, divided into
   large florets
2 eggs
juice of 1 lemon
5ml/1 tsp cornflour (cornstarch),
   mixed to a cream with a little
   cold water
30ml/2 tbsp chopped fresh flat
   leaf parsley
salt

1 Heat the olive oil in a large, heavy pan, add the cauliflower florets and sauté over a medium heat until they start to brown.

2 Pour in enough hot water to almost cover the cauliflower florets, add salt to taste, bring to the boil, then cover the pan and cook for 7–8 minutes until the florets are just soft.

3 Remove the pan from the heat and leave to stand, retaining the hot water and covering the pan tightly to keep in the heat. Meanwhile, make the sauce.

4 Beat the eggs in a bowl, add the lemon juice and cornflour and beat until well mixed. While beating, add a few tablespoons of the hot liquid from the cauliflower. Pour the egg mixture slowly over the cauliflower, then stir gently.

5 Place the pan over a very gentle heat for 2 minutes to thicken the sauce. Spoon into a warmed serving bowl, sprinkle the chopped parsley over the top and serve.

Cook's Tip
This refreshing sauce is also excellent with carefully boiled or steamed broccoli.

Mushrooms: Energy 44kcal/181kJ; Protein 1.4g; Carbohydrate 2.1g, of which sugars 1.7g; Fat 1.8g, of which saturates 0.3g, of which polyunsaturates 0.3g; Cholesterol 0mg; Calcium 9mg; Fibre 0.9g; Sodium 14mg.
Cauliflower with Egg: Energy 211kcal/874kJ; Protein 8g; Carbohydrate 5.2g, of which sugars 3.4g; Fat 17.8g, of which saturates 3g; Cholesterol 95mg; Calcium 63mg; Fibre 2.8g; Sodium 51mg.

Greek Beans with Tomato Sauce

This is a standard summer dish in Greece, and is made with different kinds of fresh beans according to what is available. When the beans are tender and the tomatoes sweet, the dish, although frugal, can have an astoundingly good flavour, particularly if you use a good quality olive oil, whose flavour will permeate the vegetables. It is usually accompanied by slices of salty feta cheese and good fresh bread.

Serves 4

800g/1¾ lb green
    beans, trimmed
150ml/¼ pint/⅔ cup extra virgin
    olive oil
1 large onion, thinly sliced
2 garlic cloves, chopped
2 small potatoes, peeled and cubed
675g/1½lb tomatoes or
    a 400g/14oz can
    chopped tomatoes
150ml/¼ pint/⅔ cup hot water
45–60ml/3–4 tbsp chopped
    fresh parsley
salt and ground black pepper
slices of feta cheese, to garnish

1 If the green beans are very long, cut them in half. Drop them into a bowl of cold water so that they are completely submerged, and leave them for a few minutes to absorb some of the water.

2 Heat the olive oil in a large pan, add the onion and sauté until translucent. Add the garlic, then, when it becomes aromatic, stir in the pieces of potato and sauté the mixture for a few minutes. Do this over a moderate heat, otherwise the garlic may burn.

3 Add the tomatoes and the hot water and cook for 5 minutes. Drain the beans, rinse them and drain again, then add them to the pan with a little salt and pepper to season. Cover and simmer for 30 minutes.

4 Stir in the chopped parsley, with a little more hot water if the mixture looks dry. Cook for 10 minutes more, until the beans are very tender.

5 Serve hot, topped with a few slices of feta cheese or crisply-fried halloumi.

Provençal Beans

In the traditional cuisine of Provençe, flavourful tomatoes, ripened in the abundant summer sun, are as important as they are in neighbouring Italy. Here, a tangy sauce based on tomatoes and garlic transform a mixture of green beans into a memorable dish.

Serves 4

5ml/1 tsp olive oil
1 small onion
1 garlic clove, crushed
225g/8oz runner beans,
    trimmed and sliced
225g/8oz French beans,
    trimmed and sliced
2 tomatoes, peeled and chopped
salt and ground black pepper

1 Finely chop the onion. Heat the oil in a heavy pan. Add the onion and sauté over a medium heat until softened but not browned.

2 Add the garlic and sauté for 1–2 minutes, then stir in the sliced runner beans, French beans and chopped tomatoes. Season generously with salt and pepper, then cover the pan tightly with a lid.

3 Cook over a fairly low heat, shaking the pan occasionally, for about 30 minutes, or until the beans are tender.

4 Remove from the heat and serve hot.

> **Variation**
> *Try adding fresh chopped herbs, such as parsley, to this dish.*

> **Cook's Tip**
> • *When runner beans are not available, just use double the quantity of French beans.*
> • *Look for beans that are bright green and crisp-textured and keep in the refrigerator for no more than a day or two.*
> • *Green beans are a good source of protein and fibre.*

Green Beans: Energy 350kcal/1448kJ; Protein 6.6g; Carbohydrate 21.9g, of which sugars 13.4g; Fat 26.9g, of which saturates 4g; Cholesterol 0mg; Calcium 121mg; Fibre 7.7g; Sodium 25mg.
Provençal Beans: Energy 47kcal/195kJ; Protein 2.5g; Carbohydrate 6.3g, of which sugars 5.3g; Fat 1.4g, of which saturates 0.3g; Cholesterol 0mg; Calcium 46mg; Fibre 3.1g; Sodium 5mg.

Eastern Mediterranean Okra

Okra is frequently combined with tomatoes and mild spices in Mediterranean cooking. Look for fresh okra that is soft and velvety, not dry and shrivelled.

Serves 4

450g/1lb fresh tomatoes
or 400g/14oz can
chopped tomatoes
450g/1lb okra
20ml/4 tsp olive oil
2 onions, thinly sliced
10ml/2 tsp coriander
seeds, crushed
3 garlic cloves, crushed
2.5ml/½ tsp sugar
finely grated rind and juice of
1 lemon
salt and freshly ground
black pepper

1 If using fresh tomatoes, cut a cross in the base of each tomato, plunge them into a bowl of boiling water for 30 seconds, then refresh them in cold water. Peel off and discard the skins and roughly chop the tomato flesh. Set aside.

2 Trim off and discard any stalks from the okra and leave the pods whole. Heat the oil in a non-stick frying pan and cook the onions and coriander seeds for 3–4 minutes, or until the onions are beginning to colour.

3 Add the okra and garlic to the pan and cook for 1 minute. Gently stir in the chopped fresh or canned tomatoes. Add the sugar, which will bring out the flavour of the tomatoes. Simmer gently for 20–30 minutes, stirring once or twice, or until the okra is tender.

4 Stir in the lemon rind and juice, and add salt and pepper to taste, adding more sugar if necessary. Serve warm or cold.

> **Cook's Tip**
> *When okra pods are sliced, they ooze a sticky, somewhat mucilaginous liquid which, when cooked, acts as a thickener. It gives dishes a very distinctive texture, which not everyone appreciates. If the pods are left whole, however, as here, all you get is the delicious flavour.*

Slow-Cooked Okra with Tomatoes

Okra makes a deliciously sweet casserole and this is one of the best vegetable stews you will taste. Made with fresh tomatoes, at the height of the summer, it is certainly a favourite lunch, especially when served with a fresh-tasting feta cheese and crusty bread. It can be served hot or at room temperature.

Serves 6

675g/1½lb fresh okra
150ml/¼ pint/⅔ cup extra virgin
olive oil
1 large onion, sliced
675g/1½lb fresh tomatoes, sliced
2.5ml/½ tsp sugar
30ml/2 tbsp finely chopped flat
leaf parsley
salt and ground black pepper

1 Cut off the conical head from each okra pod, carefully removing the stalk without cutting into the body of the okra.

2 Heat the oil in a large, deep pan or sauté pan. Add the onion slices and fry until they are softened and a light golden colour.

3 Add the fresh or canned tomatoes to the pan, stir to mix, then add the sugar, and salt and pepper to taste. Cook for a further 5 minutes.

4 Add the okra and shake the pan to distribute them evenly and coat them in the sauce. The okra should be immersed in the sauce, so add a little hot water if necessary, to cover.

5 Cook gently for a further 20–30 minutes, depending on the size of the okra. Shake the pan occasionally, but do not stir.

6 Remove from the heat, transfer to a serving dish and add the chopped parsley just before serving.

> **Cook's Tip**
> *Okra are known as ladies' fingers, because of their shape.*

Mediterranean Okra: Energy 88kcal/370kJ; Protein 4.1g; Carbohydrate 8.6g, of which sugars 7.7g; Fat 4.5g, of which saturates 0.9g; Cholesterol 0mg; Calcium 192mg; Fibre 5.8g; Sodium 20mg.
Slow-cooked Okra: Energy 326kcal/1350kJ; Protein 6.5g; Carbohydrate 14.8g, of which sugars 12.8g; Fat 27.3g, of which saturates 4.3g; Cholesterol 0mg; Calcium 295mg; Fibre 9.1g; Sodium 30mg.

Pomegranate Yogurt with Grapefruit

Ruby red or salmon pink, the jewel-like seeds of the pomegranate make any dessert look beautiful. Here they are stirred into luscious Greek yogurt to make a delicate sauce for a fresh-tasting grapefruit salad. This pretty dish is flecked with green thanks to the addition of finely chopped fresh mint, which complements the citrus flavours perfectly. Serve this refreshing combination for breakfast, as a light snack during the day, or as a dessert after a spicy main course.

Serves 3–4
300ml/½ pint/1¼ cups natural (plain) Greek yogurt
2–3 ripe pomegranates
small bunch of fresh mint, finely chopped
clear honey or caster (superfine) sugar, to taste (optional)

For the grapefruit salad
2 red grapefruits
2 pink grapefruits
1 white grapefruit
15–30ml/1–2 tbsp orange flower water

To decorate
handful of pomegranate seeds
fresh mint leaves

1 Put the yogurt in a small bowl and beat well. Cut open the pomegranates and scoop out the seeds, removing and discarding all the bitter pith.

2 Fold the pomegranate seeds and chopped mint into the yogurt. Sweeten with a little honey or sugar, if using, then chill until ready to serve.

3 Peel the red, pink and white grapefruits, cutting off and discarding all the pith. Cut between the membranes to remove the segments, holding the fruit over a bowl to catch the juices.

4 Discard the membranes and mix the fruit segments with the reserved juices. Sprinkle with the orange flower water and add a little honey or sugar, if using. Stir gently then decorate with a few pomegranate seeds.

5 Decorate the chilled yogurt with a sprinkling of pomegranate seeds and mint leaves, and serve with the grapefruit salad.

Orange and Date Salad

Dates grow abundantly in the eastern Mediterranean and are now widely available fresh in supermarkets. Fresh dates are best for this sweet, fragrant salad. It is popular throughout the Arab world, and can be served as a dessert, though it also makes an unusual and delicious accompaniment to savoury dishes.

Serves 4–6
6 oranges
15–30ml/1–2 tbsp orange flower water or rose water (optional)
lemon juice (optional)
115g/4oz/⅔ cup stoned (pitted) dates
50g/2oz/⅓ cup pistachio nuts
icing (confectioners') sugar, to taste
a few whole or split blanched almonds

1 Peel the oranges with a sharp knife, removing all the pith, and cut into segments, catching the juices in a bowl. Place the orange segments in a serving dish.

2 Stir in the juice caught in the bowl together with a little orange flower or rose water, if using, and sharpen with lemon juice, if necessary.

3 Chop the dates and pistachio nuts and sprinkle over the salad with a little sifted icing sugar. Chill in the refrigerator for about 1 hour.

4 Dry-fry the almonds in a small pan until lightly toasted.

5 Just before serving, sprinkle over the toasted almonds and a little extra icing sugar and serve.

Cook's Tip
Dried dates can be used in this salad, but fresh dates are preferable if available. The fresh fruits are plump and sweet, with a rich, chewy texture, and there are many different varieties. To remove the stones (pits), squeeze each date until the stone appears at one end, then push it through the fruit until it emerges at the other end.

Pomegranate Yogurt: Energy 188Kcal/784kJ; Protein 8.8g; Carbohydrate 18g, of which sugars 18g; Fat 10.5g, of which saturates 5.2g; Cholesterol 0mg; Calcium 202mg; Fibre 3.6g; Sodium 82mg.
Orange and Date Salad: Energy 343Kcal/1437kJ; Protein 14.3g; Carbohydrate 32.5g, of which sugars 16.8g; Fat 17.9g, of which saturates 3.8g; Cholesterol 13mg; Calcium 327mg; Fibre 2.1g; Sodium 140mg.

Moroccan Dried Fruit Salad

While fresh fruit ends most Mediterranean meals in summer, in winter assorted dried fruits, together with nuts, are put on the table for guests to enjoy. This fruit salad is a wonderful combination of fresh and dried fruit and makes an excellent light dessert throughout the year. Use frozen raspberries or blackberries in winter.

Serves 4

115g/4oz/½ cup dried apricots
115g/4oz/½ cup dried peaches
1 fresh pear
1 fresh apple
1 fresh orange
115g/4oz/⅔ cup mixed
  raspberries and blackberries
1 cinnamon stick
50g/2oz/¼ cup caster
  (superfine) sugar
15ml/1 tbsp clear honey
30ml/2 tbsp lemon juice

1 Soak the apricots and peaches in a bowl of water for 1–2 hours or until plump, then drain and halve or quarter them. Set aside.

2 Peel and core the pear and apple and cut the flesh into cubes. Peel the orange with a sharp knife, removing all the white pith, and cut the flesh into wedges. Place all the fruit in a large pan with the raspberries and blackberries.

3 Add 600ml/1 pint/2½ cups water, the cinnamon stick, sugar and honey and bring to the boil, stirring constantly. Reduce the heat, cover and simmer very gently for 10–12 minutes, then remove the pan from the heat.

4 Stir the lemon juice into the fruit. Allow to cool, then pour the mixture into a bowl and chill in the refrigerator for 1–2 hours before serving.

Variations
- *Omit the soft fruits, or add them to the fruit mixture after cooking and cooling for a fresher tasting salad.*
- *Soak prunes and dried apples and pears and use them instead of the fresh fruit.*

Italian Fruit Salad and Ice Cream

In Italy in the summer, little pavement fruit shops sell dishes of macerated soft fruits, which are delectable on their own, but also make wonderful ice-cream.

Serves 6
900g/2lb mixed summer fruits
  such as strawberries,
  raspberries, redcurrants,
  blueberries, peaches, apricots,
  plums, melons

juice of 3–4 oranges
juice of 1 lemon
15ml/1 tbsp liquid pear and
  apple concentrate
60ml/4 tbsp whipping cream
30ml/2 tbsp orange liqueur
  (optional)
fresh mint sprigs, to decorate

1 Prepare the fruit according to type. Cut it into reasonably small pieces. Put it into a serving bowl and pour over enough orange juice just to cover. Add the lemon juice and chill the fruit for 2 hours.

2 Set half the macerated fruit aside to serve as it is. Purée the remainder in a blender or food processor.

3 Gently warm the pear and apple concentrate and stir into the fruit purée. Whip the cream and fold it in, then add the liqueur, if using.

4 Churn the mixture in an ice cream maker. Alternatively, place it in a suitable container for freezing, freeze until ice crystals form around the edge, then beat the mixture until smooth. Repeat the process once or twice, then freeze until firm.

5 Allow to soften slightly in the refrigerator before serving with the fruit in scoops decorated with sprigs of mint.

Cook's Tip
The macerated fruit also makes a delicious drink. Purée in a blender or food processor, then press through a sieve (strainer).

Moroccan Fruit Salad: Energy 160kcal/682kJ; Protein 2.6g; Carbohydrate 38.9g, of which sugars 38.9g; Fat 0.4g, of which saturates 0g; Cholesterol 0mg; Calcium 57mg; Fibre 4.8g; Sodium 10mg.
Fruit Salad and Ice Cream: Energy 69kcal/289kJ; Protein 2.2g; Carbohydrate 15.2g, of which sugars 15.2g; Fat 0.2g, of which saturates 0g; Cholesterol 0mg; Calcium 38mg; Fibre 1.7g; Sodium 18mg.

Apricot and Amaretti Ice Cream

Prolong the very short season of fresh apricots by using them for this superb and very simple ice cream made with whipped cream. Crushed amaretti, flavoured with apricot kernels, add a contrasting texture.

Serves 4–6

500g/1¼lb fresh apricots, halved and stoned (pitted)
juice of 1 orange
50g/2oz/¼ cup caster (superfine) sugar
300ml/½ pint/1¼ cups whipping cream
50g/2oz amaretti biscuits

1 Put the apricots, orange juice and sugar in a saucepan. Cover and simmer for 5 minutes until the fruit is tender. Leave to cool.

2 Lift out one-third of the fruit and set it aside on a plate. Transfer the remaining contents of the pan into a food processor or blender and process to a smooth purée.

3 Whip the cream until just thick but still soft enough to fall from a spoon. Gradually fold in the fruit purée.

4 Pour into a freezerproof container and freeze for 4 hours, beating once with a fork, electric mixer or in a food processor. Alternatively, use an ice cream maker to churn the apricot purée until it is slushy, then gradually add the whipped cream. Continue to churn until the ice cream is thick, but not yet firm enough to scoop.

5 Beat the ice cream for a second time and crumble in the amaretti biscuits. Add the reserved apricots and gently fold the extra ingredients into the ice cream. (Scrape the ice cream into a tub to do this if you are using an ice cream maker.) Freeze for 2–3 hours or until firm enough to scoop.

Cook's Tip
Chill the fruit purée if you have time; this will speed up the churning or freezing process. If you have some amaretto liqueur, fold in 45ml/3 tbsp with the biscuits.

Turkish Chewy Ice Cream

There are many delicious ice creams made in Turkey, but this stands out. Pine-scented mastic provides the chewy consistency, while salep, or ground orchid root, acts as a thickening agent. Mastic and salep are both available in Middle Eastern stores.

Serves 4

900ml/1½ pints/3¾ cups full-fat (whole) milk
300ml/½ pint/1¼ cups double (heavy) cream
225g/8oz/generous 1 cup sugar
45ml/3 tbsp ground salep
1–2 pieces of mastic crushed with a little sugar

1 Put the milk, cream and sugar into a heavy pan and bring to the boil, stirring all the time, until the sugar has dissolved. Lower the heat and simmer for 10 minutes.

2 Put the salep into a bowl. Moisten it with a little cold milk, add a spoonful of the hot, sweetened milk, then tip it into the pan, stirring all the time. Beat the mixture gently and stir in the mastic, then continue simmering for 10–15 minutes.

3 Pour the liquid into a freezer container, cover with a dry dish towel and leave to cool.

4 Remove the towel, cover the container with foil and place it in the freezer. Leave to set, beating it at intervals to disperse the ice crystals. Alternatively, churn it in an ice cream maker.

5 Before serving, allow the ice cream to sit out of the freezer for 5–10 minutes so that it becomes soft enough to scoop.

Cook's Tip
Mastic is the aromatic gum from a tree, Pistacia lentiscus, that grows wild in the Mediterranean. It is sold in clear crystal form, and its aroma indicates the strength of the resinous taste it will impart to the dish, along with a chewy texture. Before using it, the crystals must be pulverized with a little sugar, using a mortar and pestle.

Apricot Ice Cream: Energy 289kcal/1202kJ; Protein 2.3g; Carbohydrate 23.4g, of which sugars 19.8g; Fat 21.3g, of which saturates 13.1g; Cholesterol 53mg; Calcium 58mg; Fibre 1.6g; Sodium 43mg.
Turkish Ice Cream: Energy 742kcal/3093kJ; Protein 8.9g; Carbohydrate 70.2g, of which sugars 70.2g; Fat 49.1g, of which saturates 30.7g; Cholesterol 134mg; Calcium 332mg; Fibre 0g; Sodium 117mg.

Fresh Figs Baked with Honey

Baking fruit with honey is an ancient cooking method, perhaps devised when local fruit harvests were so abundant there was too much to eat fresh. This is a dish most often made with apricots or figs in rural homes, where it is sometimes served as a sweet snack for everyone to share, with bread to mop up the yogurt and honey. Spices and herbs, such as aniseed, cinnamon, rosemary and lavender, are often used for flavouring. Choose ripe figs with a sweet, pink interior, and an aromatic honey.

Serves 3–4
12 ripe figs
30ml/2 tbsp vanilla sugar
3–4 cinnamon sticks
45–60ml/3–4 tbsp clear honey
225g/8oz/1 cup chilled thick and creamy natural (plain) yogurt, or clotted cream

1 Preheat the oven to 200°C/400°F/Gas 6. Wash the figs and pat them dry. Using a sharp knife, cut a deep cross from the top of each fig to the bottom, keeping the skin at the bottom intact.

2 Fan each fig out, so it looks like a flower, then place them upright in a baking dish, preferably an earthenware one.

3 Sprinkle the vanilla sugar over each fig, tuck in the cinnamon sticks and drizzle with honey. Bake for 15–20 minutes, until the sugar is slightly caramelized but the honey and figs are still moist.

4 Eat the figs straight away. Spoon a dollop of yogurt or cream into the middle of each one and scoop them up with your fingers, or serve them in bowls and let everyone help themselves to the yogurt or cream.

Cook's Tip
To make the vanilla sugar for this recipe, split a vanilla pod (bean) lengthways in half, scrape out the seeds and mix them with 30ml/2 tbsp caster (superfine) sugar.

Poached Pears in Honey Syrup

Mediterranean fruit has been poached in honey-sweetened syrup since ancient times. The Moroccans continue the tradition enjoyed by the Persians, Arabs, Moors and Ottomans in the past. They sometimes add a little orange rind or aniseed, or even a few sprigs of lavender, to give the poaching liquid a subtle flavouring. Delicate and pretty to look at, these scented pears would provide an exquisite finishing touch to any meal with a Middle Eastern or North African theme.

Serves 4
45ml/3 tbsp clear honey
juice of 1 lemon
250ml/8fl oz/1 cup water
pinch of saffron threads
1 cinnamon stick
2–3 dried lavender heads
4 firm pears

1 Heat the honey with the lemon juice in a heavy pan that will hold the pears snugly. Stir the mixture over a gentle heat until the honey has dissolved.

2 Add the water, saffron threads, cinnamon stick and the flowers from 1–2 of the dried lavender heads.

3 Bring the mixture to the boil, then reduce the heat and simmer for 5 minutes.

4 Peel the pears, leaving the stalks attached. Add the pears to the syrup in the pan and simmer gently for 20 minutes, turning and basting at regular intervals, until they are tender.

5 Leave the pears to cool in the syrup and serve at room temperature, decorated with a few lavender flowers.

Variations
• *Use whole, peeled nectarines or peaches instead of pears.*
• *Omit the saffron, cinnamon and lavender and flavour the syrup with a split vanilla pod (bean).*

Fresh Figs Baked with Honey: Energy 198kcal/845kJ; Protein 2.3g; Carbohydrate 48.2g, of which sugars 48.2g; Fat 1g, of which saturates 0g; Cholesterol 0mg; Calcium 155mg; Fibre 4.5g; Sodium 39mg.
Poached Pears: Energy 66kcal/278kJ; Protein 0.5g; Carbohydrate 16.5g, of which sugars 16.5g; Fat 0.2g, of which saturates 0g; Cholesterol 0mg; Calcium 17mg; Fibre 3.3g; Sodium 5mg.

Apricots with Pain Perdu

Pain perdu is a French invention that literally translates as "lost bread". Americans call it French toast, while a British version is known as Poor Knights.

Serves 4
75g/3oz/6 tbsp unsalted
  butter, clarified
450g/1lb apricots, stoned (pitted)
  and thickly sliced
115g/4oz/½ cup caster
  (superfine) sugar

150ml/¼ pint/⅔ cup double
  (heavy) cream
30ml/2 tbsp apricot brandy

For the pain perdu
600ml/1 pint/2½ cups milk
1 vanilla pod (bean)
50g/2oz/¼ cup caster
  (superfine) sugar
4 large eggs, beaten
115g/4oz/½ cup unsalted
  butter, clarified
6 brioche slices, diagonally halved
2.5ml/½ tsp ground cinnamon

1 Heat a heavy frying pan and melt a quarter of the butter. Add the apricot slices and cook for 2–3 minutes until golden. Using a slotted spoon, transfer them to a bowl. Heat the rest of the butter with the sugar, stirring, until golden.

2 Pour in the cream and brandy and cook gently until the mixture forms a smooth sauce. Boil for 2–3 minutes until thickened, then pour the sauce over the apricots and set aside.

3 To make the pain perdu, pour the milk into a saucepan and add the vanilla pod and half the sugar. Heat gently until almost boiling, then set aside to cool.

4 Remove the vanilla pod and pour the milk into a shallow dish. Whisk in the eggs.

5 Heat a sixth of the butter in the clean frying pan. Dip a slice of brioche into the milk mixture and fry until golden brown on both sides. Add the remaining butter as needed. As the pain perdu is cooked, remove the slices and keep hot.

6 Warm the apricot sauce and spoon it on to the pain perdu. Mix the remaining sugar with the cinnamon and sprinkle a little over each portion.

Stuffed Peaches with Amaretto

Both amaretti biscuits and amaretto liqueur, made with bitter almonds or apricot kernels, have an intense almond flavour, and make good partners for peaches.

Serves 4
4 ripe but firm peaches
50g/2oz amaretti biscuits

25g/1oz/2 tbsp butter, softened
25g/1oz/2 tbsp caster
  (superfine) sugar
1 egg yolk
60ml/4 tbsp amaretto liqueur
250ml/8fl oz/1 cup dry
  white wine
8 tiny sprigs of basil, to decorate
ice cream or pouring cream,
  to serve

1 Preheat the oven to 180°C/350°F/Gas 4. Following the natural indentation line on each peach, cut in half down to the central stone (pit), then twist the halves in opposite directions to separate them. Remove the peach stones, then cut away a little of the central flesh to make a larger hole for the stuffing. Chop this flesh finely and set aside.

2 Put the amaretti biscuits in a bowl and crush them finely with the end of a rolling pin.

3 Cream the butter and sugar together in a separate bowl until smooth. Stir in the reserved chopped peach flesh, the egg yolk and half the amaretto liqueur with the amaretti crumbs.

4 Lightly butter a baking dish that is just large enough to hold the peach halves in a single layer. Spoon the stuffing into the peaches, then stand them in the dish.

5 Mix the remaining liqueur with the wine, pour over the peaches and bake for 25 minutes or until the peaches feel tender when tested with a skewer. Decorate with basil and serve immediately, with ice cream or cream.

> **Cook's Tip**
> *Amaretto and amaretti get their name from the Italian word amaro, which means "bitter".*

Caramelized Apricots: Energy 1071kcal/4471kJ; Protein 18.5g; Carbohydrate 92.1g, of which sugars 69.2g; Fat 70.9g, of which saturates 41.6g; Cholesterol 353mg; Calcium 343mg; Fibre 3.3g; Sodium 634mg.
Peaches with Amaretto: Energy 255kcal/1068kJ; Protein 2.6g; Carbohydrate 29.4g, of which sugars 24g; Fat 8.2g, of which saturates 4.4g; Cholesterol 64mg; Calcium 40mg; Fibre 1.7g; Sodium 87mg.

Peach and Apple Compote

This delicious dessert starts as a lovely fruit compote and becomes a syrupy jam, perfect with soft bread.

Serves 10
3 firm peaches
1kg/2¼lb/5 cups sugar
3 large eating apples
finely grated rind of 1 lemon
3 firm pears
finely grated rind of 1 orange
1 small sweet potato, 150g/5oz prepared weight
200g/7oz butternut squash, peeled, prepared weight
250ml/8fl oz/1 cup dark rum
30ml/2 tbsp clear honey

1 Cut the peaches into eighths, without peeling, and place in a large flameproof casserole. Sprinkle with 15ml/1 tbsp of the sugar. Peel and core the apples and cut into 16 segments, then arrange on top of the peaches. Sprinkle with the lemon rind and 15ml/1 tbsp of the sugar.

2 Prepare the pears in the same way and add to the casserole. Sprinkle over the orange rind and 15ml/1 tbsp of the sugar.

3 Slice the sweet potato into small pieces and spread over the top, followed by the sliced squash. Sprinkle with 15ml/1 tbsp of the sugar. Cover with a plate that fits inside the rim, weight it and leave for 2–12 hours for juice to form.

4 Put the casserole over a fairly low heat and bring to a simmer. Cook for 20 minutes, stirring once or twice. Add the remaining sugar, in three or four batches, stirring to dissolve. Bring the mixture up to a rolling boil and boil very steadily for 45 minutes. Stir and lift off any scum.

5 Test the reduced syrup by pouring a spoonful on a plate. It should wrinkle when a spoon is pulled across it. Off the heat, stir in the rum and honey. Return the casserole to a moderate heat and cook for a further 10 minutes, stirring frequently to prevent the fruit sticking. The colour will deepen to russet brown.

6 Remove the pan from the heat and set aside to cool. If the resulting compote is a little too stiff, stir in some more rum before serving.

Moroccan-style Plum Pudding

There's a strong French influence in Moroccan cooking, as evidenced by this North African version of the French batter pudding known as clafouti, which is usually made with cherries. In this pudding, ground rice and flaked almonds are used instead of eggs, cream and flour to thicken the milk mixture, which is flavoured with orange flower water.

Serves 4
450g/1lb fresh plums or other fruit (see Variation)
600ml/1 pint/2½ cups skimmed or semi-skimmed (low-fat) milk
45ml/3 tbsp ground rice
30–45ml/2–3 tbsp caster (superfine) sugar
75g/3oz/¾ cup flaked almonds
30ml/2 tbsp orange flower water or rose water, to taste
icing (confectioners') sugar, to decorate

1 Preheat the oven to 190°C/375°F/Gas 5. Stone and halve the plums. Bring the milk to the boil in a pan.

2 Blend the ground rice with 30–45ml/2–3 tbsp cold water, beating well to make a smooth paste and avoid lumps.

3 Pour the hot milk over the rice and stir until smooth, then pour the mixture back into the pan. Simmer over a low heat for 5 minutes, until it thickens, stirring all the time.

4 Add the caster sugar and flaked almonds and cook gently for a further 5 minutes. Stir in the orange flower or rose water and simmer for 2 minutes.

5 Butter a shallow ovenproof dish and pour in the almond milk mixture. Arrange the prepared fruit on top and then bake in the oven for about 25–30 minutes, until the fruit has softened. Dust with sifted icing sugar and serve.

Variation
Apricots, cherries or greengages can be used instead of plums for this pudding.

Moroccan Plum Pudding: Energy 186kcal/790kJ; Protein 1.8g; Carbohydrate 45.9g, of which sugars 45.9g; Fat 0.7g, of which saturates 0g; Cholesterol 0mg; Calcium 110mg; Fibre 4.7g; Sodium 30mg.
Peach and Apple Compote: Energy 308kcal/1291kJ; Protein 11g; Carbohydrate 38.1g, of which sugars 28.6g; Fat 13.2g, of which saturates 2.4g; Cholesterol 9mg; Calcium 246mg; Fibre 2.4g; Sodium 69mg.

Coeur à la Crème with Oranges

This zesty dessert is the ideal choice to follow a rich main course such as roast pork. The little sweetened cream cheese puddings are traditionally made in pierced heart-shaped moulds, hence their name.

Serves 4
225g/8oz/1 cup cottage cheese
250g/9oz/generous 1 cup
   mascarpone cheese
50g/2oz/¼ cup caster
   (superfine) sugar
grated rind and juice of 1 lemon
spirals of orange rind, to decorate

For the Cointreau oranges
4 oranges
10ml/2 tsp cornflour (cornstarch)
15ml/1 tbsp icing
   (confectioner's) sugar
60ml/4 tbsp Cointreau

1 Put the cottage cheese in a food processor or blender and whizz until smooth. Add the mascarpone, caster sugar, lemon rind and juice and process briefly to mix the ingredients.

2 Line four coeur à la crème moulds with muslin, then divide the mixture among them. Level the surface of each, then place all the moulds on a plate to catch any liquid that drains from the cheese. Cover and chill overnight.

3 To make the Cointreau oranges, squeeze the juice from two oranges and pour into a measuring jug. Make the juice up to 250ml/8fl oz/1 cup with water, then pour into a small saucepan.

4 Blend a little of the juice mixture with the cornflour and add to the pan with the icing sugar. Heat the sauce gently, stirring, until it has thickened.

5 Using a sharp knife, peel and segment the remaining oranges. Add the orange segments to the pan, stir well to coat, then set aside. When cool, stir in the Cointreau. Cover and chill in the refrigerator overnight.

6 Turn the cream cheese moulds out on to plates and surround with the oranges. Decorate with spirals of orange rind and serve immediately.

Leche Frita with Black Fruit Sauce

The name of this Spanish dessert means "fried milk", but it is really custard squares with a creamy centre and crunchy, golden coating. Here, it is served hot with fruit sauce, but it is also good cold.

Serves 4–6
550ml/18fl oz/2½ cups full-fat
   (whole) milk
3 finely pared strips of lemon rind
½ cinnamon stick
90g/3½oz/½ cup caster
   (superfine) sugar, plus extra
   for sprinkling
60ml/4 tbsp cornflour (cornstarch)
30ml/2 tbsp plain
   (all-purpose) flour
3 large (US extra large) egg yolks
2 large (US extra large) eggs
90–120ml/6–8 tbsp stale
   breadcrumbs or dried crumbs
sunflower oil, for frying
ground cinnamon, for dusting

For the sauce
450g/1lb blackcurrants
   or blackberries
90g/3½oz/½ cup granulated
   sugar, plus extra for dusting

1 Put the milk, lemon rind, cinnamon stick and sugar in a pan and bring to the boil, stirring gently. Cover and leave to infuse for 20 minutes.

2 Put the cornflour and flour in a bowl and beat in the egg yolks with a wooden spoon. Add a little of the milk and beat to make a smooth batter.

3 Strain the remaining hot milk into the batter, then pour back into the pan. Cook over a low heat, stirring constantly. (The mixture won't curdle, but it will thicken unevenly if you don't stir it.) Cook for a couple of minutes, until it thickens and separates from the side of the pan.

4 Beat the mixture hard to ensure a really smooth consistency. Pour into an 18–20cm/7–8in, 1cm/½in-deep rectangular dish, and smooth the top. Cool, then chill until firm.

5 Meanwhile, make the fruit sauce. Cook the blackcurrants or blackberries with the sugar and a little water for about 10 minutes until soft. Reserve 30–45ml/2–3 tbsp whole currants or berries, then put the rest in a food processor and blend to a smooth purée. Return the purée and the whole berries to the pan and keep warm.

6 Cut the chilled custard into eight or twelve squares. Beat the eggs in a shallow dish and spread the breadcrumbs on a plate. Lift half of the squares with a metal spatula into the egg. Coat on both sides, then lift into the crumbs and cover all over. Repeat with the second batch of squares.

7 Pour about 1cm/½in oil into a deep frying pan and heat until very hot. Lift two or three coated squares with a metal spatula into the oil and fry for a couple of minutes, shaking or spooning the oil over the top, until golden. Reserve on kitchen paper while you fry the other batches.

8 To serve, arrange the custard squares on plates and sprinkle with sugar and cinnamon. Pour a circle of warm fruit sauce round the custard squares, distributing the whole berries evenly.

Coeur à la Crème: Energy 333kcal/1400kJ; Protein 14.3g; Carbohydrate 36.8g, of which sugars 34.5g; Fat 11.4g, of which saturates 7g; Cholesterol 35mg; Calcium 137mg; Fibre 2.1g; Sodium 178mg.
Leche Frita: Energy 257kcal/1089kJ; Protein 6.9g; Carbohydrate 45.9g, of which sugars 30.6g; Fat 6.4g, of which saturates 2.7g; Cholesterol 133mg; Calcium 159mg; Fibre 2.3g; Sodium 143mg.

Festive Semolina Helva

In Turkey, this soft semolina helva signifies good fortune and is made for events such as moving house or starting a new job, but it is also traditional for a bereaved family to offer it to friends when someone dies. It is also associated with religious festivals, and makes a regular appearance at holiday celebrations.

It is sweet and rich, with a texture rather like that of Italian polenta.

Serves 6–8
225g/8oz/1 cup butter
450g/1lb/scant 2¾cups semolina
45ml/3 tbsp pine nuts
900ml/1½ pints/3¾ cups milk
225g/8oz/generous 1 cup sugar
*5–10ml/1–2 tsp ground
    cinnamon*

1 Melt the butter in a heavy pan, stir in the semolina and pine nuts and cook over a medium heat, stirring all the time, until lightly browned.

2 Lower the heat and pour in the milk. Mix well, cover the pan with a dish towel and press the lid down tightly. Pull the flaps of the dish towel up and over the lid and simmer gently for about 10–12 minutes, until all the milk has been absorbed.

3 Add the sugar to the pan and stir well until the sugar has completely dissolved. Cover the pan with the dish towel and lid again, remove the pan from the heat and leave to stand for at least 1 hour.

4 To serve, mix well with a wooden spoon and spoon into individual bowls, then dust with a little ground cinnamon.

> **Cook's Tip**
> *Helva, or halva, is a sweet confection made in Greece, Turkey, Bulgaria and the Middle East, as well as in India and Pakistan. There are various forms. The type made with tahini, or sesame paste, is dry and crumbly, usually flavoured with honey, and often contains pistachio nuts.*

Chocolate Ravioli

This spectacular Italian dessert is made from sweet pasta. The little packets contain a creamy white chocolate filling.

*30ml/2 tbsp icing
    (confectioner's) sugar*
2 eggs
*single (light) cream and grated
    dark (bitter sweet) and white
    chocolate, to serve*

Serves 4
*175g/6oz/1½ cups plain
    (all-purpose) flour*
pinch of salt
25g/1oz/¼ cup cocoa powder

For the filling
175g/6oz white chocolate
350g/12oz/3 cups cream cheese
1 egg, plus 1 beaten egg to seal

1 Put the flour, salt, cocoa and icing sugar into a food processor, add the eggs, and process until the dough begins to come together. Tip out the dough and knead until smooth. Wrap in clear film (plastic wrap) and rest for 30 minutes.

2 To make the filling, break up the white chocolate and melt in a basin over a pan of barely simmering water. Cool slightly, then beat into the cream cheese with the egg. Spoon into a piping bag fitted with a plain nozzle.

3 Cut the dough in half and wrap one portion. Roll out the rest thinly to a rectangle on a lightly floured surface, or use a pasta machine. Cover with a clean, damp dish towel and repeat with the remaining pasta.

4 Pipe small mounds (about 5ml/1 tsp) of filling in even rows, spacing them at 4cm/1½in intervals, across one piece of dough. Brush the dough between the mounds with beaten egg. Using a rolling pin, lift the remaining sheet of pasta over the dough with the filling. Press down firmly between the pockets, pushing out any trapped air. Cut into rounds with a serrated cutter or knife. Transfer to a floured dish towel. Cover and rest for 1 hour.

5 Bring a large pan of water to the boil and add the ravioli a few at a time, stirring to prevent them sticking. Simmer gently for 3–5 minutes, then remove with a slotted spoon. Serve with a generous splash of single cream and some grated chocolate.

Semolina Helva: Energy 568kcal/2388kJ; Protein 10.2g; Carbohydrate 78.3g, of which sugars 34.7g; Fat 26g, of which saturates 15.9g; Cholesterol 67mg; Calcium 165mg; Fibre 1.2g; Sodium 227mg.
Chocolate Ravioli: Energy 894kcal/3722kJ; Protein 16.2g; Carbohydrate 68.1g, of which sugars 34g; Fat 63.9g, of which saturates 36.5g; Cholesterol 226mg; Calcium 299mg; Fibre 2.1g; Sodium 424mg.

Italian Chocolate Ricotta Tart

This luxurious tart makes a rich afternoon treat.

Serves 6
2 egg yolks
115g/4oz/¹/₂ cup caster
  (superfine) sugar
500g/1¹/₄ lb/2¹/₂ cups
  ricotta cheese
finely grated rind of 1 lemon
90ml/6 tbsp dark (bittersweet)
  chocolate chips
75ml/5 tbsp chopped mixed peel
45ml/3 tbsp chopped angelica

For the pastry
225g/8oz/2 cups plain
  (all-purpose) flour
30ml/2 tbsp cocoa powder
60ml/4 tbsp caster
  (superfine) sugar
115g/4oz/¹/₂ cup butter, diced
60ml/4 tbsp dry sherry

1 Preheat the oven to 200°C/400°F/Gas 6. To make the pastry, sift the flour and cocoa into a bowl, then stir in the sugar. Rub in the butter until the mixture resembles fine breadcrumbs, then work in the dry sherry, using your fingertips, until the mixture binds to a firm, smooth dough.

2 Roll out three-quarters of the pastry on a lightly floured surface and use to line a 24cm/9¹/₂ in loose-based flan tin (quiche pan). Chill for 20 minutes.

3 Beat the egg yolks and sugar in a bowl, then beat in the ricotta cheese. Stir in the lemon rind, chocolate chips, mixed peel and angelica. Turn the mixture into the pastry case and level the surface. Roll out the remaining pastry thinly and cut into narrow strips, then arrange these in a lattice over the filling.

4 Bake for 15 minutes, then lower the oven temperature to 180°C/350°F/Gas 4 and bake for 30–35 minutes more until golden brown. Leave to cool in the tin.

Cook's Tip
This chocolate tart is best served at room temperature, so if made in advance, chill it when cool, then, when needed, bring to room temperature before serving.

Chocolate Salami

This after-dinner sweetmeat resembles a salami in shape, hence its curious name. It is very rich and will serve a lot of people. Slice it very thinly and serve with espresso coffee and amaretto liqueur.

Serves 8–12
24 Petit Beurre biscuits, broken
350g/12oz dark (bittersweet)
  chocolate, broken into squares
225g/8oz/1 cup unsalted
  butter, softened
60ml/4 tbsp amaretto liqueur
2 egg yolks
50g/2oz/¹/₂ cup flaked (sliced)
  almonds, lightly toasted and
  thinly shredded lengthways
25g/1oz/¹/₄ cup ground almonds

1 Place the biscuits in a food processor fitted with a metal blade and process until coarsely crushed.

2 Place the chocolate in a large heatproof bowl over a saucepan of barely simmering water, add a small chunk of the butter and all the liqueur and heat until the chocolate melts, stirring occasionally. Remove from the heat.

3 Allow the chocolate to cool a little, then stir in the egg yolks followed by the remaining butter, a little at a time. Tip in most of the crushed biscuits, reserving a good handful, and stir well to mix. Stir in the shredded almonds. Leave the mixture in a cold place for about 1 hour until it begins to stiffen.

4 Process the remaining crushed biscuits in the food processor until they are very finely ground. Tip into a bowl and mix with the ground almonds. Cover and set aside until serving time.

5 Turn the chocolate and biscuit mixture on to a sheet of lightly oiled greaseproof (waxed) paper, then shape into a 35cm/14in sausage with a palette knife, tapering the ends slightly so that the roll looks like a salami. Wrap in the paper and freeze for at least 4 hours until solid.

6 To serve, unwrap the "salami". Spread the ground biscuits and almonds out on a clean sheet of greaseproof paper and roll the salami in them until evenly coated. Transfer to a board and leave to stand for about 1 hour before serving in slices.

Chocolate Ricotta Tart: Energy 701kcal/2938kJ; Protein 14.2g; Carbohydrate 83.4g, of which sugars 54.1g; Fat 35.6g, of which saturates 21.3g; Cholesterol 144mg; Calcium 115mg; Fibre 3g; Sodium 223mg.
Chocolate Salami: Energy 453kcal/1885kJ; Protein 4.5g; Carbohydrate 36.6g, of which sugars 26.9g; Fat 32.3g, of which saturates 16.8g; Cholesterol 96mg; Calcium 47mg; Fibre 1.4g; Sodium 173mg.

Ricotta Cheesecake

In this Sicilian-style dessert, ricotta cheese is enriched with eggs and cream and enlivened with tangy orange and lemon rind.

Serves 8
450g/1lb/2 cups ricotta cheese
120ml/4fl oz/½ cup double (heavy) cream
2 eggs
1 egg yolk
75g/3oz/⅓ cup caster (superfine) sugar
finely grated rind of 1 orange
finely grated rind of 1 lemon

For the pastry
175g/6oz/1½ cups plain (all-purpose) flour
45ml/3 tbsp caster (superfine) sugar
pinch of salt
115g/4oz/8 tbsp chilled butter, diced
1 egg yolk

1 To make the pastry, sift the flour, sugar and salt on to a cold surface. Make a well in the centre, add the diced butter and egg yolk and gradually work in the flour with your fingertips. Gather the dough together, reserve about a quarter for the lattice, then press the rest into a 23cm/9in fluted tart tin (quiche pan) with a removable base. Chill the pastry case for 30 minutes.

2 Meanwhile, preheat the oven to 190°C/375°F/Gas 5 and make the filling. Put the ricotta, cream, eggs, egg yolk, sugar and orange and lemon rinds in a large bowl and beat together.

3 Prick the bottom of the pastry case, then line with foil and fill with baking beans. Bake blind for 15 minutes, then transfer to a wire rack, remove the foil and beans and allow the tart shell to cool in the tin.

4 Spoon the cheese and cream filling into the pastry case and level the surface. Roll out the reserved dough and cut into strips. Arrange the strips on the top of the filling in a lattice pattern, sticking them in place with water.

5 Bake for 30–35 minutes until golden and set. Transfer to a wire rack and leave to cool, then carefully remove the side of the tin, leaving the cheesecake on the base.

Bitter Chocolate Mousse

The Spanish introduced the rest of Europe to chocolate, and chocolate mousse remains a favourite. This one is laced with liqueur.

Serves 8
225g/8oz dark (bittersweet) chocolate, chopped
30ml/2 tbsp orange liqueur or good Spanish brandy
50g/2oz/¼ cup unsalted (sweet) butter, cut into small pieces
4 eggs, separated
90ml/6 tbsp whipping cream
45ml/3 tbsp caster (superfine) sugar

1 Place the chocolate and 60ml/4 tbsp water in a heavy pan. Melt over a low heat, stirring. Off the heat whisk in the orange liqueur or brandy and butter. Beat the egg yolks until thick and creamy, then slowly beat into the melted chocolate.

2 Whip the cream until soft peaks form, then stir a spoonful into the chocolate mixture to lighten it. Gently fold in the remaining whipped cream.

3 In a clean, grease-free bowl, use an electric mixer to slowly whisk the egg whites until frothy. Increase the speed and continue until the egg whites form soft peaks. Gradually sprinkle the sugar over the egg whites and continue beating until the whites are stiff and glossy.

4 Using a rubber spatula or large metal spoon, stir a quarter of the egg whites into the chocolate mixture to lighten it, then gently fold in the remaining whites, cutting down to the bottom of the bowl, along the sides and up to the top in a semicircular motion until they are just combined.

5 Gently spoon the mixture into eight individual dishes or a 2 litre/3½ pint/8 cup bowl. Chill for at least 2 hours until set.

> **Cook's Tip**
> The addition of 1.5ml/¼ tsp cream of tartar to the egg whites helps them to stabilize and hold the volume.

Chocolate Mousse: Energy 236kcal/988kJ; Protein 5.5g; Carbohydrate 25.7g, of which sugars 25.4g; Fat 12.2g, of which saturates 6.2g; Cholesterol 121mg; Calcium 31mg; Fibre 0.8g; Sodium 46mg.
Ricotta Cheesecake: Energy 449kcal/1873kJ; Protein 9.9g; Carbohydrate 34.8g, of which sugars 18.1g; Fat 31.1g, of which saturates 18.4g; Cholesterol 173mg; Calcium 62mg; Fibre 0.7g; Sodium 112mg.

Ladies' Navels

This is a classic Turkish fried pastry, an invention from the Ottoman palace kitchens.

60g/2oz/¹⁄₃ cup semolina
2 eggs
sunflower oil, for deep-frying

Serves 4–6
50g/2oz/¹⁄₄ cup butter
2.5ml/¹⁄₂ tsp salt
175g/6oz/1¹⁄₂ cups plain
   (all-purpose) flour

For the syrup
450g/1lb/scant 2¹⁄₄ cups
   granulated (white) sugar
juice of 1 lemon

1 To make the syrup, put the sugar and 300ml/¹⁄₂ pint/1¹⁄₄ cups water into a heavy pan and bring to the boil, stirring all the time. When the sugar has dissolved, stir in the lemon juice and lower the heat, then simmer for about 10 minutes, until the syrup has thickened a little. Leave to cool.

2 Put the butter, salt and 250ml/8fl oz/1 cup water in another pan and bring to the boil. Remove from the heat and add the flour and semolina, beating all the time, until the mixture becomes smooth and leaves the side of the pan. Leave to cool. Beat the eggs into the cooled mixture so that it gleams. Add 15ml/1 tbsp of the cooled syrup and beat well.

3 Pour enough oil for deep-frying into a wok or other deep-sided pan. Heat until just warm, then remove the pan from the heat. Wet your hands and take an apricot-sized piece of dough in your fingers. Roll it into a ball, flatten it in the palm of your hand, then use your finger to make an indentation in the middle to resemble a lady's navel.

4 Drop the dough into the pan of warmed oil. Repeat with the rest of the mixture to make about 12 navels.

5 Place the pan back over the heat. As the oil heats up, the pastries will swell, retaining the dip in the middle. Swirl the oil, until the navels turn golden all over. Remove the navels from the oil with a slotted spoon, then toss them in the cooled syrup. Leave to soak for a few minutes, arrange in a serving dish and spoon some of the syrup over.

Semolina and Nut Halva

Hazelnuts and almonds top this soft halva. Pistachio nuts, walnuts or toasted pine nuts would also work well.

Makes 24
115g/4oz/¹⁄₂ cup unsalted
   (sweet) butter, softened
115g/4oz/generous ¹⁄₂ cup caster
   (superfine) sugar
finely grated rind of 1 orange,
   plus 30ml/2 tbsp juice
3 eggs 175g/6oz/1 cup semolina
10ml/2 tsp baking powder
115g/4oz/1 cup ground hazelnuts

To finish
350g/12oz/1³⁄₄ cups caster
   (superfine) sugar
2 cinnamon sticks, halved
juice of 1 lemon
60ml/4 tbsp orange flower water
50g/2oz/¹⁄₂ cup unblanched
   hazelnuts, toasted and chopped
50g/2oz/¹⁄₂ cup blanched
   almonds, toasted and chopped
shredded rind of 1 orange
whipped cream, clotted cream
   or Greek (US strained plain)
   yogurt, to serve

1 Preheat the oven to 220°C/425°F/Gas 7. Grease and line the base of a 23cm/9in square deep solid-based cake tin (pan). Cream the butter in a bowl. Add the sugar, orange rind and juice, eggs, semolina, baking powder and hazelnuts and beat until smooth.

2 Turn into the prepared tin and level the surface. Bake for 20–25 minutes until just firm and golden. Leave to cool in the tin.

3 For the syrup, put the caster sugar in a pan with 575ml/19fl oz/2¹⁄₄ cups water and the cinnamon sticks. Heat gently, stirring, until the sugar has dissolved completely. Bring to the boil and boil fast, without stirring, for 5 minutes. Measure half the syrup and add the lemon juice and orange flower water to it. Pour over the halva. Reserve the remainder of the syrup in the pan.

4 When the halva has absorbed the syrup, turn it out on to a plate and cut diagonally into diamond-shaped portions. Sprinkle with the nuts.

5 Boil the remaining syrup until slightly thickened, then pour it over the halva. Sprinkle the shredded orange rind over the cake. Serve with lightly whipped or clotted cream, or Greek yogurt, if you like.

Ladies' Navels: Energy 517kcal/2190kJ; Protein 6.3g; Carbohydrate 108.8g, of which sugars 78.9g; Fat 9.3g, of which saturates 4.9g; Cholesterol 81mg; Calcium 93mg; Fibre 1.1g; Sodium 80mg.
Semolina Halva: Energy 4910kcal/20601kJ; Protein 74.5g; Carbohydrate 638.2g, of which sugars 498g; Fat 247g, of which saturates 74.5g; Cholesterol 816mg; Calcium 738mg; Fibre 18.1g; Sodium 976mg.

Gazelle's Horns

These pastries filled with orange-scented almond paste are a real sweet treat.

Makes 16
200g/7oz/1¾ cups plain (all-purpose) flour
25g/1oz/2 tbsp butter, melted
about 30ml/2 tbsp orange flower water or water
1 large egg yolk, beaten
pinch of salt

icing (confectioners') sugar, to serve

For the almond paste
200g/7oz/1 cups ground almonds
115g/4oz/1¾ cups icing (confectioners') sugar or caster (superfine) sugar
30ml/2 tbsp orange flower water
25g/1oz/2 tbsp butter, melted
2 egg yolks, beaten
2.5ml/½ tsp ground cinnamon

1 First make the almond paste, mixing together all the ingredients until smooth. Set aside.

2 To make the pastry, mix the flour with a pinch of salt then stir in the melted butter, orange flower water or water, and about three-quarters of the egg yolk. Stir in enough cold water, little by little, to make a fairly soft dough. Knead for about 10 minutes, until smooth and elastic, then roll out very thinly on a floured surface and cut long strips about 7.5cm/3in wide.

3 Preheat the oven to 180°C/350°F/Gas 4. Take small pieces of the almond paste and roll them between your hands into thin "sausages" about 7.5cm/3in long with tapering ends. Place these in a line along one side of the strips of pastry, about 3cm/1¼in apart. Dampen the pastry edges with water and then fold the other half of the strip over the filling and press the edges together firmly to seal.

4 Using a pastry wheel, cut around each "sausage" (as for ravioli) to make a crescent shape. Make sure that the edges are firmly pinched together. Prick the crescents with a fork and place on a buttered baking tray. Brush with the remaining beaten egg yolk and then bake in the oven for 12–16 minutes, until lightly coloured.

5 Remove to a wire rack, cool and then dust with icing sugar.

Butter and Almond Shortbreads

Dazzling white *kourabiethes* are traditionally made at Christmas and Easter, but are also an important feature of many other Greek celebrations. They are traditionally crescent-shaped, but here have been cut into stars.

Makes 20–22
225g/8oz/1 cup unsalted butter
150g/5oz/⅔ cup caster (superfine) sugar

2 egg yolks
5ml/1 tsp vanilla extract
2.5ml/½ tsp bicarbonate of soda (baking soda)
45ml/3 tbsp brandy
500g/1¼lb/5 cups plain (all-purpose) flour sifted with a pinch of salt
150g/5oz/1¼ cups blanched almonds, toasted and coarsely chopped
350g/12oz/3 cups icing (confectioners') sugar

1 Cream the butter, beat in the caster sugar gradually, until light and fluffy. Beat in the egg yolks one at a time, then the vanilla. Mix the soda with the brandy and stir into the mixture.

2 Add the flour and salt and mix to a firm dough. Knead lightly, add the almonds and knead again. Cover half the dough with clear film (plastic wrap) and set aside.

3 Preheat the oven to 180°C/350°F/Gas 4. Roll out the remaining dough until about 2.5cm/1in thick. Press out star or half-moon shapes, using pastry cutters. Repeat with the remaining dough.

4 Place the shortbread shapes on baking sheets and bake for 20–25 minutes, or until they are pale golden – do not let them brown.

5 Meanwhile, sift a quarter of the icing sugar on to a platter. As soon as the shortbreads come out of the oven, dust them generously with icing sugar. Let them cool for a few minutes, then place them on the sugar-coated platter.

6 Sift the remaining icing sugar over them. The aim is to give them a generous coating, so they are pure white.

Almond Shortbreads: Energy 325kcal/1363kJ; Protein 4.4g; Carbohydrate 46.1g, of which sugars 26.9g; Fat 14.3g, of which saturates 6.4g; Cholesterol 44mg; Calcium 71mg; Fibre 1.3g; Sodium 72mg.
Gazelle's Horns: Energy 163kcal/682kJ; Protein 4g; Carbohydrate 18.1g, of which sugars 8.2g; Fat 8.8g, of which saturates 1.5g; Cholesterol 16mg; Calcium 53mg; Fibre 1.3g; Sodium 13mg.

Crunchy-topped Fresh Apricot Cake

Almonds are perfect partners for fresh apricots as they come from trees of the same family, and this is a great way to use up fruits that are a little too firm to eat raw. In Greece this cake is eaten as a snack at any time of the day.

Serves 8
175g/6oz/1½ cups self-raising (self-rising) flour
175g/6oz/¾ cup butter, softened
175g/6oz/scant 1 cup caster (superfine) sugar
115g/4oz/1 cup ground almonds
3 eggs
5ml/1 tsp almond extract
2.5ml/½ tsp baking powder
8 firm apricots, stoned (pitted) and chopped

For the topping
30ml/2 tbsp demerara (raw) sugar
50g/2oz/½ cup slivered (sliced) almonds

1 Preheat the oven to 160°C/325°F/Gas 3. Grease an 18cm/7in round cake tin (pan) and line the base with baking parchment.

2 Put all the cake ingredients, except the apricots, in a large mixing bowl and whisk until creamy. Fold the chopped apricots into the cake mixture.

3 Spoon the mixture into the prepared tin. Make a hollow in the centre with the back of a spoon. Sprinkle 15ml/1 tbsp of the demerara sugar evenly over the surface, together with the slivered almonds.

4 Bake for about 1½ hours, or until a skewer inserted into the centre of the cake comes out clean. Sprinkle the remaining sugar over the top and cool for 10 minutes in the tin, then remove the cake from the tin and leave on a wire rack to cool completely.

> **Variation**
> When fresh apricots are not in season, replace them with 125g/4oz ready-to-eat dried apricots, chopped.

Twelfth Night Bread

This special cake is baked in Spain for Epiphany on 6 January. Traditionally it contains a bean, coin or tiny china doll, and whoever finds it is king of the party.

Serves 12
450g/1lb/4 cups unbleached strong white bread flour
2.5ml/½ tsp salt
25g/1oz fresh yeast
140ml/scant ¼ pint/scant ⅔ cup mixed warm milk and water
75g/3oz/6 tbsp butter
75g/3oz/6 tbsp caster (superfine) sugar
10ml/2 tsp grated lemon rind
10ml/2 tsp grated orange rind
2 eggs
15ml/1 tbsp brandy
15ml/1 tbsp orange flower water
silver coin or dried bean (optional)
1 egg white, lightly beaten

For the decoration
mixed candied fruit slices
flaked (sliced) almonds

1 Lightly grease a large baking sheet. Sift together the flour and salt into a large bowl. Make a well in the centre. Mix the yeast with the milk and water until dissolved. Pour into the well and stir in enough of the flour to make a thick batter. Sprinkle a little of the remaining flour over the top and leave in a warm place, for about 15 minutes or until frothy.

2 Beat the butter and sugar until soft and creamy. Add the citrus rinds, eggs, brandy and orange flower water to the flour mixture and mix to a sticky dough. Gradually add the butter mixture and beat until smooth and elastic. Cover with lightly oiled clear film (plastic wrap) and leave in a warm place, for about 1½ hours, or until doubled in size.

3 Knock back (punch down) the dough and turn on to a floured surface. Knead gently for 2 or 3 minutes, adding the coin or bean, if using, then roll out into a long strip measuring about 65 × 13cm/26 × 5in. Roll up from one long side, join the ends and place seam side down on the baking sheet. Cover and leave in a warm place for 1–1½ hours until doubled in size.

4 Preheat the oven to 180°C/350°F/Gas 4. Brush the ring with lightly beaten egg white and decorate with glacé fruit slices. Sprinkle with flaked almonds and bake for 30–35 minutes.

Greek Yogurt and Fig Cake

Baked fresh figs, thickly sliced, make a delectable topping for a featherlight sponge, baked upside-down. Figs that are a bit on the firm side work best for this particular recipe, retaining their shape and flavour.

Serves 6–8

6 firm fresh figs, thickly sliced
45ml/3 tbsp clear honey,
   plus extra for glazing
200g/7oz/scant I cup
   butter, softened
175g/6oz/³/₄ cup caster
   (superfine) sugar
grated rind of I lemon
grated rind of I orange
4 eggs, separated
225g/8oz/2 cups plain
   (all-purpose) flour
5ml/I tsp baking powder
5ml/I tsp bicarbonate of soda
250ml/8fl oz/I cup natural
   (plain) Greek yogurt

I Preheat the oven to 180°C/350°F/Gas 4. Grease a 23cm/ 9in cake tin (pan) and line the base with baking parchment. Arrange the figs over the base of the tin and drizzle over the honey.

2 In a large mixing bowl, cream the butter and caster sugar with the lemon and orange rinds until the mixture is pale and fluffy, then gradually beat in the egg yolks.

3 Sift the dry ingredients together. Add a little to the creamed mixture, beat well, then beat in a spoonful of Greek yogurt. Repeat this process until all the yogurt and the dry ingredients have been incorporated.

4 Whisk the egg whites in a grease-free bowl until they form stiff peaks. Stir half the whites into the cake mixture to slacken it slightly, then fold in the rest.

5 Pour the mixture over the figs in the tin, then bake for 1¼ hours or until golden and a skewer inserted in the centre of the cake comes out clean.

6 Turn the cake out on to a wire rack, peel off the lining paper carefully, to avoid dislodging the figs, and leave to cool. Drizzle the figs with extra honey before serving.

Pear and Polenta Cake

In this rustic Italian-style cake, the additional of polenta gives the light sponge a slightly nutty texture and a lovely corn flavour that complements the topping of honeyed, sliced pears perfectly. You can serve the cake while still warm as a dessert, accompanied by custard or cream.

Makes 10 slices

175g/6oz/³/₄ cup golden caster
   (superfine) sugar
4 ripe pears
juice of ¹/₂ lemon
30ml/2 tbsp clear honey
3 eggs
seeds from I vanilla pod (bean)
120ml/4fl oz/¹/₂ cup sunflower oil
115g/4oz/I cup self-raising
   (self-rising) flour
50g/2oz/¹/₃ cup instant polenta

I Preheat the oven to 180°C/350°F/Gas 4. Generously grease and line a 21cm/8½in round cake tin (pan). Scatter 30ml/2 tbsp of the golden caster sugar over the base of the prepared tin.

2 Peel and core the pears. Cut them into chunky slices and toss them in the lemon juice. Arrange across the base of the cake tin. Drizzle the honey over the pears and set aside.

3 Mix together the eggs, seeds from the vanilla pod and the remaining golden caster sugar in a bowl.

4 Beat the egg mixture until thick and creamy, then gradually beat in the oil. Sift together the flour and polenta and fold into the egg mixture.

5 Pour the mixture carefully into the tin over the pears. Bake for about 50 minutes or until a skewer inserted into the centre comes out clean. Cool in the tin for 10 minutes, then turn the cake out on to a plate, peel off the lining paper, invert and slice.

> **Cook's Tip**
> Use the tip of a small, sharp knife to scrape out the vanilla seeds. If you do not have a vanilla pod, use 5ml/I tsp pure vanilla extract instead.

Yogurt and Fig Cake: Energy 473kcal/1981kJ; Protein 8.2g; Carbohydrate 59.4g, of which sugars 38g; Fat 24.3g, of which saturates 14g; Cholesterol 149mg; Calcium 167mg; Fibre 2g; Sodium 225mg.
Pear Cake: Energy 205kcal/862kJ; Protein 2.9g; Carbohydrate 31.1g, of which sugars 21.4g; Fat 8.4g, of which saturates 1.2g; Cholesterol 46mg; Calcium 52mg; Fibre 1.4g; Sodium 53mg.

Polenta Bread

Polenta is combined with pine nuts to make an Italian bread with a fantastic flavour.

Makes I loaf

50g/2oz/1/2 cup polenta
300ml/1/2 pint/1 1/4 cups
  lukewarm water
15g/1/2 oz fresh yeast
2.5ml/1/2 tsp clear honey

225g/8oz/2 cups unbleached
  white bread flour
25g/1oz/2 tbsp butter
45ml/3 tbsp pine nuts
7.5ml/1 1/2 tsp salt

For the topping
1 egg yolk
15ml/1 tbsp water
pine nuts, for sprinkling

1 Lightly grease a baking sheet. Mix the polenta and 250ml/ 8fl oz/1 cup of the water in a pan and slowly bring to the boil, stirring continuously, then simmer for 2–3 minutes, stirring occasionally. Set aside to cool for 10 minutes, or until just warm.

2 Mix the yeast with the remaining water and honey until creamy. Sift 115g/4oz/1 cup of the flour and beat in the yeast mixture, then stir in the polenta mixture. Turn on to a floured surface and knead for 5 minutes until smooth and elastic.

3 Put the dough in a lightly oiled polythene bag and leave in a warm place, for about 2 hours, or until it has doubled in bulk. Meanwhile, melt the butter, add the pine nuts and cook over a medium heat, stirring, until pale golden. Set aside to cool.

4 Add the remaining flour and salt to the dough and mix to a soft dough. Knead in the pine nuts. Turn out on to a floured surface and knead for 5 minutes until smooth and elastic. Place in a lightly oiled bowl, cover and leave in a warm place, for 1 hour, or until doubled in bulk.

5 Knock back (punch down) the dough and turn it out on to a floured surface. Divide into 2 equal pieces and roll each piece into a fat sausage about 38cm/15in long. Plait together and place on the prepared baking sheet. Cover again and leave to rise in a warm place for 45 minutes. Preheat the oven to 200°C/400°F/Gas 6. Mix the egg yolk and water and brush over the loaf. Sprinkle with pine nuts and bake for 30 minutes.

Warm Herby Bread

This Italian-style bread is flavoured with basil, rosemary, olive oil and sun-dried tomatoes.

Makes 3 loaves

5ml/1 tsp caster (superfine) sugar
900ml/1 1/2 pints/3 3/4 cups
  warm water
15ml/1 tbsp dried yeast
1.3kg/3lb/12 cups strong white
  flour, plus extra for dusting

15ml/1 tbsp salt
75ml/5 tbsp mixed fresh chopped
  basil and rosemary leaves
50g/2oz/1 cup drained sun-dried
  tomatoes, roughly chopped
150ml/1/4 pint/2/3 cup extra virgin
  olive oil, plus extra for greasing
  and brushing

To finish
15ml/1 tbsp rosemary leaves
sea salt flakes

1 Put the sugar into a bowl, pour on 150ml/1/4 pint/2/3 cup warm water, then sprinkle the dried yeast over the top. Leave in a warm place for 10–15 minutes, or until frothy.

2 Put the flour, salt, chopped basil and rosemary leaves, and sun-dried tomatoes into a large mixing bowl. Add the olive oil together with the yeast mixture, then gradually stir in the remaining warm water. As the mixture becomes stiffer, bring it together with your hands. Mix to a soft but not sticky dough, adding a little extra water if needed.

3 Turn the dough out on to a lightly floured surface and knead for 5 minutes until smooth and elastic. Put back into the bowl, cover loosely with oiled clear film (plastic wrap) and leave in a warm place for 30–40 minutes, or until doubled in size.

4 Knead again until smooth and elastic, then cut into three pieces. Shape each into an oval loaf about 18cm/7in long, and arrange on oiled baking sheets. Slash the top of each loaf with a knife in a criss-cross pattern.

5 Loosely cover and leave in a warm place for 15–20 minutes, or until well risen. Preheat the oven to 220°C/425°F/Gas 7. Brush the loaves with a little olive oil and sprinkle with rosemary leaves and salt flakes. Cook for about 25 minutes. The bases should sound hollow when they are tapped.

Polenta Bread: Energy 1994kcal/8427kJ; Protein 50.5g; Carbohydrate 366.8g, of which sugars 7.1g; Fat 44.7g, of which saturates 15g; Cholesterol 53mg; Calcium 1085mg; Fibre 14.9g; Sodium 2337mg.
Warm Herby Bread: Energy 1789kcal/7563kJ; Protein 41.5g; Carbohydrate 338.2g, of which sugars 7.9g; Fat 39.3g, of which saturates 5.7g; Cholesterol 0mg; Calcium 643mg; Fibre 14.6g; Sodium 1987mg.

French Baguettes

Baguettes made by an artisan baker are difficult to reproduce at home, but by using less yeast and triple fermentation you can produce bread far superior to mass-produced loaves.

Makes 3 loaves

500g/1¼lb/5 cups unbleached strong white bread flour
115g/4oz/1 cup fine French plain (all-purpose) flour
10ml/2 tsp salt
15g/½oz fresh yeast

1 Sift the flours and salt into a large bowl. Add the yeast to 550ml/18fl oz/2½ cups lukewarm water in a separate bowl and stir until combined. Gradually beat in half the flour mixture to form a batter. Cover with clear film (plastic wrap) and leave for about 3 hours, or until nearly trebled in size.

2 Add the remaining flour a little at a time, beating with your hand. Turn out on to a lightly floured surface and knead for 8–10 minutes to form a moist dough. Place the dough in a lightly oiled bowl, cover with lightly oiled clear film and leave to rise, in a warm place, for about 1 hour.

3 Knock back (punch down) the dough, turn out on to a floured surface and divide into three equal pieces. Shape each into a ball and then into a 15 × 7.5cm/6 × 3in rectangle. Fold the bottom third up lengthways and the top third down and press down. Seal the edges. Repeat two or three more times until each loaf is an oblong. Leave to rest for a few minutes between foldings.

4 Stretch each piece of dough into a 35cm/14in long loaf. Pleat a floured dish towel on a baking sheet to make three moulds for the loaves. Place the loaves between the pleats, cover with lightly oiled clear film and leave to rise in a warm place for 45–60 minutes.

5 Preheat the oven to maximum. Roll the loaves on to a baking sheet, spaced apart. Slash the top of each diagonally several times. Place at the top of the oven, spray the inside of the oven with water and bake for 20–25 minutes. Spray the oven twice during the first 5 minutes of baking. Allow to cool.

Sicilian Scroll

A wonderful pale yellow, crusty loaf, enhanced with a nutty flavour from the sesame seeds. It's perfect for serving with cheese.

Makes 1 loaf

450g/1lb/4 cups finely ground semolina
115g/4oz/1 cup unbleached white bread flour
10ml/2 tsp salt
20g/¾oz fresh yeast
360ml/12½fl oz/generous 1½ cups lukewarm water
30ml/2 tbsp extra virgin olive oil
sesame seeds, for sprinkling

1 Lightly grease a baking sheet. Mix the semolina, white bread flour and salt in a large bowl and make a well in the centre.

2 Cream the yeast with half the water, then stir in the remainder. Add the creamed yeast to the centre of the semolina mixture with the olive oil and gradually incorporate the semolina and flour to form a firm dough.

3 Turn out the dough on to a lightly floured surface and knead for 8–10 minutes until smooth and elastic. Place in a lightly oiled bowl, cover with lightly oiled clear film and leave to rise, in a warm place, for 1–1½ hours, or until doubled in bulk.

4 Turn out on to a lightly floured surface and knock back (punch down). Knead gently, then shape into a fat roll about 50cm/20in long. Form into an "S" shape.

5 Carefully transfer the dough to the prepared baking sheet, cover with lightly oiled clear film and leave to rise, in a warm place, for 30–45 minutes, or until doubled in size.

6 Meanwhile, preheat the oven to 220°C/425°F/Gas 7. Brush the top of the scroll with water and sprinkle with sesame seeds. Bake for 10 minutes. Spray the inside of the oven with water twice during this time.

7 Reduce the temperature to 200°C/400°F/Gas 6 and bake for a further 25–30 minutes, or until golden. Transfer to a wire rack to cool.

French Baguettes: Energy 233kcal/991kJ; Protein 6.4g; Carbohydrate 53.1g, of which sugars 1g; Fat 0.9g, of which saturates 0.1g; Cholesterol 0mg; Calcium 96mg; Fibre 2.1g; Sodium 439mg.
Sicilian Scroll: Energy 2344kcal/9922kJ; Protein 64.4g; Carbohydrate 438.4g, of which sugars 1.8g; Fat 49g, of which saturates 5.9g; Cholesterol 0mg; Calcium 443mg; Fibre 15.4g; Sodium 63mg.

Italian Country Bread

This classic Italian open-textured bread is moistened and flavoured with fruity olive oil. Its floured top gives it a true country feel.

Makes 1 large loaf
For the starter
175g/6oz/1½ cups unbleached
white bread flour
7g/¼oz fresh yeast
90ml/6 tbsp lukewarm water

For the dough
225g/8oz/2 cups unbleached
white bread flour, plus extra
for dusting
225g/8oz/2 cups unbleached
wholemeal bread flour
5ml/1 tsp caster (superfine) sugar
10ml/2 tsp salt
15g/½oz fresh yeast
275ml/9fl oz/generous 1 cup
lukewarm water
75ml/5 tbsp extra virgin olive oil

1 Sift the flour for the starter into a large bowl. Make a well in the centre. Cream the yeast with the water and pour into the well. Gradually mix in the flour to form a firm dough. Turn out on to a lightly floured surface and knead for 5 minutes until smooth and elastic. Return to the bowl, cover with lightly oiled clear film (plastic wrap) and leave in a warm place for 8–10 hours, or until well risen and starting to collapse.

2 Lightly flour a baking sheet. Mix the flours, sugar and salt for the dough in a large bowl. Cream the yeast and the water in another large bowl, then stir in the starter. Stir in the flour mixture a little at a time, then add the olive oil in the same way, and mix to a soft dough. Turn out on to a lightly floured surface and knead for 8–10 minutes until smooth and elastic. Place in a lightly oiled bowl, cover with lightly oiled clear film and leave in a warm place for 1–1½ hours, or until doubled in bulk.

3 Turn out on to a floured surface and knock back (punch down). Gently pull out the edges and fold under to make a round. Transfer to the baking sheet, cover again and leave in a warm place for 1–1½ hours, or until almost doubled in size.

4 Preheat the oven to 230°C/450°F/Gas 8. Lightly dust the loaf with flour and bake for 15 minutes. Reduce the temperature to 200°C/400°F/Gas 6 and bake for a further 20 minutes, or until the loaf sounds hollow when tapped on the base.

Ciabatta

This irregular-shaped Italian bread is so called because it looks like an old slipper. It is made with a very wet dough flavoured with olive oil, producing a bread full of holes with a chewy crust.

Makes 3 loaves
For the starter
7g/¼oz fresh yeast
175–200ml/6–7fl oz/¾–scant
1 cup lukewarm water

350g/12oz/3 cups unbleached
plain (all-purpose) flour, plus
extra for dusting

For the dough
15g/½oz fresh yeast
400ml/14fl oz/1⅔ cups
lukewarm water
60ml/4 tbsp lukewarm milk
500g/1¼lb/5 cups unbleached
strong white bread flour
10ml/2 tsp salt
45ml/3 tbsp extra virgin olive oil

1 Cream the yeast for the starter with a little of the water. Sift the flour into a large bowl. Gradually mix in the yeast mixture and enough of the remaining water to form a firm dough. Turn out on to a floured surface and knead for about 5 minutes, or until smooth and elastic. Return the dough to the bowl, cover with lightly oiled clear film (plastic wrap) and leave in a warm place for 12–15 hours, until risen and starting to collapse.

2 Sprinkle three baking sheets with flour. Mix the yeast for the dough with a little of the water until creamy, then mix in the rest. Add this mixture to the starter and gradually mix in. Mix in the milk, beating thoroughly with a wooden spoon. Using your hand, gradually beat in the flour, lifting the dough as you mix. This will take 15 minutes or more and form a very wet dough.

3 With a spoon, carefully tip one-third of the dough at a time on to the baking sheets without knocking it back in the process. Using floured hands, shape into rough oblong loaves, about 2.5cm/1in thick. Flatten slightly with splayed fingers. Sprinkle with flour; leave to rise in a warm place for 30 minutes.

4 Meanwhile, preheat the oven to 220°C/425°F/Gas 7. Bake the loaves in the oven for 25–30 minutes, or until golden brown and sounding hollow when tapped on the base. Transfer to a wire rack to cool.

Italian Country Bread: Energy 2502kcal/10567kJ; Protein 71.9g; Carbohydrate 430.4g, of which sugars 11.8g; Fat 66.7g, of which saturates 9.5g; Cholesterol 0mg; Calcium 468mg; Fibre 43g; Sodium 3949mg.
Ciabatta: Energy 985kcal/4176kJ; Protein 25g; Carbohydrate 202.8g, of which sugars 4.8g; Fat 13.8g, of which saturates 2.2g; Cholesterol 1mg; Calcium 386mg; Fibre 8.1g; Sodium 1217mg.

Onion, Parmesan and Olive Bread

This bread is great served warm with olive oil.

Makes 1 large or 2 small loaves
350g/12oz/3 cups unbleached strong bread flour, plus a little extra
115g/4oz/1 cup yellow cornmeal, plus a little extra
rounded 5ml/1 tsp salt
15g/½oz fresh yeast or 10ml/2 tsp active dried yeast
5ml/1 tsp muscovado sugar
270ml/9fl oz/1 cup warm water
5ml/1 tsp chopped fresh thyme
30ml/2 tbsp olive oil
1 onion, finely chopped
75g/3oz/1 cup freshly grated Parmesan cheese
90g/3½oz/scant 1 cup black olives, stoned (pitted)

1 If using fresh yeast, cream it with the sugar and stir in 120ml/4fl oz/½ cup of the warm water. If using dried yeast, stir the sugar into the water, then sprinkle the dried yeast on the surface. Leave in a warm place for 10 minutes, until frothy.

2 Mix the flour, cornmeal and salt, in a warmed bowl. Make a well in the centre and add the yeast liquid and 150ml/ ¼ pint/ ⅔ cup of the remaining warm water. Add the thyme and 15ml/1 tbsp of olive oil and mix thoroughly. Add a dash more warm water, if necessary, to make a soft, but not sticky, dough.

3 Knead the dough on a lightly floured work surface for 5 minutes, until smooth and elastic. Place in a lightly oiled bowl and cover with oiled clear film. Set aside to rise in a warm, not hot place for 1–2 hours or until well risen.

4 Fry the onion until soft, not browned. Once they have cooled, knead them, the Parmesan and olives into the dough.

5 Shape the dough into one or two loaves. Sprinkle cornmeal on the work surface and roll the bread in it, then place on an oiled baking sheet. Make slits across the top. Cover with oiled clear film and leave in a warm place for 1 hour, or until risen.

6 Preheat the oven to 200°C/400°F/Gas 6. Bake for 30–35 minutes, or until the bread sounds hollow when tapped on the base. Cool on a wire rack.

Walnut Bread

This delicious butter-and-milk-enriched wholemeal bread is filled with walnuts. It is the perfect companion for cheese.

Makes 2 loaves
50g/2oz/¼ cup butter
350g/12oz/3 cups wholemeal bread flour
115g/4oz/1 cup unbleached white bread flour
15ml/1 tbsp light brown muscovado (molasses) sugar
7.5ml/1½ tsp salt
20g/¾oz fresh yeast
275ml/9fl oz/generous 1 cup lukewarm milk
175g/6oz/1½ cups walnut pieces

1 Lightly grease two baking sheets. Heat the butter in a pan until starting to brown, then set aside to cool. Mix the flours, sugar and salt in a large bowl and make a well in the centre. Cream the yeast with half the milk and pour into the well with the remaining milk.

2 Pour the melted butter through a fine strainer into the well with the other liquids. Using your hand, mix the liquids together in the bowl and gradually draw in small amounts of flour to make a batter. Continue until the mixture forms a moist dough. Knead on a lightly floured surface for 6–8 minutes. Place in a lightly oiled bowl, cover with oiled clear film (plastic wrap) and leave in a warm place for 1 hour, or until doubled in bulk.

3 Turn out the dough on to a floured surface and gently knock back (punch down). Flatten and sprinkle with the nuts. Gently press the nuts into the dough, then roll it up. Return to the oiled bowl, re-cover and leave in a warm place for 30 minutes.

4 Turn out on to a lightly floured surface, divide in half and shape each piece into a ball. Place on the baking sheets, cover with lightly oiled clear film and leave in a warm place for 45 minutes or until doubled in bulk.

5 Meanwhile, preheat the oven to 220°C/425°F/Gas 7. Using a sharp knife, slash the top of each loaf 3 times. Bake for about 35 minutes, or until the loaves sound hollow when tapped on the base. Transfer to a wire rack to cool.

Onion and Olive Bread: Energy 571kcal/2402kJ; Protein 18.7g; Carbohydrate 91.3g, of which sugars 3.2g; Fat 16.2g, of which saturates 5.2g; Cholesterol 19mg; Calcium 367mg; Fibre 4.2g; Sodium 714mg.
Walnut Bread: Energy 1620kcal/6782kJ; Protein 45.4g; Carbohydrate 173.9g, of which sugars 21.3g; Fat 87.4g, of which saturates 20.1g; Cholesterol 61mg; Calcium 403mg; Fibre 20.6g; Sodium 224mg.

Portuguese Corn Bread

The Portuguese make corn bread with a mixture of cornmeal and white flour. It has a hard crust with a moist crumb.

Makes I large loaf
20g/³⁄₄oz fresh yeast
250ml/8fl oz/I cup
   lukewarm water

225g/8oz/2 cups cornmeal
450g/1lb/4 cups unbleached
   white bread flour
150ml/¼ pint/²⁄₃ cup
   lukewarm milk
30ml/2 tbsp olive oil
7.5ml/1½ tsp salt
polenta, for dusting

I Dust a baking sheet with a little cornmeal. Put the yeast in a large bowl and gradually mix in the lukewarm water until smooth. Stir in half the cornmeal and 50g/2oz/½ cup of the flour and mix to a batter. Cover the bowl with lightly oiled clear film (plastic wrap) and leave in a warm place for about 30 minutes, or until bubbles appear on the surface.

2 Stir the milk into the batter, then stir in the olive oil. Gradually mix in the remaining cornmeal, flour and salt to form a pliable dough. Turn out on to a lightly floured surface and knead for about 10 minutes until smooth and elastic.

3 Place the dough in a lightly oiled bowl, cover with lightly oiled clear film and leave to rise, in a warm place, for 1½–2 hours, or until doubled in bulk.

4 Turn out the dough on to a lightly floured surface and knock back (punch down). Shape into a round ball, flatten slightly and place on the prepared baking sheet. Dust with polenta, cover with a large upturned bowl and leave in a warm place for about 1 hour, or until doubled in size. Meanwhile, preheat the oven to 230°C/450°F/Gas 8.

5 Bake for 10 minutes, spraying the inside of the oven with water 2–3 times. Reduce the oven temperature to 190°C/375°F/Gas 5 and bake for a further 20–25 minutes, or until golden and hollow sounding when tapped on the base. Transfer to a wire rack to cool.

Onion, Chive and Ricotta Bread

Ricotta cheese and chives make a moist, well-flavoured loaf that is excellent for sandwiches. Shape the dough into rolls or one large loaf.

Makes I loaf or 16 rolls
5ml/1 tsp caster (superfine) sugar
270ml/9fl oz/generous I cup
   lukewarm water
10ml/2 tsp active dried yeast

450g/1lb unbleached strong white
   flour, plus a little extra
7.5ml/1½ tsp salt
I large egg, beaten
115g/4oz/½ cup ricotta cheese
I bunch spring onions (scallions),
   thinly sliced
30ml/2 tbsp extra virgin olive oil
45ml/3 tbsp snipped fresh chives
15ml/1 tbsp milk
10ml/2 tsp poppy seeds
coarse sea salt

I Stir the sugar into 120ml/4fl oz/½ cup of the water, then sprinkle the dried yeast over the surface. Leave in a warm place for 10 minutes. Sift the flour and salt into a bowl. Make a well in the centre and pour in the yeast liquid and the remaining water. Reserve a little beaten egg, then put the rest in the bowl. Add the ricotta and mix to a dough. Add more flour if it is sticky.

2 Knead the dough on a floured work surface until smooth and elastic. Put an oiled bowl covered with lightly oiled clear film (plastic wrap) and leave in a warm place for 1–2 hours, until doubled in size. Meanwhile, cook the spring onions in the oil for 3–4 minutes, until soft. Set aside to cool.

3 Punch down the dough and knead in the onions, with their oil from cooking, and the chives. Shape into rolls or a loaf.

4 Grease a baking sheet or loaf tin (pan) and place the rolls or bread on it. Cover with oiled film and leave in a warm place to rise for about 1 hour. Preheat the oven to 200°C/400°F/Gas 6.

5 Beat the milk into the reserved beaten egg and use to glaze the rolls or loaf. Sprinkle with poppy seeds and a little coarse sea salt, then bake rolls for about 15 minutes or a loaf for 30–40 minutes, or until golden and well risen. When tapped firmly on the base, the bread should feel and sound firm. Cool on a wire rack.

Corn Bread: Energy 3008kcal/12539kJ; Protein 52.7g; Carbohydrate 303.3g, of which sugars 87.7g; Fat 179.8g, of which saturates 46.1g; Cholesterol 561mg; Calcium 696mg; Fibre 7.4g; Sodium 1672mg.
Ricotta Bread: Energy 2042kcal/8626kJ; Protein 61.6g; Carbohydrate 356.9g, of which sugars 13.8g; Fat 50.8g, of which saturates 16.3g; Cholesterol 239mg; Calcium 716mg; Fibre 15.4g; Sodium 97mg.

French Dimpled Rolls

A French speciality, these attractive white rolls are distinguished by the split down the centre. They have a crusty finish while remaining soft and light inside thanks to the steaming technique used to bake them – they taste lovely, too.

Makes 10 rolls

400g/14oz/3½ cups unbleached
   white bread flour
7.5ml/1½ tsp salt
5ml/1 tsp caster (superfine) sugar
15g/½oz fresh yeast
120ml/4fl oz/½ cup
   lukewarm milk
175ml/6fl oz/¾ cup
   lukewarm water

1 Lightly grease 2 baking sheets. Sift the flour and salt into a large bowl. Stir in the sugar and make a well in the centre.

2 Cream the yeast with the milk until dissolved, then pour into the centre of the flour mixture. Sprinkle over a little of the flour from around the edge. Leave at room temperature for 15–20 minutes, or until the mixture starts to bubble.

3 Add the water and gradually mix in the flour to form a fairly moist, soft dough. Turn out on to a lightly floured surface and knead for 8–10 minutes until smooth and elastic. Place in a lightly oiled bowl, cover with lightly oiled clear film (plastic wrap) and leave at room temperature for about 1½ hours, or until doubled in bulk.

4 Turn out on to a floured surface and knock back (punch down). Re-cover and leave to rest for 5 minutes. Divide the dough into 10 pieces. Shape into balls, then roll into ovals. Lightly flour the tops. Space well apart on the baking sheets, cover with lightly oiled clear film and leave to rise for about 30 minutes, or until almost doubled in size.

5 Lightly oil the side of your hand and press the centre of each roll to make a deep split. Re-cover and leave to rest for 15 minutes. Meanwhile, place a roasting pan in the bottom of the oven and preheat the oven to 230°C/450°F/Gas 8. Pour 250ml/8fl oz/1 cup water into the pan and bake the rolls for 15 minutes, or until golden. Cool on a wire rack.

Petit Pains au Lait

These classic French round milk rolls have a delicate crust and a sweet crumb. They are great for breakfast and don't last long!

Makes 12 rolls

450g/1lb/4 cups unbleached
   white bread flour
10ml/2 tsp salt

15ml/1 tbsp caster
   (superfine) sugar
50g/2oz/¼ cup butter, softened
15g/½oz fresh yeast
280ml/9fl oz/generous 1 cup
   lukewarm milk, plus
15ml/1 tbsp extra, to glaze

1 Lightly grease 2 baking sheets. Sift the flour and salt together into a bowl. Stir in the sugar. Rub the butter into the flour. Cream the yeast with 60ml/4 tbsp of the milk. Stir in the remaining milk. Pour into the flour and mix to a soft dough.

2 Turn out on to a lightly floured surface and knead for 8–10 minutes until smooth and elastic. Place in a lightly oiled bowl, cover with lightly oiled clear film (plastic wrap) and leave to rise, in a warm place, for 1 hour, or until doubled in bulk.

3 Turn out the dough on to a lightly floured surface and gently knock back (punch down). Divide into 12 equal pieces. Shape into balls and space on the baking sheets.

4 Using a sharp knife, cut a cross in the top of each roll. Cover with lightly oiled clear film and leave to rise, in a warm place, for about 20 minutes, or until doubled in size.

5 Preheat the oven to 200°C/400°F/Gas 6. Brush the rolls with milk and bake for 20–25 minutes. Cool on a wire rack.

> ### Variations
> *These can also be made into long rolls. To shape, flatten each ball of dough and fold in half. Roll back and forth, using your hand to form a 13cm/5in long roll, tapered at either end. Just before baking, slash the tops horizontally several times.*

French Dimpled Rolls: Energy 145kcal/614kJ; Protein 4.4g; Carbohydrate 31.9g, of which sugars 1.4g; Fat 0.8g, of which saturates 0.3g; Cholesterol 1mg; Calcium 77mg; Fibre 1.2g; Sodium 9mg.
Petit Pains au Lait: Energy 169kcal/714kJ; Protein 4.3g; Carbohydrate 30.2g, of which sugars 1.6g; Fat 4.3g, of which saturates 2.5g; Cholesterol 10mg; Calcium 79mg; Fibre 1.2g; Sodium 36mg.

Ricotta and Oregano Knots

Ricotta adds a wonderful moistness to these rolls, made using a breadmaker. They are best served warm.

Makes 12 rolls

60ml/4 tbsp ricotta cheese
225ml/8fl oz/scant 1 cup water
450g/1lb/4 cups unbleached
  white bread flour
45ml/3 tbsp skimmed
  milk powder

10ml/2 tsp dried oregano
5ml/1 tsp salt
10ml/2 tsp caster
  (superfine) sugar
25g/1oz/ 2 tbsp butter
5ml/1 tsp easy-blend (rapid-rise)
  dried yeast

For the topping

1 egg yolk
15ml/1 tbsp water
freshly ground black pepper

1 Spoon the cheese into the bread machine pan and add the water. (Reverse the order in which you add the liquid and dry ingredients if the instructions for your machine specify this.)

2 Sprinkle over the flour to cover the cheese and water. Add the skimmed milk powder and oregano. Place the salt, sugar and butter in separate corners of the pan. Make a small indent in the centre of the flour and add the yeast. Set the machine to the basic dough setting (if available). Start.

3 Oil two baking sheets. When the dough cycle has finished, remove the dough and place it on a lightly floured surface. Knock back (punch down) gently, then divide it into 12 pieces and cover these with oiled clear film (plastic wrap).

4 Roll each piece of dough on a floured surface into a rope 25cm/10in long. Lift one end over the other to make a loop. Push the end through the hole in the loop to make a knot.

5 Place the knots on the baking sheets, cover them with oiled clear film and leave in a warm place for about 30 minutes, or until doubled in size. Preheat the oven to 220°C/425°F/Gas 7.

6 Mix the egg yolk and water for the topping and brush over the rolls. Sprinkle some with pepper and leave the rest plain. Bake for about 15–18 minutes, or until golden brown.

Wholemeal and Rye Pistolets

Unless your bread maker has a programme for wholemeal dough, it is worth the extra effort of the double rising, because this gives a better flavour.

Makes 12

300ml/½ pint/1¼ cups water
280g/10oz/2½ cups stoneground
  wholemeal (whole-wheat)
  bread flour
50g/2oz/½ cup unbleached white
  bread flour, plus extra for dusting

115g/4oz/1 cup rye flour
30ml/2 tbsp skimmed milk powder
10ml/2 tsp salt
10ml/2 tsp caster (superfine) sugar
25g/1oz/2 tbsp butter
7.5ml/1½ tsp easy-blend
  (rapid-rise) dried yeast

For the glaze

5ml/1 tsp salt
15ml/1 tbsp water

1 Pour the water into the bread pan and sprinkle over all three types of flour, covering the water completely. Add the skimmed milk powder. Then add the salt, sugar and butter in separate corners of the pan. Make a small indent in the centre of the flour and add the dried yeast.

2 Set the machine to the dough setting; use wholewheat dough setting (if available), otherwise repeat the programme to allow sufficient rising time. Start. Lightly oil two baking sheets.

3 When the dough cycle has finished, remove the dough and place it on a floured surface Knock back (punch down)gently, then divide it into 12. Cover with oiled clear film (plastic wrap). Shape each piece into a ball and roll into an oval. Place the rolls on the baking sheets. Cover with oiled clear film and leave in a warm place for about 30–45 minutes, or until almost doubled in size. Preheat the oven to 220°C/425°F/Gas 7.

4 Mix the salt and water for the glaze and brush over the rolls. Dust the tops with flour. Using the oiled handle of a wooden spoon held horizontally, split each roll almost in half, along its length. Replace the clear film and leave for 10 minutes. Bake the rolls for 15–20 minutes, until the bases sound hollow when tapped. Turn out on to a wire rack to cool.

Ricotta Knots: Energy 146kcal/620kJ; Protein 4.7g; Carbohydrate 30g, of which sugars 1.4g; Fat 1.7g, of which saturates 0.7g; Cholesterol 19mg; Calcium 70mg; Fibre 1.2g; Sodium 9mg.
Wholemeal Pistolets: Energy 120kcal/511kJ; Protein 4.2g; Carbohydrate 25.3g, of which sugars 0.6g; Fat 0.9g, of which saturates 0.2g; Cholesterol 0mg; Calcium 18mg; Fibre 3.4g; Sodium 330mg.

Spanish Picos

These small knotted bread shapes, dusted with salt and sesame seeds, are often eaten in Spain with drinks, but can also be served with a starter or soup. In this recipe they are made using a breadmaker.

Makes about 70
200ml/7fl oz/⅞ cup water
45ml/3 tbsp extra virgin olive oil

350g/12½oz/3 cups unbleached
  white bread flour
5ml/1 tsp salt
2.5ml/½ tsp granulated sugar
5ml/1 tsp easy-blend (rapid-rise)
  dried yeast

For the topping
30ml/2 tbsp water
15ml/1 tbsp sea salt
15ml/1 tbsp sesame seeds

1 Pour the water and oil into the pan and sprinkle over the flour, ensuring that it covers the liquid. (If necessary, reverse the order in which you add the liquid and dry ingredients.) Add the salt and sugar, in separate corners of the pan. Make a small indent in the centre of the flour and add the yeast.

2 Set the machine to the dough setting, using the basic dough setting if available, and start. Lightly oil two baking sheets.

3 When the cycle has finished, place the dough on a floured surface. Knock back (punch down) gently, then roll it out to a rectangle measuring 30 × 23cm/12 × 9in. Cut lengthways into three strips, then cut each strip into 2.5cm/1in wide ribbons.

4 Preheat the oven to 200°C/400°F/Gas 6. Tie each ribbon into a loose knot and space well apart on the prepared baking sheets. Cover with oiled clear film (plastic wrap) and leave in a warm place for 10–15 minutes to rise. Leave the picos plain or brush with water and sprinkle with salt or sesame seeds. Bake for 10–15 minutes, or until golden.

> **Cook's Tip**
> *Make these tasty nibbles up to a day in advance. Re-heat in a moderate oven for a few minutes, to refresh.*

Cashew and Olive Scrolls

These attractively shaped rolls have a crunchy texture and ooze with the flavours of olives and fresh herbs. In this recipe they are made using a breadmaker.

Makes 12 rolls
140ml/5fl oz/⅝ cup milk
120ml/4fl oz/½ cup water
30ml/2 tbsp extra virgin olive oil
450g/1lb/4 cups unbleached
  white bread flour

5ml/1 tsp salt
2.5ml/½ tsp caster
  (superfine) sugar
7.5ml/1½ tsp easy-blend
  (rapid-rise) dried yeast
5ml/1 tsp finely chopped fresh
  rosemary or thyme
50g/2oz/½ cup salted cashew
  nuts, finely chopped
50g/2oz/½ cup stoned (pitted)
  green olives, finely chopped
45ml/3 tbsp freshly grated
  Parmesan cheese, for sprinkling

1 Pour the milk, water and oil into the pan. If your bread machine specifies it, reverse the order in which you add the liquid and dry ingredients.

2 Sprinkle over the flour, ensuring that it covers the liquid. Add the salt and sugar, placing them in separate corners of the bread pan. Make a small indent in the centre of the flour (but not down as far as the liquid) and add the yeast.

3 Set the machine to the dough setting; use basic raisin dough setting (if available). Press Start. Add the herbs, cashew nuts and olives when the machine beeps, or five minutes before the end of the kneading period. Lightly oil two baking sheets.

4 When the dough cycle has finished, remove it from the machine and place it on a lightly floured surface. Knock it back gently, then divide int 12 pieces of equal size and cover with oiled clear film. Take one piece, leaving the rest covered, and roll into a rope about 23cm./9 in long, tapering the ends. Shape this into an 's; shape. Repeat with the reamining 11 rolls. Leave to rise in a warm place for 30 minues, until doubled in size.

5 Preheat the oven to 200°C/400°F/Gas 6. Sprinkle the rolls with Parmesan and bake for 18–20 minutes, or until risen and golden. Cool on a wire rack.

Spanish Picos: Energy 23kcal/95kJ; Protein 0.5g; Carbohydrate 4.2g, of which sugars 0.1g; Fat 0.5g, of which saturates 0.1g; Cholesterol 0mg; Calcium 8mg; Fibre 0.2g; Sodium 28mg.
Cashew Scrolls: Energy 196kcal/828kJ; Protein 6.3g; Carbohydrate 30.5g, of which sugars 1.3g; Fat 6.3g, of which saturates 1.7g; Cholesterol 4mg; Calcium 116mg; Fibre 1.4g; Sodium 153mg.